P. 188  Bach-Vivaldi

P. 197  Connectise Marile...

P. 198 – 199

    Maritain

P. 208 ...

P. 195 Times is only
phenomenon of perspective

P. 195 Perfect friendship
is a creation by two...

P. 196 To start a work I
should have to receive the
command. This command
must come from myself

P. 223 Aragon – Cocteau
Cocteau affirmed that
art was a reflection of
individual, while Aragon
declared that it was
a reflection of the Epoch

# JEAN COCTEAU:
# THE MAN AND THE MIRROR

*By Elizabeth Sprigge:*

THE STRANGE LIFE OF AUGUST STRINDBERG
Hamish Hamilton, London
Macmillan, New York
1949

GERTRUDE STEIN. HER LIFE AND WORK
Hamish Hamilton, London
Harper, New York
1957

*By Jean-Jacques Kihm:*

JEAN COCTEAU
Gallimard, Paris
1960

MARCEL BEALU
Seghers, Paris
1966

# JEAN COCTEAU:
# THE MAN AND THE MIRROR

by

## ELIZABETH SPRIGGE
### AND
## JEAN-JACQUES KIHM

## COWARD-McCANN INC.
### NEW YORK

*Frontispiece:* Silhouette of Jean Cocteau, during the filming of
*Le Testament d'Orphée (Lucien Clergue)*

# CONTENTS

# LIST OF ILLUSTRATIONS

## DRAWINGS BY JEAN COCTEAU

* These portraits are reproduced with the permission of the S.P.A.D.E.M.

# ACKNOWLEDGEMENTS

The authors wish to express their warm thanks to the following for giving them the benefit of their personal memories of Jean Cocteau:

CECIL BEATON

REGINALD BRIDGEMAN

PHILIPPE ERLANGER

ANDRÉ FRAIGNEAU

STANISLAS FUMET

JEAN HUGO

VALENTINE HUGO

MADAME KANDAOUROFF

R. P. YVES LE CREURER

RAOUL LEVEN

MILORAD

JACQUES NICOLAU

JACQUES QUELLENNEC

FRANCIS ROSE

MARIANNE SINGER

SUZY SOLIDOR

And to HENRI BEHAR for his invaluable aid.

Our thanks are due to the following authors and publishers for permission to quote certain passages from their publications:

MARGARET CROSLAND　　MARY HOECK　　GEORGE D. PAINTER

SINCLAIR ROAD　　VIRGIL THOMSON

ALBIN-MICHEL

AMIOT-DUMONT

ANDRÉ BONNE

BUCHET-CHASTEL

GEORGE BRAZILLER

BRUCKMANN

CALMANN-LÉVY

FERENCZI

FLAMMARION

GALLIMARD

GRASSET

HAMISH HAMILTON

HARPER-ROW

JULLIARD

PETER OWEN

PLON

EDITIONS DU ROCHER

EDITIONS DU SEUIL

STOCK

And to EDOUARD DERMIT for his kind cooperation.

# NOTE

THE authors of this biography met on Whit Sunday 1965 by chance—an event that they feel would have pleased Jean Cocteau —standing beside his tomb in the Chapelle Saint-Blaise-des-Simples at Milly-la-Forêt. Jean-Jacques Kihm was there to interview tourists for the Radio Française, Elizabeth Sprigge was there to pay homage to Jean Cocteau on the publication of her translation of *La Difficulté d'Etre*,\* which she had made with the author's permission during his lifetime.

Jean-Jacques Kihm knew Cocteau well during the last years of his life and is the author of the most comprehensive book about Cocteau, and particularly about his work, to have so far appeared.† He also adapted *Thomas l'Imposteur* for radio and *La Farce du Château* for television and wrote the scenario and the text for a short film of the chapel at Milly-la-Forêt.

Elizabeth Sprigge first met Jean Cocteau in 1953, when she was living in Paris, writing her biography of Gertrude Stein.‡ He had already given his permission for a production in 1950 by Val May of Ronald Duncan's translation of *The Typewriter* at the little Watergate Theatre, of which Elizabeth Sprigge was a director.

When the radio interviews were over Elizabeth Sprigge and Jean-Jacques Kihm continued to talk among the sweet-smelling herbs in the chapel garden. Before the end of the conversation they had decided to write this biography together.

---

\* *The Difficulty of Being* (Peter Owen 1965).
† *Jean Cocteau* (Gallimard 1960).
‡ *Gertrude Stein. Her Life and Work* (Hamish Hamilton 1957, Harpers 1957)

JEAN COCTEAU:
THE MAN AND THE MIRROR

NOTE

Much of the material in the early chapters of this book comes from *Portraits-Souvenir* by Jean Cocteau (Bernard Grasset, 1935)

## CHAPTER I

# PREMIERS SPECTACLES! PREMIERS VERTIGES!

At ten minutes to four on the morning of 5 July 1889, a little boy was born with a silver spoon in his mouth. He was, so his grandmother said, a beautiful child with fine limbs and a remarkably well-shaped head covered with springy black hair, and he greeted his arrival in a world of pleasure and leisure with a strong gay shout. *"C'est un joli petit vieux,"* wrote Madame Lecomte.

Indeed it would be difficult to imagine a more charming place in which to gain one's first impressions of life than this small town of leafy streets and fountained squares, some twenty kilometres from Paris on the edge of the Forest of Saint-Germain. Maisons-Laffitte was largely designed by Mansard and is studded with his deep-roofed houses, while Place Sully, where this little boy's family lived, is in a kind of large park a short way from the town, and is itself a spacious grassy square surrounded by small mansions with hidden gardens, set among lime trees, chestnuts and flowering shrubs, close to a fine racecourse below which runs the Seine. Thus it was into a world of leaf and blossom that this happy child was born, with the vivid life of horse-trainers on his doorstep, and inside and outside the house captivating shapes and colours, sounds and smells.

The little Château, which was roomy and light and full of elegant furniture and pictures, had been bought by the baby's grandfather—his mother's father, Monsieur Eugène Lecomte—a well-to-do stockbroker whose family came from Champagne. At one end of the old house were excellent stables and to this Monsieur Lecomte had added a brick wing for his married children. His daughter, Eugénie, the mother of the new baby, had been born there, and she and her family spent every summer at Maisons-Laffitte.

The little boy was duly registered as Clément Eugène Jean Maurice. Nobody ever called him Clément and the name Eugène meant his grandfather, so the child was known as Jean-Maurice, but the Maurice was soon dropped and he became quite simply Jean Cocteau. As he grew a little older he treasured this name and he was very happy when he found that the cocks crowing around Place Sully kept on saying: "Cocteau, twice over." The name derives from the low Latin *"cocinarius, coctus"*, a cook, and Jean Cocteau was destined to become a chef in the kitchen of the arts. Through the Lecomtes the Cocteaus were well-connected members of that *grande bourgeoisie française* that produced Gide, Proust and many other writers of their generation. General Catroux and Admiral Darlan were later to emerge as their relatives, besides various members of the Diplomatic Corps; but as Jean's grandfather, Athanase Cocteau, had died before his son married and his widow had continued to live in Le Havre, the Cocteau family played a smaller part in Jean's life than did the Lecomtes, although he used to go to visit his grandmother during the summer holidays.

Two children had already been born when Jean made his entry: Marthe, twelve years his senior, and Paul, four years younger than Marthe. When they were not at Maisons-Laffitte, Monsieur Georges Cocteau, a man of independent means who had briefly practised as a lawyer, and his wife and children occupied a large private apartment in his father-in-law's Paris house, 45 Rue la Bruyère—a street of dignified bourgeois houses, close to the informalities of Clichy and Montmartre.

Jean's uncle, Maurice Lecomte, a diplomat with two small children, lived in a nearby street, besides occupying the second floor at Place Sully, Maisons-Laffitte. His son, Pierre, was only four years older than Jean, and little Marianne was two years younger than her brother, so these cousins were more natural playmates for Jean than were Marthe and Paul. Marianne was constantly in their grandfather's house, and the grown-ups of both families met for dinner every Wednesday. Indeed Marianne was like a devoted sister to Jean, and although he loved his mother and was fond too of his father—his was a most affectionate nature—it was with Marianne that he chiefly shared his early life, Marianne and "Jéphine", as he called Fräulein Josephine, the dear ugly German nurse whom he loved best of all. "Josephine use to lay me across her knees," he wrote, "and I would curl up under the tablecloth. How delightful it was while digesting my soup to listen to the sounds of her jaws and her stomach in the half-sleep of childhood!"

There was also Uncle André, a much younger Lecomte son, who often came to stay at Place Sully and enjoyed playing with the children. A piece of land at the far end of the property, comprising the kitchen gardens and the lawn, where the older members of the family played tennis and the younger ones croquet under the supervision of Fräulein Josephine, was known as "le clos André". Jean Cocteau had an obsessive memory and he was never to forget that "kitchen garden of discoveries", "for it is in such places," he wrote, "that childhood seeks to understand the secrets of the grown-up people's universe." And how he longed to understand these secrets and to share in older people's activities, particularly his brother's. Childhood is concerned with one thing only, he was to write later in Opium, "to escape from childhood".

Whether in town or in the country these people led an enchanted existence, in which the arts were recognised as an essential part of good living. Eugène Lecomte was an amateur of music; he had once lived in the same house as Rossini and Jean's mother had grown up in this atmosphere and was an accomplished pianist. Monsieur Lecomte played the violin himself and greatly enjoyed the quartet that met to play in rue la Bruyère—for the pure joy of making music, not as a performance—his fellow

players all being professional musicians, including the famous
Spanish violinist Sarasate. For these evenings the precious
Stradivarius violins were taken from their royal-blue velvet beds
in the billiard room, and while their elders were safely absorbed
in the music, Jean, Marianne and her brother pursued a favourite
game of exploration. The Paris house was perfect for the purpose—the grandparents' part of it being full of passages and steep
staircases and seeming to Jean quite remote from the one in
which he lived himself and vastly exciting and mysterious. There
were endless treasures to be visited, for his grandfather collected
Greek busts, drawings by Ingres, paintings by Delacroix, Floren-
tine coins, vases from Cyprus and, most interesting of all to Jean,
the masks of Antinoüs with their enamel eyes, their pallid terracotta cheeks and horseshoe beards, nestling in red velvet like, as
he was to write later, a theatre-box by Manet. There was too, in
an oval green box in Monsieur Lecomte's dressing-room, a wig
that had belonged to Rossini which became one of Jean's fetishes
and, joy of joys to all the children, there was a silver bath full of
shoes and books that rang like a gong when you struck it.

But music was not the only art in which the family was interested. Georges Cocteau was an accomplished amateur painter
and Jean used to sit enthralled, watching him at work, and ever
afterwards the smell of oil paints brought his father back to him.
He began to draw himself at a very early age—a talent that his
sister Marthe shared.

Indeed, although Jean wrote his childish pieces and charming
little letters, the only art in which the members of this gifted
family took small interest was literature, except inasmuch as it
contributed to the theatre. They went frequently to concerts, but
they also enjoyed the theatre and most of all the highly fashionable opera. Later in life Jean Cocteau made drawings of his
mother's toilette and of the departure of his parents for these
entertainments in full regalia. His own passion for the theatre
that he more than once described as "the fever of crimson and

gold", started in these tender years as he watched his mother being dressed by her maid for these magical adventures. Clothes fascinated Jean Cocteau all his life and on these evenings Madame Cocteau sometimes wore a gown of jet-embroidered red velvet, which merged in the little boy's imagination with the pictures of the theatre that he saw and the descriptions that he heard, chiefly from his brother Paul, who was old enough "to have embarked on the red river". And when at last Madame Cocteau was ready with her glittering jewels and her aigrette and the long kid gloves, so difficult to put on, had changed from dead skins to living creatures on her hands, Jean would kiss the bare palm in the "little skylight" above her wrist and go to bed to dream of theatre.

Everything he heard, everything he saw—including the décor of rue la Bruyère with its ivory and ebony tables, its chocolate and café-au-lait dining-room chairs, the Persian wallpaper in his mother's room, the treasures of his grandfather's collection, everything—the circus, the puppet-shows, magic lanterns and Mass at the Church of La Trinité—merged into one fantastic spectacle, and before long he was building theatres in the court-yard out of cardboard boxes from Old England, that interesting store that provided the little boys' sailor-suits and whistles and horribly scratchy gaiters. When they were not playing indoors or in the courtyard of their grandfather's house, Jean and Marianne would be taken out for walks by Fräulein Josephine, most often—like all well-to-do children of the period—to the Champs-Elysées and the Parc Monceau.

But delightful as all this was, it never ceased to be the greatest joy to Jean to be back at Maisons-Laffitte. He and Marianne and the older children too, were wild with excitement when that summer day arrived on which they piled into the horse-bus with their parents, to arrive a few hours later in that paradise of trees, fountains, white gates, race-horses with their trainers and grooms, and cyclists too, for cycling had now become a luxury sport and

Paul was already the proud owner of a bicycle. Young Jean was always jealous of the things his elder brother could do. Although he was often ill, he was himself a lean and wiry youngster. He could run like the wind and, as soon as he was old enough, he too had first a tricycle and then a bicycle on which he pedalled round the wide roads of the park and off with a young friend to the forest of Saint-Germain, where they smoked pipes hollowed out of horse chestnuts with elder twigs for stems, and then went down on all fours to chew the grass to get rid of the smell of the horrible concoctions that they smoked.

There was never a dull moment in these holiday months. There was Max Lebaudy, the little sugar millionaire who had his carriages washed in champagne, to spy upon; there were gymkhanas (with countless amusements like sack races), which ladies in enormous hats would attend with beribboned rabbits on leads, and best of all there were fairs. The little Jean adored fairs and whenever there was one at Maisons-Laffitte he and Marianne went to it as often as permitted. Although on the whole Jean did not get on well with his grandfather, who found his irrepressible nature exasperating, the old man did on occasion buy some of the little boy's drawings to provide funds for the fair, where Jean would visit all the side-shows while Marianne rode on the merry-go-rounds.

At Maisons-Laffitte there was music too, for Monsieur Lecomte could not bear to be long separated from his beloved quartet. On Sunday mornings, wearing a tussore jacket and a straw hat on the back of his head, with a little bunch of flowers in his hand, he would wait in the *Place*, watching the roads leading up from the race-course until at last the fiacre of the *virtuosi* arrived. Then there would be music and feasting and once again the children would take the opportunity to explore forbidden parts of the house, and be banished for their dinner to a room by themselves.

In spite of having everything a child could want, Jean was

given to sudden fits of temper and was fiercely obstinate when told to do things that displeased him—such as putting on a flannel waistcoat because he was developing a cold, or taking the Sunday purge in spite of the bribe of a peppermint. He would go limp as a sack and be carried upstairs with his feet dragging behind him, or he would work off his rages by some *"tour de force"*, like making his way round the garden standing upright in a barrel, for he was agile as a monkey. In fact, Fräulein Josephine found him very difficult to manage; he was tremendously excitable and his mother spoiled him and predicted from very early days that this son of hers would be a genius.

He enjoyed his illnesses, for adventurous as he was in some ways, he was also extremely sensitive. "A child needs a room," he wrote, "in which to keep his toys and his loves safe. He detests anything that scatters them."

This feeling made him hate going away, particularly to places where he could not imagine the people whom he loved. It was not so bad when he went on journeys, such as to Biarritz, with his mother. The same feeling made him welcome illnesses which gathered his loved ones about him and left him free to cut out and paste paper figures, to build his miniature theatres, to do the cross-stitch that Marianne had taught him. The gentle rolling of thunder, "furniture moving in heaven", enchanted him because it meant that outings would be cancelled, that the family would stay at home, that his cousins would help him play with his bricks, that the nurses would sit in a circle, sewing, that he would hear below first music and then the sound of billiard balls clicking, a reassuring proof that grown-up people were still like children.

He would not, however, have liked any thunderstorm to interfere with him being taken by his faithful "Jéphine" to the circus—the New Circus at the Faubourg Saint-Honoré, to which he went first at the age of seven. ". . . I closed my eyes and I smelt that marvellous great smell."

Jean Cocteau's memories of childhood were full of smells—the smell of the paste for the pictures he cut out, of burnt-out fireworks (he and Marianne had earned the wrath of their grandfather one day by setting the house on fire with the squibs they had bought), of geraniums, the smell of hothouses, of dung, and best of all, of the circus.

Wonderful as were other aspects of the circus, it was the acrobats and the clowns who dominated the show for the young Jean—Footit and his negro partner Chocolat were his idols then. He would sit gazing at the ring, deaf and blind to the rest of life, and Josephine would have to tell him to move or to lift his feet—it was just as if he were hypnotised. He was to keep this passion for the circus all his life and later to share it with Picasso and other artists of the day.

By this time Jean had also been to the Châtelet to see *La Biche au Bois* and *Round the World in Eighty Days*. *Premiers spectacles! Premiers vertiges!* Now he had seen with his own eyes the crimson boxes and crimson gold-tasselled curtains and experienced that foretaste of fairyland, wavering between the edge of the curtain and the boards before the glorious moment when the curtain rose. Thirty years later when he produced *Parade* at the Châtelet he complained of the lighting and demanded such as there had been for *La Biche au Bois* when he was a small child.

"That lighting was of your own making," they told him. "They hadn't got a proper switchboard in those days."

He always looked back with nostalgia on those days when, before he knew anything of the backstage he was to come to know so well, he had been wholly a member of the audience, his imagination untrammelled by any mundane considerations.

Skating was another favourite pastime for the young—Paul skated at Le Pôle Nord in the rue de Clichy, and Jean found its red illuminated letters glamorous and filled the place with icebergs, polar bears and brigs in distress, but the prospect of skating was spoiled for him by watching Paul being taught this skill.

"The prospect of lessons took all the poetry out of it for me . . .
Dunce as I was by nature, the fear of a lesson spoilt the dream, and
the magic of Christmas was destroyed by useful presents."

But soon, however unwillingly, the young Jean Cocteau would
have to endure many lessons, for the time had come for him to
go to school. At present there had only been the agreeable classes
for very young children and Josephine's kindly casual tuition;
but before long he would have to start his proper education. He
would learn many things at school that were not in the textbooks
and Marianne had already begun his education in human behaviour. Shutting him into the big old carriage in the coach-
house, the "omnibus" in which the family at Place Sully used to
go to Mass, and the smell of which was one of the childhood
smells he always remembered, she said:

Listen, I know everything. There are grown-ups who go to bed in
the day time. The men are called *lapins* and the women *cocottes*.
Oncle André is a *lapin*. If you tell anybody, I'll beat you to death
with a spade.

## CHAPTER II

## THE SNOWBALL

WHEN Jean Cocteau was nine years old his father suddenly died. He appears to have taken his own life because of financial difficulties. Jean was immediately sent to stay at his uncle Maurice Lecomte's house, and the most important aspect of this event for him was the chance to pay a visit to his adored little cousin Marianne. Indeed her nurse even felt obliged to reprove him for laughing so gaily when his father was dead.

On 1 January 1899 Jean wrote to his grandmother Madame Lecomte, who was now an invalid and had a nun to take care of her, describing his prowess in the junior section of the Petit Lycée Condorcet. His letter was written on black-edged mourning paper with a little decoration in the corner.

> Ma chère grand'mère
> Je t'embrasse bien fort pour la nouvelle année.
> Je suis bien triste d'être si loin de toi et je te remercie beaucoup de tes étrennes. J'ai été Ier en dessin et 3e en récitation, cela fait que j'ai ma St. Charlemagne. J'ai reçu beaucoup de livres très jolis. Je t'embrasse tendrement et je fais bien des amitiés à la soeur.
>
> ton petit fils
> Jean Cocteau.

Very shortly after this Madame Lecomte too died, but the thought of death cast no shadows on these early years, although later it was to become the dearest of Cocteau's obsessions. His family's way of living was little changed; the only apparent difference was that both at Maisons-Laffitte and in Paris the Cocteaus were more completely absorbed into the ménage of Monsieur Lecomte. It was one of Jean's pleasures to accompany his grandfather to *la petite salle du Conservatoire* and have his horizon widened by hearing the music of Beethoven, Liszt, Berlioz and Wagner. Altogether life remained beautiful and safe.

By now to the small boy's geography of 45 rue la Bruyère had been added the still more important geography of la Cité Monthiers, that high, oblong, cobbled courtyard, bounded on one side by the rue de Clichy and on the other by the rue d'Amsterdam, its archway here being almost opposite the doors of Jean Cocteau's first school. Twice a day now the eleven-year-old boy crossed the Cité, only a few moments' walk from his grandfather's house, and this small section of old Paris, with its quiet aged houses, its flight of steps at one end and the Théâtre de l'Oeuvre at the other, became the arena of his most poignant schoolboy experiences and the setting for one of those "legends" that he compounded, half of fact half of fantasy, as he balanced precariously between stern reality and the enchantment of dreams. The Cité Monthiers was real enough—its peace disturbed twice a day, at the end of morning and afternoon school, by hordes of noisy schoolboys, trading stamps and marbles and pursuing the secret and often cruel rites of childhood; but for Jean, released with the rest from those hated lessons, it was a "courtyard of miracles", a "battle-field of knights in woollen armour", and he was to reconstruct it vividly for the novel *Les Enfants Terribles* and the film *Le Sang d'un Poète*.

The hours in class were wasted hours—the only lessons in which Jean excelled were drawing, gymnastics and, because of Fräulein Josephine, German—and what he was to remember of them were his fears and tears, the smell of gas, the squeak of chalk, blots of ink, raps over the knuckles with a ruler, detentions and having to write out countless times: "Eight plus eight does not make fourteen."

There was nothing to do but suffer and know himself a dunce, but once released into the Cité Monthiers he was full of life again and his imagination soared.

How enchanting the courtyard was in those brief moments of

freedom, whatever the season, whatever the weather—though most magical of all under snow—but for the scene to be complete, the star, the hero, must appear—Dargelos! Jean had known beauty all his life—in his mother and other women, in pictures, in the theatre and in nature; but here suddenly was a new kind of beauty that was such a revelation that once again he was hypnotised as he had been when he first saw the marvels of the circus and the theatre. Every time he saw Dargelos he was "moved and astonished", and he was never to recover from this shock to his heart, which he symbolised in *Les Enfants Terribles* by the snowball with which Paul was felled by Dargelos—even in fiction Cocteau gave him his real name.

Pierre Dargelos was the same age as Cocteau and joined the Petit Lycée soon after him, but they did not share the same class-rooms and they were never close friends. Indeed Dargelos des-pised most of his schoolfellows—Cocteau observed that the name Dargelos "stood for arrogance"; but he quite simply worshipped his image.

Dargelos was in no way a classic beauty; he had rather thick lips, a snub-nose and deep-set, dark-circled eyes over which fell a lock of inky hair. His "bruised and noble knees", which figure in all Cocteau's descriptions were conspicuous, as most of the schoolboys, including Jean himself, wore long stockings, while Dargelos had thick socks that ended just below his knees:

> . . . he was beautiful; he had the beauty of an animal, a tree or a river, that insolent beauty that dirt only accentuates . . .

and he made Jean realise for the first time "the havoc that could be caused to sensitive natures by *'le sexe surnaturel de la beauté'*."

These were the words that Cocteau used first in 1926 when writing of Barbette, the boy *equilibriste* who performed in the guise of a girl, "*plus femme que femme*". Cocteau revived the phrase when writing later of Dargelos, evoking that adolescent age when masculine and feminine forces walk the tight-rope together in one being and arouse in the sensitive beholder a passion having little or nothing to do with sexual desire. Jean Cocteau was to have this immediate response to human beauty all his life.

Something like that famous scene of the snowball that Dargelos throws at Paul in the beginning of *Les Enfants Terribles* clearly did happen during Jean Cocteau's time at the Petit Condorcet. A snowball was thrown and the boy hit in the chest fainted, staining the snow with his blood. Whether the snowball really contained a stone as was suggested was never discovered, but in Cocteau's mind the incident became a symbol of the irresistible power of his idol. "Contact with a Dargelos would be enough in itself to turn a snowball into a lump of marble."

Cocteau was not alone in being bewitched by Dargelos. Professors, porters and pupils alike fell under his spell and the latter indulged in endless vain intrigues to win his favour; he was cock of the walk and could break all rules with impunity.

Thus was born the myth of beauty that Jean Cocteau was for ever to pursue, that androgynous beauty that pervades his work, the love for a boy so often becoming the love for a girl resembling the boy or the other way round. Again and again he declares his passion for beautiful bodies and beautiful faces to whichever sex they belong: *"Les privilèges de la beauté sont immenses."*

As he became a "myth" in Cocteau's treasury of obsessions, the real Dargelos was lost in the imaginary one. Cocteau remembered him, for instance, as a poor scholar, always bottom of the class, and found it hard to believe when, much later, he was told that the records of the school showed that Dargelos had in fact won the *Prix d'Excellence* each year and also excelled in mathematics. Indeed he was to become a successful engineer.

"Where does he live?" Cocteau was to ask himself. "Does he live? Will he materialise?"

On the whole he hoped not. He preferred to keep him as a symbol of youth, of beauty, of arrogance, of untamed power, Dargelos of the "marble heart", *"plus vrai que vrai"*.

This inaccuracy about Dargelos was by no means the only case of Cocteau's memory playing him false. He said himself that it was impossible to write memoirs—although he often did—because he constantly confused the dates and put people in settings belonging to others. But he kept Dargelos always in one setting, although at the age of thirteen they had moved together from the Petit Condorcet to the Grand Condorcet, exchanging the rue d'Amsterdam for the rue du Havre and their satchels for bookstraps. The Cité Monthiers was no longer their playground, yet there in "the courtyard of miracles", Dargelos lived for ever for Jean Cocteau, and there he was constantly to portray him in drawings, book and film, his beret aslant on his dark hair, his splendid legs emerging from his shorts beneath his cape bulging with the satchel on his hip.

Although he was in fact a good-looking boy, with a delightful wide smile, Cocteau was displeased by his own appearance—with, as he put it, hair and teeth growing in every direction. As Jacques, in the partly autobiographical novel *Le Grand Ecart*, he describes himself at Mürren, the Swiss resort that he visited with his mother at the age of eleven, falling wildly in love with a young couple, a brother and sister (androgynous beauty again), who danced as partners and spent all their time together—as the couple in the novel *Les Enfants Terribles* were to do. The girl was tubercular and coughed and had holes in her slippers; the brother collected stamps, cooked sweets over a spirit lamp and developed a limp from a skating accident. Jacques—or Jean—made holes in his tennis shoes, tormented his mother by coughing and in private limped. When he looked in the glass and compared his appearance with that of his idols he wanted to die. This was always Jean Cocteau's desire—not to be loved, but to become like those whom he admired—to be able to see himself in the mirror of their being.

*Spectacles*, shows of every kind, were still the schoolboy Jean's chief delight, and those who shared this taste were his chosen companions. His cousin Marianne remained always close to him

Jean Cocteau's mother, gouache and crayon by Georges Cocteau, after a photograph by Nadar, 1875 (*Collection Marianne Singer, photo Simon Guillot*)

Jean Cocteau about 1899 (*Collection Marianne Singer, photo Simon Guillot*)

Jean Cocteau with his schoolfellows at the Petit Condorcet
(*Collection Edouard Dermit*)

Dargelos, centre, in the same photograph

and among his schoolfellows his foremost friend was Réné Rocher, later to make his name as a theatre director. With him he had built his model theatres, first from cardboard boxes and then with pieces of wood and nails found in the old stable and coach-house. With him he decorated these models, lighted them with a batten of candles and devised endless fantastic scenes, and with him he visited every theatre they could devise the means of reaching.

To everything Jean Cocteau gave his excited attention except to lessons, and by the time he had been at the Grand Condorcet for a few terms, his mother and grandfather began to despair of him attaining the proper scholastic standard for his age. And indeed early in 1904, after only two years, his family was invited to remove him, partly no doubt because of his habit of playing truant with his friends in order to visit such places as the fun-fair "Looping the Loop" or the Palais de Glace. But he was also often absent from school on account of ill-health; an operation for appendicitis, for instance, keeping him away for weeks, which also put him back in his studies.

He was now fifteen and Madame Cocteau decided to take him for a trip abroad. In *Le Grand Ecart* Cocteau describes the time they spent in Venice. He was aghast, seeing the city as a great gaudy fair and the elegant crowds in the theatrical setting of the Piazza San Marco as guests at a vast masked ball, their very souls unmasked. He did his sight-seeing conscientiously, but after some hours of walking and observing, the splendours would pall and he would take refuge in one of his intermittent fevers. He went about with a group of young people involved in emotional crises; his mother being always nervous about his health and about accidents, but never considering the dangers that his own over-excitable, over-sensitive nature might meet at this impres-sionable age. He says himself that during this trip he crossed that delicate age-line at which spirit and body make their own choice. Madame Cocteau, he explains, thought that she was bringing back to Paris the same boy that she took away, but this was not so. He tells the tale of the imprudent mother who allowed her small son to be put in a chest by a Chinese conjuror. The chest was closed and opened—no child. Closed and opened again and there he was, restored to her. But he was not the same boy.

On his return to Paris his education had to be continued, so he was sent to study for his *baccalauréat*, first at the Ecole Fénelon and then at Monsieur Dietz's private classes. This was certainly no place to cure him of his "fever of crimson and gold", for Monsieur Dietz's son was an actor at the Comédie-Française and his grandson was to become the well-known actor Pierre Fresnay. Monsieur Dietz took a few boarders, among whom was Jean, and taught literature at the Ecole Alsacienne where André Gide had been his pupil some twenty years before. Gide describes this professor fondly in his autobiographical book *Si le Grain ne meurt*:

> Dietz before his class was like an organist at his keyboard; this *maestro* drew from us at will the most unexpected sounds, ones to which we did not even aspire. Sometimes perhaps he fooled a bit too much, as does happen with *virtuosi*. But how amusing his classes were! I came out over-fed, blown-out. And how I loved his warm voice and that affectation of indolence that made him almost lie down in the seat of his chair—across it—one leg hanging over an arm, the knee on a level with his nose.

And in *Portraits-Souvenir* Cocteau gives this little caricature:

> . . . this master who amazed us by the contrast between his protestantism and his odalisque poses. He sprawled, he crept, he tied himself in knots and untied himself, threw an arm out here, a leg out there, watching us over the rim of his pincenez, shaking with ironic laughter.

Cocteau also gives us a somewhat bizarre description of Monsieur Dietz, his wife and their establishment as *Les Berlins* in *Le Grand Ecart*. Dietz had originally been a Protestant pastor, but he took pains to keep his pension undenominational and received foreign pupils as well as native ones. He was, according to this book, easy to deceive. He saw nothing that went on and did not wish to see anything, so his pupils were able to pursue their romantic adventures and stay out half the night with impunity. Cocteau still spent a large part of his time amusing himself—skating had now become a "fetish" and roller-skating was all the rage. He adored the Palais de Glace in the Champs-Elysées and described the rink as an enormous peppermint-cream. Here he consorted with the sons and daughters of little-known actresses, a milieu of which his family did not know much, but of which they strongly disapproved. At five o'clock the young skaters were supposed to leave, but Jean often managed to remain and enjoyed watching the *"grandes cocottes"* who now took possession of the Palais. "You go," he would say to Marianne, "but I'll stay. I'm a man." Here too he saw many celebrities, among them Colette with her first husband Willy and her bull-dog—not the robust Colette who was later to become such a friend of Cocteau's, but a "thin, thin Colette, like a little red fox in skirts". Here too he met Madeleine Carlier and her sister, a pair of pretty, unsophisticated girls, older than himself, who created something of a sensation at the Palais. *"La Môme Carlier"*, Cocteau calls Madeleine in *Portraits-Souvenir*; in *Le Grand Ecart* these girls appear again, and significantly one of them, after a series of intrigues, becomes "Jacques's" mistress. The real Jean Cocteau met Madeleine Carlier again in Mistinguett's company, by which time she was making spasmodic appearances as a music-hall singer. Cocteau was now going through the normal development of an adolescent—it was at this period that he had his first affair—and he did not take long to fall in love with Madeleine Carlier, although she was quite ten years his senior, and to announce her at one of the regular Wednesday evening family dinners, to which Marianne and her brother always came, as his prospective fiancée—to the consternation of his mother's arch-bourgeois soul. Later he was to reproduce this situation in the play *Les Parents Terribles*.

B

Cocteau and his friends all adored Mistinguett, *"princesse de l'Eldo"*. They would pool their money and take the cheapest box at the Eldorado, from which they peered at the stage between the necks of the musical instruments. Thence they pelted Mistinguett with bouquets and afterwards waited for her at the stage-door. Writing her biography in old age, she said that it was not her first appearance at the Café de Paris that she remembered with most pleasure, but the bunches of violets brought her by the students, "a charming lot". She particularly mentioned Jean Cocteau and Madeleine Carlier, whom she used to meet in the evenings at the Café de l'Eldo. "We didn't talk about things of much importance. We were happy to be together and did not imagine we were the centre of the world."

Cocteau's infatuation for Madeleine Carlier did not last long, but it is perhaps not surprising that with all these distractions he failed his *"bachot"*.

During this period, in 1906, Monsieur Lecomte died in his seventy-eighth year, the establishment at 45 rue la Bruyère, which had contributed so much to Jean's rich childhood, came to an end, and Madame Cocteau moved with her children to 62 Avenue Malakoff, where she kept up the tradition of Wednesday night family dinners, to which Marianne and her brother still came. Jean continued to go abroad occasionally with his mother, and he would sometimes amuse himself and the other guests in the hotels by putting on scenes from plays. His histrionic tastes and talents had steadily developed; he could learn a part very rapidly and devise a décor with great originality. At Caux, above the lake of Geneva, when he was still in his teens, his performance of Tristan Bernard's *Triplepatte* earned him much admiration.

Speaking on the radio with his biographer André Fraigneau in 1951, Jean Cocteau made this interesting observation about his bourgeois upbringing:

Je n'ai conservé de mon milieu natal qu'une espèce de bonne éduca-
tion néfaste grâce à laquelle j'ai toujours eu l'air de traverser
légèrement une vie lourde et dramatique.

This was Cocteau's way of saying that people without a good
bourgeois upbringing respond tragically to tragic events, whereas
bourgeois etiquette insists that one should speak lightly of serious
matters and present a serene façade disguising their importance.
This then it became Cocteau's life-long habit to do, although it
was entirely alien to his histrionic nature. He was to become the
reflection of the sophisticated and artistic circles in which he
moved, but always among the many facets of his mirror, the
image of his early years would remain. Cocteau had now left his
childhood behind, but he was never to escape from its influence.
All his life he would champion the individual against the masses,
but all his life too he would be bound to that powerful bourgeois
milieu into which he had been born.

## CHAPTER III

## THE DEBUT OF A DANDY

HATED lessons over and examinations cast aside, the young Cocteau was now in a state of bliss. He remained delicate, but his great vitality and the unremitting care he took of himself kept any serious trouble at bay. His temper too was less fiery than it had been in childhood, and although he did sometimes have painful scenes with his mother, these were quickly over and forgotten.

His relatives might have been expected to consider the way that Jean's education had ended a disaster, but in fact they took it in their stride. They were rich; there was no need for Jean to seek a career, still less for him to find a job. He did not even have to do his military service; he was considered too delicate. The silver spoon was still in his mouth; his mother was prepared to pay for him to live as he chose and he would never in his life know what it was to be short of money.

He had failed his examinations, but he had made the delightful discovery that far from being a dunce he was exceptionally talented. Besides drawing and in one way and another playing at theatre, he was now writing poetry. The world was his study and his studio and he flung himself headfirst into it.

He had known the actor Edouard de Max now for a year or so. René Rocher had proudly led Cocteau to his house, which was not far from the Grand Condorcet, and the boys had been effusively welcomed by this ebullient man. On his first visit de Max gave Cocteau a signed photograph bearing the dedication: "*A vos seize ans en fleur, mes quarante ans en pleurs*", although it does not seem that de Max had much to weep about. In those early years of the century, in spite of his eccentricities, he was playing opposite

Sarah Bernhardt and other leading actresses of the day, and his wildly untidy apartment full of strange *objets d'art* and theatrical props, signs of his luxuriant nature, was also always full of a great assortment of visitors. This was the very place to appeal to the young Jean and although de Max was justly considered a dangerous friend for youths, "*redouté des mères à genoux*", Madame Cocteau herself remained as unaware as she had been in Venice of the influences to which her son might be subjected, while Cocteau wrote later that in that apartment, so much laughed at and warned against, he and his friends had met with nothing short of nobility. The appreciation was mutual and de Max took his young friends everywhere.

From the first Jean adored the rich unconventionality of the theatre—what have they, "*les monstres sacrés*", to do with the *comme-il-faut*, he wrote later, with Sarah Bernhardt, de Max and Isadora Duncan in mind, ". . . *ces princes du comme-il-ne-faut-pas?*"

Everything about de Max delighted Cocteau, his extravagances and his absurdity and not least the pearl-grey electric brougham which was matched by his hat, his gloves and his powdered chin. Occasionally he led his young companions into scrapes, as, for instance, when he took them all uninvited and ridiculously apparelled to a formal fancy-dress ball, but Jean could forgive him anything.

On 4 April 1908 de Max arranged for a reading of Cocteau's first poems at the Théâtre Femina. The readers were de Max, René Rocher and several other prominent actors and actresses, all the expenses being met by de Max himself. It was a brilliant occasion, attended by Jean's mother, brother, sister and Marianne, besides the whole of de Max's wide circle of friends and many of the élite of Paris. The slender young poet was praised to the skies by a leading critic and the audience was enthusiastic. These early poems were graceful, skilful and conventional verses, and everyone spoke of Ronsard and de Musset. When the curtain

fell, Cocteau was so overcome with emotion that instead of
staying behind with de Max and the other stars he fled home with
his relatives and kept on embracing them all. He was still closely
attached to his family.

This early recognition put the young Jean Cocteau in the limelight. He was not slow in acclimatising himself to his new milieu.
His hair was sleek and his clothes grew more elegant. He read
Oscar Wilde, admired Aubrey Beardsley's drawings and wore
butterfly ties and a flower in his button-hole, although perhaps
he had not yet achieved true elegance, for this as, paraphrasing
Beau Brummel, he later observed, is never noticeable. His man-
ners also acquired a polish that they were never to lose. Jean
Cocteau was now known everywhere, invited everywhere, and
without doubt his success went straight to his head. Later he was
to deplore the performance at the Théâtre Femina and to try
so hard to forget the occasion that he made it quite unforgettable.
He also came to despise the poems themselves and to refuse to
have them republished; however, he graciously acknowledged
his debt to the generous actor:

> But by and large de Max helped me. He saw further than my follies,
> sensed a hidden strength in me, forcing me to conquer myself and
> teaching me that *"la grandeur s'accommode mal de nuances délicates"*,

which was de Max's way of trying to persuade his young friend
to jettison his bourgeois niceties.

For the moment Dargelos was forgotten, put away in Cocteau's
treasury of obsessions, like the photograph in *Les Enfants Terribles*,
to be brought out and gloated over from time to time for the
rest of his life. He was constantly casting aside one set of interests
for another. He remained faithful to his friendship with René
Rocher, but the friend of the moment, who claimed his first
attention, was Lucien Daudet, the son of the late Alphonse.
Madame Daudet, Lucien's mother, and Madame Cocteau knew
one another, so their sons met in the normal course of social

visits. At Madame Daudet's too he met the writers Francis Jammes and Paul Claudel, already famous as a diplomat and a poet, but not yet as a playwright. These men were some twenty years older than Cocteau, and Lucien Daudet was about eleven years his senior, very handsome and highly talented, but suffering from being put in the shade by his famous father and his brother Léon, so that although he had already published a couple of novels he never became a serious writer, but gravitated uncertainly between literature and painting. Lucien was not, like Léon, anti-semitic, but had in company with Marcel Proust strongly supported Dreyfus. The Dreyfus case had, in Cocteau's own words, "split the bourgeois world in two" throughout his childhood—Dreyfus had not been finally exonerated until 1906.

Lucien Daudet liked young men; he usually preferred those coming from the working class, but Jean Cocteau interested him and he was soon to do a portrait of him as an attractive young decadent. Although they remained perhaps nothing more than friends, there was no doubt that Lucien's tastes had a psychological influence on Cocteau. Lucien Daudet was also an exceptionally brilliant conversationalist and Cocteau envied his prowess in society and determined to emulate him. Daudet took him everywhere and through him he came to know Jules Lemaître, the foremost theatre critic of Paris, who was amused by Cocteau, called him Ariel and invited him alone to his apartment every Sunday morning. Lemaître, with his red face and snow-white beard looked, said Cocteau, "like a hothouse strawberry nestling in January on a bed of cotton-wool".

Daudet also introduced Cocteau to Marcel Proust whose intimate friend he had been since 1895, when the former was described by Jules Renard as "a beautiful youth, waved, pomaded, painted and powdered, who spoke in a tiny voice from his waistcoat pocket". Proust was in his late thirties. He had already published two books: *Les Plaisirs et les Jours* and *Jean Santeuil* and was beginning to work on *A la Recherche du Temps Perdu*, but he was still only known as an author to a small circle of admirers, among whom Lucien Daudet was paramount. They would meet him at Larue's, that café in the Place de la Madeleine that was such a centre for the stars of Paris, or go up to his room at 102 Boulevard Haussmann, which smelt of anti-asthmatic powder and spoke of the night-life of its occupant, where Proust would read passages of his manuscript to them.

Proust was, on the other hand, already well known in society, his background being—unlike Gide's protestant upbringing—much the same as Cocteau's own. Proust had been greatly influenced by Lucien Daudet's brilliance (the aristocrat of the family as his brother Léon called him); but he did not think much of his young friend Jean Cocteau, who seemed to him vain and frivolous.

He used Cocteau, although not exclusively, as his model for Octave, the brilliant *mondain*, "*jeune homme sportif*", at the beginning of *A la Recherche du Temps Perdu*, and perhaps it was not quite by chance that he gave this young man the name of a de Musset character, for Cocteau had already been called "*un Musset de boulevard*". In a later volume Proust admitted that he had changed his mind about Octave. By this time, in 1918, Cocteau had become a brilliant exponent of the *avant-garde*.

However, although Proust was cool towards Cocteau, this did not prevent him from giving the young man an emerald at some point—he liked to present people with costly gifts in the manner of a *grand seigneur*—and their relations were not improved when Cocteau sent the emerald back. There is no doubt, however, that the young Jean was deeply impressed by meeting him—he was bent on raising himself through knowing the élite—but he also sincerely loved Marcel Proust and was to portray him appreciatively many times, from the first occasion on which he saw him at Madame Daudet's (at this period without a beard, then with a black beard, "he seemed to put it on and take it off again like a comedian in a provincial music-hall"), on the red benches

Jean Cocteau at seventeen (*Private Collection*)

Jean Cocteau and the Comtesse Anna de Noailles, about 1912 (*Private Collection*)

Jean Cocteau in the garden at Offranville, oil painting by Jacques-Emile
Blanche, 1912 (*Rouen museum, photo Ellebé*)

of the Café Larue, where everyone met for supper after the theatre—and again and again until the end of Proust's life. And Proust thought highly enough of Cocteau to send him, as well as Lucien Daudet, a set of proofs of the first chapters of *Du côté de chez Swann*. Both young men at once offered to review the book. Cocteau's article appeared in *Excelsior* in November 1913. Like Daudet he saw *Swann* as a new classic.

> "*Swann* is a gigantic miniature," he wrote, "full of mirages, superimpositions of gardens, plays on space and time, broad cool touches in the style of Manet."

Lucien Daudet also presented Cocteau, during a visit with both their mothers to Cap Martin, to the Empress Eugénie, who had a villa there. This pleased Cocteau inordinately, and although he never became one of her intimate circle, he went from time to time in Paris to pay his respects to the remarkable old lady. Lucien, on the other hand, was to give up all ambition to become a painter or a writer and be the Empress's "*chevalier servant*" until she died in 1920 in her native Madrid.

Another event of importance for Jean Cocteau at this time was the meeting with Princess Bibesco, an intimate member of Marcel Proust's circle, who was to become a life-long friend. Still more important was his introduction to the Comtesse de Noailles and to Edmond Rostand, for with them he entered the special world of poets. He was introduced to Anna de Noailles, as she was leaving some event in her carriage, by the accomplished actress and society figure Madame Simone, the wife of Claude Casimir-Périer, who was the Countess's devoted slave and used to give public recitations of her poetry. It was Madame Simone too who introduced Cocteau to the writer Alain-Fournier.

Jean Cocteau lost his head and his heart at first sight of Madame de Noailles. He called on her constantly, when she would receive him lying on an enormous Louis XV bed.

"Come in, my little Jean," she would say, "here we are among the cretonnes,"

by which she meant the cretonne-covered cork behind which, like Proust, she sheltered herself from noise.

The influence of Anna de Noailles over Cocteau is incalculable; he passed quickly from idolisation to emulation and his poems always retained some echo of her own. He drew her, he described her endlessly; the beauty of her small person and of her adornments, the charm of her voice, of her movements, of her gestures, and the wittiness of her descriptions. She and Jean Cocteau were held together not only by their poetry but by their laughter. He adored laughter. "The ability to burst out laughing," he wrote, "is proof of a fine character." She was also a great talker—Cocteau quotes Baudelaire when writing of her: "Hugo is starting on one of those monologues he calls conversation."

Anna talked, her guests listened and did not interrupt, and everybody was enchanted. So for years Cocteau sat at her feet and tried to write poetry like hers. When people mocked her behind her back he was deeply hurt and resolved only to see her in private. And when many years later she died, he was desolate:

"*Elle est morte. La vie est morte* . . ."

After his own death, he said, he would go to see Anna de Noailles. He would open the door and hear the discursive voice:

You see, my dear, there is nothing afterwards, nothing. You remember . . . I told you so!

And to his eternal joy everything would begin again. The Countess was talking.

The whole Rostand family fascinated Jean Cocteau and he paid frequent visits to their splendid house at Cambo in the Pays

Basque. There was Edmond, famous for his *Cyrano de Bergerac*, his wife and their two sons Maurice, the poet, and Jean, the biologist. It was Maurice, who was Jean's contemporary and also a disciple of the Comtesse de Noailles, who became his particular friend, and with him he shared an entirely new enterprise when, in 1909, with another friend they launched *Schéhérazade*, the first "*revue de luxe*" to be entirely dedicated to poetry and music. In those days one could produce such a magazine quite cheaply and although *Schéhérazade* did not endure for more than a couple of years, it had time to publish a fair number of Cocteau's poems and to win him further recognition.

Another extraordinary character to whom de Max introduced Cocteau was Catulle Mendès, the poet and influential critic who had invited Cocteau to luncheon after his Théâtre Femina success. Cocteau became a regular visitor at the Saturday luncheon parties Catulle Mendès and his wife, a pair of ornate figures, gave at their house in Saint-Germain-en-Laye.

It was at about this time that Jean Cocteau chanced upon the Hôtel Biron, a vast building, once a convent, just off the Boulevard des Invalides, set in a great wilderness of a garden. Here Rodin had his studio and here, unknown to his mother, Cocteau rented a large room at a very modest price. The place was a haven amid the clatter of the city—and here, having decorated the room himself and furnished it with a stove, a piano, a divan, some chairs and packing cases which transformed it into a palace, Cocteau secretly and joyfully entertained his astonished circle of friends—among whom Reynaldo Hahn was a constant visitor. According to Cocteau's own rather fanciful account, which does not quite tally with his cousin Marianne's memories, his hide-out was discovered by accident. Madame Cocteau, he says, was a member of *La Société des Amis du Louvre*, and one day the Society decided to visit the Hôtel Biron. Madame Cocteau was asked if she would obtain her son's permission for the Society to make use of his premises. She replied that neither

of her sons had anything to do with the Hôtel Biron, although
when she found that Jean had a room there she graciously provided cakes and orangeade which were served on the packing
cases, but because of her disapproval he was obliged to give up
the luxury of a *garçonnière* and henceforth content himself with
his room looking on to the courtyard in Avenue Malakoff.

One thing remained, however, to give him satisfaction. Having
heard from the concierge that the magical garden of the Hôtel
Biron was to be destroyed by a road leading to building-lots, he
alerted the press. His friends wrote ardent articles, Ministers
called and were moved almost to tears. As Cocteau put it, fate
had willed that this poetic retreat should be saved by a poet.

Years afterwards Jean Cocteau was to learn that the lamp he
saw burning every night in a window of the Hôtel Biron was
the lamp of Rodin's secretary, Rainer-Maria Rilke. In the arrogance of youth Cocteau had thought that he knew so much, but
of this great poet's proximity he remained unaware.

Nor did I know that one far off day the friendship of R.-M. Rilke
would console me for having seen his lamp shining without understanding that it was signalling to me to approach and burn my wings.

In fact when, in 1926, Rilke died, he was about to translate
*Orphée* into German. "To think of such good fortune," Jean
Cocteau wrote, "what a loss this was to me!"

Perhaps, however, without knowing who owned the lamp
glowing in those enchanted nights, it inspired the young writer,
for Jean Cocteau was to call his first published volume of poems
*La Lampe d'Aladin*.

And now, as if Paris had not enough entertainment of its own,
the "Russian barbarians" arrived. The Comtesse de Greffulhe
and Madame Edwards (later Misia Sert) gave a dinner for
Diaghilev and his company, including Nijinsky and Karsavina,
at the Hôtel Crillon and were astonished to find them such "drab
provincials"; but the moment *Les Ballets Russes* went into action

Paris was captivated. The old Châtelet Theatre, where Cocteau had seen his first shows in childhood, was now altered and re-decorated at Diaghilev's command; the seats were covered in new red plush and potted plants abounded. Workmen, journalists and artists swarmed round the place, among them Jacques-Emile Blanche who was already making portraits of the members of *Les Ballets Russes* and with whom Cocteau was often to stay at Offranville in Normandy, where Blanche painted both him and Madame Cocteau.

The first ballet that Cocteau saw was Fokine's *Le Pavillon d'Armide*, with story and décor by Benois and music by Tcherep-nine. This was not one of Diaghilev's best productions, although it was well received in Paris and given a gala performance at Covent Garden for the Coronation of King George V in 1911; but in any case it was splendid enough—with Karsavina dancing—to give Jean Cocteau one of those shocks dealt him from time to time throughout his life by art and beauty.

"The red curtain rises," he wrote, "on performances instinct with such joy that they will revolutionise France, and ecstatic crowds will follow the chant of Dionysos."

To crown all this brilliance Cocteau now came to know Misia Edwards, that fabulous Polish woman whose beauty, wit and accomplishments—she was among other things a fine pianist—won her the friendship of so many great men of her day. Renoir, Vuillard and Toulouse-Lautrec had all loved and painted her—Cocteau described her as a young beribboned tiger with a soft and cruel face like a pink cat—and the amazing circle of her admirers included Verlaine, Mallarmé, Debussy and Alfred Jarry, who had recently caused a sensation with *Ubu Roi* and certainly influenced Cocteau by his preposterousness. Misia, who was only about four years older than Cocteau, was already nearing the end of her second marriage with the millionaire Alfred Edwards, a man much older than herself who had fought like a madman to get her and then in spite of her fascination had deserted her for a young actress. Misia's first husband, a friend of her childhood, Thadée Natanson and his brother had founded the *Revue Blanche*, an avant-garde magazine devoted to the arts, and she had now fallen deeply in love with the brilliant young Spanish architect and painter José-Maria Sert, who would eventually become her third husband.

Among Misia's countless friends now, when Jean Cocteau met her at *Les Ballets Russes*, were Proust, Vollard—in whose shop Leo and Gertrude Stein had recently discovered Picasso—Lugné-Poë, who had introduced Ibsen and Strindberg to the Paris Theatre, and Sacha Guitry, who called on Misia daily with other theatre friends to try to persuade her to go on the stage. But most exciting of all her new admirers was Serge Diaghilev. It was Sert who had already known him and introduced him to Misia at Prunier's one evening, when she had already been deeply impressed by his production of Boris Godounov in 1908. They became life-long friends and in spite of violent disputes Diaghilev never ceased to ask Misia's advice about anything that he undertook. And she, at her salon on the Quai Voltaire—"bathed", to quote Cocteau, "in green light on one side by the Seine, and in orange light on the other by Bonnard murals"—put him in touch with many French musicians and artists, which contacts were invaluable to Diaghilev, who was determined that *Les Ballets Russes* should not lead an isolated existence in Paris.

Cocteau had been described to Diaghilev by his designer Léon Bakst as a very talented young man and their meeting soon took place in Misia's salon.

"From that moment," Cocteau wrote, "I became a member of the company. From then onwards I saw Nijinsky only from the wings, and from the box where, seated behind Madame Sert, crowned with her Persian aigrette, Diaghilev watched his dancers through minute opera-glasses of mother-of-pearl."★

★ *The Difficulty of Being* (Peter Owen, 1965).

Cocteau described Diaghilev as appearing to wear the smallest hat in the world—because his head was so big—and whose one white lock in his very black dyed hair earned him the nickname of Chinchilla. He also, according to Cocteau, had the smile of a young crocodile with one tooth sticking over his lip, which he chewed as a sign of pleasure or displeasure.

Cocteau's main ambition now was to work with Diaghilev. Characteristically he threw overboard all former enthusiasms and saw Diaghilev as alone blazing the lamp of twentieth-century art.

"Heavens knows that Jean was irresistible at the age of twenty," Misia Sert was to write in her memoirs, "for instance when he started dancing on the tables at Larue's at the supper that always followed a first night . . ."

Proust used often to sit at Larue's, writing, and on this occasion made up a verse ending:

*Jean sauta sur la table auprès de Nijinsky.*

Another of Cocteau's athletic feats was to run along the narrow ledge at the back of Larue's red plush benches to give Proust his overcoat when he was complaining of the draught.

"But it needed more than this of course to claim the right to collaborate with Diaghilev," Misia's memoirs continue. "Jean, whose life is one miraculous chain of successes, soon found out how to set about it."*

It was, however, some time before Diaghilev, surrounded as he was on all sides by talent, found any wide use for Cocteau's gifts, but in response to his urgent requests he gave him the job of designing a poster depicting Karsavina and Nijinsky in *Le Spectre de la Rose*. This was one of the first of Cocteau's drawings to be reproduced and not one of the best, but other posters

* *Two or Three Muses*, by Misia Sert, translated by Moura Budberg (Museum Press, 1953).

followed and also articles in ballet programmes. Cocteau complained that Diaghilev did not seem to rate him as highly as many people did, which made the maestro pronounce his famous injunction to Jeanchik, as he called Cocteau: *"Etonne-moi!"*

This Cocteau was determined to do, and in the meantime he was not idle. He had written quite a number of poems now—much as he adored the merry-go-round of his social life in Paris he sometimes shut himself up at Maisons-Laffitte to work in solitude, or went off to Dieppe with Reynaldo Hahn or to Offranville with Jacques-Emile Blanche where he sometimes visited André Gide who lived close by.

When he was living with his mother, Jean was for the first time in the very heart of Paris, for they had recently moved from Avenue Malakoff to an apartment on the top floor of 10 rue d'Anjou. It had an antiquated lift—dating from the period before lifts were invented, said Cocteau. Sacha Guitry was their next-door neighbour; the young artist-writer and the young actor-writer soon became friends and Cocteau drew a caricature of Guitry to mark his doorbell. Cocteau's room had a little balcony which he loved—it gave him light, an opening to the imagination—and here he entertained his friends. Pictures, portraits and poems were pinned up all over the walls, and near the window stood an architect's table with a sloping board at which Cocteau always worked. Madame Cocteau, who had kept on the house at Maisons-Laffitte that had meant so much to her children, was shortly to sell this property; after this there was no longer a country home.

Another great change had recently taken place in Cocteau's life. His cousin Marianne had married Monsieur Singer, a banker, and although she brought her husband faithfully to Madame Cocteau's weekly dinner parties, which Marthe and Paul also attended, and she and Jean remained on most affectionate terms, he had inevitably lost the close companion of his early years.

As a result of these bouts of work two new volumes of

Cocteau's poems appeared: *Le Prince Frivole*—a title it was only too easy for people to apply to its author—and *La Danse de Sophocle*. The first volume, *La Lampe d'Aladin*, which had appeared the previous year, received scant notice in the press, but with the publication of the further volume by this young dandy, already known in other fields as something of an infant prodigy, the critics decided to acknowledge his talents and deplore his waste of them. The author Georges Duhamel, only five years older than Cocteau himself, wrote that if he had had the poetic gifts, elegance and facility of Monsieur Cocteau, he would have made it a point of honour to jettison all this rubbish. The playwright, Henri Ghéon, wrote a long article in *La Nouvelle Revue Française*, again acknowledging Cocteau's gifts but deploring the misuse of them and the lack of originality—mentioning Anna de Noailles as one of the poets Cocteau had clearly emulated. Ghéon's article was definitely a slate, but to have three pages devoted to his poetry in *La Nouvelle Revue Française*—the leading literary publication which André Gide and later Jacques Rivière edited—was an honour for a young poet. Although Henri Ghéon had written the review, its tone, as Cocteau well knew, had been decided jointly by a group of its distinguished editors, for this was the custom of the *N.R.F.* The chance of this contact was something not to be missed. Cocteau called at the editorial offices, pleaded guilty to the charge of literary frivolity and promised to do better, whereupon the links with the *N.R.F.* were satisfactorily forged.

And now, even if Cocteau did not actually astonish him, he claimed Diaghilev's attention with his first ballet *Le Dieu Bleu*. He wrote the scenario with Frederico de Madrazo, Reynaldo Hahn's nephew, and Reynaldo Hahn composed the music. Fokine did the choreography, Bakst the décor, Diaghilev directed and Nijinsky danced the title rôle with Karsavina as his partner.

Cocteau describes Nijinsky as a very short man with a very long and very thick neck, thick legs and fingers so short that they looked as if they had been cut off at the knuckles—in fact a deformity. But on the stage he was a god:

> His figure lengthened (his heels never touching the ground), his hands became the fluttering leaves of his gestures, and his face . . . was radiant.

*Le Dieu Bleu* was a flop, although it was included in the repertoire of *Les Ballets Russes* for their London season that year. The critic of the *Illustrated London News* was right in criticising Reynaldo Hahn's score, his gentle light music was not suited to the fierce art of the Russians, but in fact it was not only the score that was soft; the whole structure of the ballet lacked the force and fire of the former Diaghilev productions. By now *Petrouchka*, *Prince Igor* and *The Firebird*, to mention only a part of the Russian repertoire, had taken Paris by storm.

Cocteau attributed the failure of his ballet entirely to the music. He now knew many composers, including Debussy, Ravel and all the new young men. But when, in 1913, Stravinsky's *Le Sacre du Printemps* was received by the first-night audience in complete hysteria, Cocteau characteristically put the thought of working with any other musician out of his head. Diaghilev had already said of Stravinsky during the rehearsals of *The Firebird*: "Mark him well. He is a man on the eve of celebrity." Now he had achieved celebrity in a manner after Cocteau's own heart—by creating a riot.

Diaghilev had conceived *Le Sacre du Printemps* as a series of dances depicting earthly joy and celestial triumph as understood by the Slavs, and had engaged Stravinsky and Roerich, as the musician and the artist most familiar with Slavic folk-lore, to create the ballet with him—incidentally Diaghilev was at this time strongly influenced by Gauguin—while Nijinsky, helped by Diaghilev and Madame Rambert, was responsible for much of the choreography.

When the first night came Stravinsky's score maddened the

audience and the critics; it was considered a devilish attempt to destroy music as an art. After a while the orchestra played almost unheard for the hissing, catcalls and fighting in the theatre. And when the performance was over Diaghilev, Nijinsky, Stravinsky and Cocteau drove for the rest of the night around the Bois to calm themselves down.

After this Cocteau haunted Stravinsky as he had formerly haunted Diaghilev. He was not unduly cast down by the failure of his own ballet or the severity of the critics in regard to his poetry. He felt that to have achieved these works was in itself a measure of success, but now he was determined to do something different. He persuaded Diaghilev to commission him to create a ballet based on the story of David and endlessly discussed the subject with Stravinsky who he hoped would compose the music.

This project came to nothing, but Cocteau did now write a book that was not in the least like anything that he had done before. This was *Le Potomak* which, like Proust, Cocteau wrote on anything that was to hand, scraps of paper, backs of envelopes and even his tennis shoes—he always played tennis enthusiastically at Maisons-Laffitte. The book itself is composed of fragments in a variety of styles, prose and verse, without head or tail and with an astonishing medley of prefaces and postscripts. The title implies some kind of edifice resembling the Madeleine, close to which Cocteau and his mother were now living, and the names he uses in the book were suggested by words that took his fancy on old jars in a chemist's shop at Offranville. *Le Potomak* is partly autobiographical, partly critical, and illustrated with caricatures—extraordinary little figures whom Cocteau calls the *Eugènes* and who are reminiscent both of Alfred Jarry's drawings and of popular newspaper cartoons of today. The book is dedicated to Igor Stravinsky and was begun in Jacques-Emile Blanche's house to the sound of Stravinsky's music, and finished at Leysin in Switzerland, where Cocteau joined the composer who had gone there to be near his wife who was ill in a sanatorium.

This was Cocteau's first really original work, in which he became determinedly modern. He jettisoned "tradition" in literature, music, art (including tradition in *Les Ballets Russes*) and was severely critical of the earlier Jean Cocteau and of everyone whom he had then admired, not least of Catulle Mendès whom, as Persicaire, he mocks a little meanly in *Le Potomak*. Later Cocteau was to regret this indiscretion and Catulle Mendès' death by falling on a Paris railway line was a great shock to him.

Jean Cocteau had now taken Henri Ghéon's advice and shed his old skin. He was at last, with all his faults and all his qualities, himself. And of himself he says in *Le Potomak*:

*Je suis parisien, je parle parisien, je prononce parisien.*

The book was finished in March 1914. By August it was already in the printers' hands, but then, in Cocteau's own words: "It slept because of the war."

## CHAPTER IV

## FROM THE THEATRE OF WAR TO
## THE THEATRE OF PARIS

"WHAT luck! Oh God, if only there really is a war!" Misia
Edwards recalled herself as exclaiming when a friend burst into
her apartment, while Erik Satie was playing one of his compositions to Diaghilev, and announced the Sarajevo assassinations.
And so as not to appear too monstrous she went on to describe
the atmosphere of exultation sweeping Paris as war approached,
and the delirious joy of the crowds on the boulevards when it
was finally declared—people singing, laughing, crying and
embracing one another, while every soldier in sight was bedecked
with flowers, *la fleur au fusil*.

This very summer Alfred Edwards had died and Misia would
be able at last to marry José-Maria Sert. She had let her apartment on the Quai Voltaire and gone to live with Sert in a suite
on the top floor of the Hôtel Meurice, which soon became a
centre not only for artists of every kind, but for politicians,
including Briand and Clémenceau, and military chiefs. Before
long Misia had found a way of bringing herself right into the
excitement of the war. The French Red Cross was not yet fully
organised and she obtained permission from General Gallieni
to form a convoy of ambulances to take first-aid to the wounded.
She managed to persuade several *couturiers* to donate their delivery
vans, which would not be needed for their normal purpose during
the war, and when these were converted she had, with her own
large Mercedes, a convoy of fourteen vehicles ready for action.
Finding volunteers to man them proved more difficult, but
among others she was able to recruit Sert, Jean Cocteau, their
friend Paul Iribe, the designer, and one professional nurse.

"My large Mercedes led the convoy," Misia wrote. "Iribe was at the wheel in something resembling a diver's outfit and Jean Cocteau was in a male nurse's costume designed by Poiret."

These preliminaries gave them all a great deal of fun, but as soon as they reached l'Haÿ-les-Roses laughter turned to tears. They came upon a group of untended German prisoners whose wounded faces were black with flies, and the road was littered with dead horses, while fragments of men's and animals' bodies hung in the trees.

Back in Paris, at one of Misia's luncheon parties, General Gallieni held forth on the danger of the situation if transport could not be immediately found to rush fresh troops to the Marne. Somebody suggested taxis and three days later, as Misia's convoy drove to Rheims, in her own words, "we passed at Meaux that glorious and interminable file of small red taxis filled with soldiers who were to strike an unexpected and decisive blow at the enemy".

Cocteau's admiration for Misia had increased tenfold. From the first he had adored her gaiety and her way of attracting amusing and interesting people to her circle, but now he also saw her as a great organiser. She began to take shape in his mind as the Princesse de Bormes, the heroine of the novel *Thomas l'Imposteur* he was to write, based on his war experiences, although in this book he makes Madame de Bormes a good deal older than Misia was at the time.

The appreciation was mutual:

"Jean Cocteau's gaiety, tenderness and wit," Misia wrote, "were precious to me during that time of my ambulances' tumultuous activity. Vitality and good humour were indispensable to compensate for the fatigue, the irritation and the sleepless nights."

At the same time Gide was writing in his *Journal* on 20 August 1914:

Jean Cocteau had arranged to meet me at a *thé anglais* at the corner of the rue de Ponthieu and the avenue d'Antin. I got no pleasure from seeing him again, in spite of his great amiability, for he cannot be serious and all his thoughts, his witticisms, his feelings, all that extraordinary *brio* of his speech shocked me like a piece of luxury displayed in a time of famine and mourning. He is dressed more or less like a soldier and the stimulus of present events has made him look healthier; he hasn't renounced anything, he has simply turned his liveliness towards war.

Nearly forty years later, at the beginning of *Gide Vivant*, Cocteau was to write:

I always seem to be decrying Gide, just as he seems to be decrying me. He likes me so much and I exasperate him. I like him so much and he exasperates me. We are quits. It's this way two people of different outlook and ways of living mislead one another that I find so interesting . . .

The situation when Misia's ambulances reached Rheims was desperate—thousands of wounded lying prostrate on beds of straw, of whom they could only transport a fraction, their task being further complicated by the fact that they were forbidden to drive into Paris except at night, for fear of the demoralising effect the sight of the wounded might have on the public. There were difficulties too with the local authorities who were unwilling to hand over their wounded to this strange organisation, all of which Cocteau retails in *Thomas l'Imposteur* with a horrifyingly vivid description of the wounded, showing how deeply and lastingly he was affected by this experience. He was more serious than Gide and many other people realised.

Between these expeditions to Rheims Cocteau paid two visits to Maurice Barrès at his great house at Neuilly. Now in his early fifties, he was at the height of his literary and political career. His articles in the *Echo de Paris* were fanatically patriotic, extolling the French army and proclaiming the suffering of Alsace-Lorraine and the glorious wounded. Cocteau had hoped to persuade Barrès to use his pen to help Misia Sert's ambulances. The mission failed, but Cocteau continued to admire and slightly envy this writer. Later he wrote an account, *Visites à Maurice Barrès*, in which he criticised the latter for sacrificing himself to his theories and for not realising that "the sincerity of each moment", even when offering apparent contradictions, was truer than any rigid consistency.

Without question, in these early months of the war Cocteau was obsessed by its horror. He made symbolic drawings of German atrocities: *les Eugènes de la Guerre*, and he tried to make Gide, among others, aware that children were being mutilated by the Germans.

On one of their frequent returns from Rheims, Misia was anxious to show General Gallieni that they had all been unharmed by their venture. To her consternation Cocteau arrived at her luncheon party on crutches. He had dislocated his hip among the rubble at Rheims, although Misia had not realised at the time how badly hurt he was. According to her account, Sert was furious and suspected Cocteau of trying to attract attention—"one must admit he was scarcely more than a child and always ready for a joke". Which reminds one of Cocteau's exclamation one night as the sirens wailed: "Someone's trodden on the Eiffel Tower's toe and it's complaining!"

The strange adventure with Misia's ambulances did not last long, for after a few months she tired of this enterprise and presented her fourteen vehicles to the Empress of Russia.

Meanwhile another of the "shocks" had occurred that was to fire Cocteau's imagination. This was the experience of flying. He had come to know the air-ace Roland Garros, already internationally famous for his flying feats. Garros was a fine-looking man with a big moustache and hairy hands, who was a great lover of music, and Cocteau was fascinated by him.

After fighting in Eastern France late in 1914, Garros had been

Jean Cocteau by Picasso, 1916 (*Collection Jean Marais*)

Jean Cocteau with Picasso in Rome, 1917 (*Private Collection*)

sent to Villacoublay to advise on the air defence of Paris. During this period he several times took Cocteau up with him and performed what seemed to the novice extraordinary acrobatic feats. Cocteau at once shared his new friend's enthusiasm for the conquest of the air and he was also thrilled by the look of Paris and the countryside from above. Before long Cocteau introduced Roland Garros to Misia who at once made him a member of her motley circle. In the evening he would come back to her apartment to dine with her friends and to sleep under the piano while she played to him.

It was on these flights with Garros that Cocteau conceived the theme of the angel which was to appear so often in his work, and his next volume of poems, *Le Cap de Bonne-Espérance*, was inspired by this experience of flying and dedicated to Roland Garros, who in 1915 was shot down in the German lines and taken prisoner. The poem *L'Invitation à la mort* includes this passage:

> De ta main d'ours Garros
> alors
> tu me signales quelque chose
>
> et je me suis penché au bord du gouffre
> et j'ai vu Paris sur la terre
>
> et plus humble ma ville
> à sa mesure
> déserte d'hommes
> faible seule sa Seine en jade
> et plus je la regardais décroître
> et plus je sentais croître mon triste amour . . .

Meanwhile Cocteau had embarked on the second and more bizarre part of his war activities. Count Etienne de Beaumont, an immensely wealthy friend of Misia's, had also organised an ambulance unit—very different from hers—with the most luxurious of vehicles, one of which was even fitted out with an

X-ray apparatus. Etienne de Beaumont's convoy was detailed for Belgium, and Cocteau readily accepted his invitation to join it, although this did not prevent him, any more than had his former expedition with Misia, from spending a great deal of time in Paris. He even continued his experience as an editor by bringing out, with Paul Iribe, the journal *Le Mot*. Twenty numbers of this magazine appeared, with poems and articles, sometimes anonymous, by Cocteau and his friends, quotations from Nietzsche, about whom they were enthusiastic at this moment, and illustrations by Paul Iribe and Cocteau, the latter's being signed "Jim", the name of Cocteau's dog which he was now using as his pseudonym.

He arrived with the ambulance corps in Nieuport, which place he describes vividly in *Thomas l'Imposteur*. In this story the young hero creates his own rôle by posing as the nephew of a famous general, a theme Cocteau developed from a true incident. Cocteau did not himself actually impersonate anybody else, yet this part of his adventure was based on a kind of deception, inasmuch as he found himself quite without authority among a company of Fusiliers Marins who adopted him as a sort of mascot.

In one of his letters to Misia Sert—Cocteau wrote to her almost every day from Nieuport—he said:

> How can I describe to you the strangeness of this bleak camp where hangars fly away like aeroplanes, explosives fall with a loud miaow like great ferocious cats of the type of M. Sert; and one passes from absolute calm to an apocalypse, and from the apocalypse to champagne?

It was a strange period indeed. These marines were a most distinguished company, among them being the Princes Xavier and Sixte de Bourbon-Parme and their lives appear to have been quite fantastic. For several months Cocteau continued to live in their midst, to wear their uniform and to share their pleasures, their perils and their eccentricities. "I had the good fortune to live with the marines," he later wrote. "An incredible freedom of thought prevailed among them."

This adventure ended as strangely as it had begun, just after, so it is said, Cocteau had been recommended for the *croix de guerre*. An inspection by a senior officer revealed that Cocteau's presence there was illegal. He was arrested, but managed to evade his guards, and while his friends, convinced that he would be put in prison, were lamenting his fate, Jean Cocteau had by some fluke come across a car carrying a general who recognised him, and was entering Dunkerque in triumph.

Scarcely a day had passed before the greater number of these marines were killed in a sudden enemy attack, and so later was Jean Leroy, the young poet, one of Cocteau's dearest friends whose poems he later managed to get published. The whole event moved him deeply, inspiring him to write *Adieu aux Fusiliers Marins*, a beautiful poem ending:

*Adieu marins, naïfs adorateurs du vent.*

This whole episode is more like one of Jean Cocteau's fantasies than real life. During his war experiences he seems to have left his own personality on one side and assumed various rôles—he did not actually lie himself in order to remain with the Fusiliers-Marins, but a lie somehow happened to him and led almost to his death. *Thomas l'Imposteur* in fact ends with the young hero being killed—a death that Cocteau invented and grieved over.

On his final return to 10 rue d'Anjou Cocteau found that the widowed Madame de Chevigné—the origin of Proust's Duchesse de Guermantes—was living in the same house. George D. Painter, tells a number of picturesque anecdotes of this time:

When Cocteau hugged her lapdog Kiss on the stairs, and the Countess shouted: "Look out! I don't want him smothered in your face-powder!" they became friends . . .*

* *Marcel Proust*, Vol. 2 (Chatto & Windus, 1965).

In August Proust called on them both and Jean found him sitting at
midnight in the darkness on the top landing. "Why didn't you wait
in my room, Marcel? You know I always leave the door ajar!"
"Dear Jean," replied Marcel, "Napoleon had a man shot for waiting
in his room."

On a later occasion Proust lamented to Cocteau:

"When I was twenty she refused to love me. Will she refuse to read
me now that I am forty?"
    "Fabre wrote a book about insects," Cocteau replied, "but he did
not expect the insects to read it."

This return marked the end of Cocteau's participation in the
war and his mind turned again wholly towards the arts, but he
still mourned the death of his friends. Alain-Fournier, the author
of the novel *Le Grand Meaulnes*, was another loved member of
the circle who had mysteriously disappeared for ever. The
theme of death would now always haunt Cocteau's work and
very poignantly he wrote, in the early prose-poem *Visite*, which
strangely calls to mind the *Tibetan Book of the Dead*:

*J'ai une grande nouvelle triste à t'annoncer: je suis mort.*

As Cocteau threw himself once more into the arms of Paris
without any further curious escapades, he found the artistic life
of the city no longer dominated by *Les Ballets Russes*. This was
not so much because of the war (for Paris still resounded with
dance and music, and theatres and restaurants were packed to
overflowing), as because Nijinsky's sudden marriage in 1915
had deeply upset Diaghilev and caused Nijinsky to leave the
company. At his wife's instigation he started a troupe of his own
and she persuaded him for "reasons of propriety" not to go back
to Diaghilev, although Nijinsky assured her that he would never
regret his relationship with the great impresario who had made
him what he was. Diaghilev went hither and thither, to Italy and

Spain and Russia, and although he still produced a few ballets in Paris his great seasons there were for the moment over.

It was natural therefore that Cocteau should turn to new enthusiasms, and the friend who played the largest part in these was Valentine Gross. He had met her at the theatre and at *Les Ballets Russes*, where she had been making drawings of the dancers, and he now set about cultivating her society. She was extremely beautiful, besides being brilliant, and she knew everyone including Picasso, the painters of Montparnasse and Erik Satie, whose music she performed on the piano for her own pleasure, so Cocteau saw in her not only a glamorous young woman, but somebody who would be of great use to him in climbing the ladder of the *avant-garde*. Valentine Gross had not liked *Le Dieu Bleu* and she was not sure at first if she liked its creator either, but he relentlessly pursued her and after a while she succumbed to his charm. Indeed, although it is doubtful if Valentine Gross ever really intended to marry him, Cocteau did present her to his mother, letting it be understood that she was his fiancée, and this time Madame Cocteau was delighted at the prospect of such a match, for not only was Valentine comely and rich, but she came of a very good family, as befitted one who was later to marry Victor Hugo's grandson, Cocteau's friend the artist Jean Hugo.

It was in this period that Cocteau became enthusiastic about the group of young musicians, *Les Nouveaux Jeunes*, who were soon to achieve fame as "*Les Six*",* and for whom to quote one of them—the brilliant composer Francis Poulenc—Cocteau was to become "a promoter of genius, a faithful and exquisite friend . . . our poetic chronicler".

The master around whom these young musicians revolved was Erik Satie, who was approaching fifty and whose close association with Debussy was on the wane. Cocteau always said

* Les Six: Georges Auric, Louis Durey, Arthur Honegger, Germaine Tailleferre, Darius Milhaud, Francis Poulenc.

that it was through Debussy and Ravel that he met Satie, but it was in fact Valentine Gross who introduced him to the "Hermit of Arcueil" as Satie was called, since nobody was ever allowed to set foot in his mysterious retreat in that little suburb of Paris, Arcueil. He was a familiar sight as he walked about Paris in his grey velvet clothes (which earned him the further nickname: "The Velvet Gentleman"), topped by a *melon* and always carrying an umbrella. Cocteau was to write of him:

> Another poet whom the angels guide, cherish and torment is Erik Satie, who walks every night from Montmartre or Montparnasse to his home in Arcueil-Cachan—a miracle which cannot be explained unless the angels carry him . . .*

When Satie and Cocteau first met, the latter had been making an adaptation of *A Midsummer Night's Dream*, from translations as he knew very little English. He invited Satie to write incidental music, but this project was not realised. Soon afterwards, however, Cocteau heard the *Morceaux en Forme de Poire* which made him more determined to collaborate with Satie.

Cocteau had also now met Picasso through Valentine Gross—he spoke of this event as "the meeting of my life". He went to Picasso's studio overlooking the Montmartre cemetery, shortly before the latter moved to Montrouge, and was overwhelmed both by the man—Picasso was then in his mid-thirties—and by the artist. After this Cocteau consorted with all these young painters—Braque, Juan Gris, Modigliani. The latter at once painted a portrait of Cocteau, who in his turn made drawings of them all. The young poets were part of the Montparnasse circle too, among them Guillaume Apollinaire, Blaise Cendrars and Max Jacob, who became one of Cocteau's most devoted friends. All these painters and writers, including the young novelist François Mauriac, who was also painted by Jacques-Emile Blanche as a *jeune homme précieux*, were symbols of the future

* *The Difficulty of Being.*

for Cocteau and once again he forgot the past and turned his dynamic attention towards what appeared to him to be the only true *avant-garde*. Other painters and writers went overboard and, where music was concerned, Cocteau dethroned Stravinsky and put Erik Satie in his place.

Although Satie was now called by his admirers the "Prince of Musicians", his work was not yet well known in Paris, and it fell to Jean Cocteau's happy lot to interest Diaghilev in both him and in Picasso and so bring fame to Satie, a new chapter to *Les Ballets Russes* and another fine leap of inspiration for himself. Erik Satie and Diaghilev both prided themselves in having a gift for spotting talent, so Satie was well pleased with the young Cocteau and Diaghilev was interested in the prospect of adding the French composer and the Spanish artist to his court of geniuses. His outlook was becoming more international and before long he had agreed to produce a ballet written by Cocteau with Picasso and Satie as his collaborators.

Gertrude Stein, another famous Paris figure whose writings Cocteau admired, wrote at this time:

One day Picasso came in and with him and leaning on his shoulder was a slim elegant youth. It is Jean, announced Pablo, Jean Cocteau, and we are leaving for Italy.

Picasso had been excited at the prospect of doing the scenery for a Russian ballet, the music to be by Satie, the drama by Jean Cocteau . . .

The creation of *Parade*, however, was fraught with difficulties. Cocteau wanted to—and indeed did—write dialogue for it, whereupon Satie refused to write the music, insisting that the ballet was to be a *parade* without words, such as is presented before a booth at a fair. Satie won his point, but meanwhile Diaghilev declared that he would not undertake the production.

Cocteau then urged Valentine Gross to induce Misia Sert to use her influence with Diaghilev and in the end agreement was

reached. Cocteau and Picasso went off to join Diaghilev, first in
Rome and then in Naples, and begin their work on *Parade*, while
Satie remained at Arcueil writing his score.

> "Picasso amazes me more and more every day," Cocteau wrote to
> Misia Sert while this work was going on. "To live beside him sets
> one an example of hard work and nobility."

And Satie wrote to her:

> I am working on a thing that I propose to show you very soon and
> which is dedicated to you while I think of it and while I write it.

This "thing" was the score for *Parade* which had sounds in it
that Cocteau, on the analogy of "*trompe-l'oeil*" called "*trompe-
l'oreille*".

In the winter of 1916 Cocteau and Picasso returned with
Diaghilev to join Satie in Paris and they finished *Parade* together.
The choreography was entrusted to Massine, the beautiful young
dancer who had now taken Nijinsky's place in Diaghilev's
company and in his heart.

> "Massine's 'finds' in *Parade*," Serge Lifar was to write in his life of
> Diaghilev, "derive directly from Cocteau, as does its literariness and
> circus stylisation. The time had come for literature too to have its
> say in the ballet, since painting and music had each had their turn.
> All this, which is now the usual currency of the ballet, was invented
> by Cocteau for *Parade*, every *pas* of which he suggested and knew by
> heart."

So, in 1917, once again *Les Ballets Russes* produced a scandal—
people even called its creators "*Les Boches*", and Cocteau said
that only Guillaume Apollinaire's bandaged head prevented them
from all being lynched on the first night. This reaction was due
not only to Cocteau's daring conception, Satie's new "noises"
and Picasso's bizarre cubist décor, which incidentally delighted
Marcel Proust, but because when the ballet was produced the

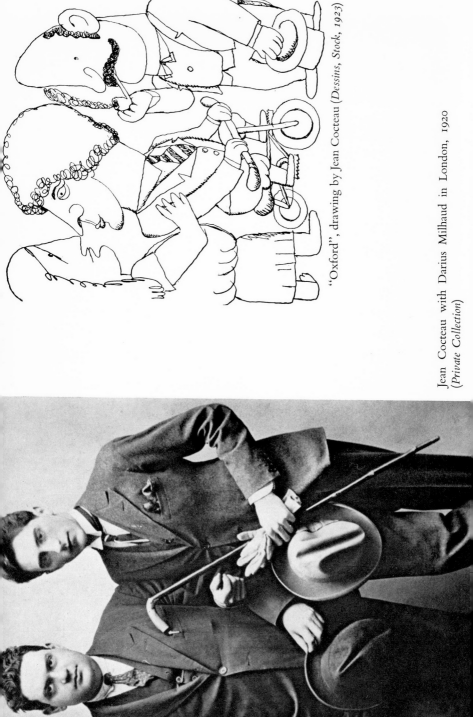

"Oxford", drawing by Jean Cocteau (*Dessins, Stock, 1923*)

Jean Cocteau with Darius Milhaud in London, 1920
(*Private Collection*)

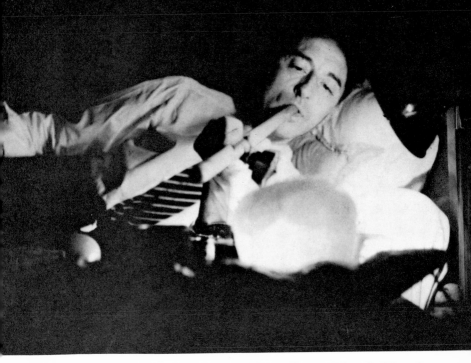

Jean Cocteau smoking opium at the Hôtel de Castille, 1929 (*photo Cecil Beaton*)

*Le Sang d'un Poète: La Cité Monthiers*, film by Jean Cocteau (*photo Sacha Masour*)

war was at a critical phase and many people, including the critics, were shocked at this frivolous display in the theatre of Paris, when in the theatre of war men were still dying in their thousands. With this ballet Cocteau had obeyed Diaghilev's injunction "*Etonne-moi*", but although the scandal enchanted Cocteau, it did not please the impresario nor improve his business. Nevertheless in bringing cubism, the most modern music and his own original conceptions into the ballet, Cocteau had done an incomparable service to this art.

It was Guillaume Apollinaire who more than anyone else converted the Paris public to *Parade*.

"It is a scenic poem," he wrote in his programme article entitled "Parade and the New Spirit", "for which Erik Satie has written the music . . . music which it would be impossible not to recognise as the pure transparent air of our France.

The cubist painter, Picasso, and the most audacious of choreographers, Massine, has made that music concrete, by bringing about for the first time, that union of painting and dancing, of plastic form and miming, which establishes the precursive signs of a yet completer art . . .

This new union . . . gives to *Parade* a semblance of surrealism, in which I see the beginning of that New Spirit which, having now found an opportunity of expressing itself, cannot fail to tempt the elect, or radically change the arts and customs of humanity, since reason demands that they must at least keep pace with scientific and industrial progress . . ."

But the poet Guillaume Apollinaire, to whom *Parade* owed so much, was himself a victim of the war. "I knew him in a pale blue uniform," Cocteau was to write, "one temple marked by a scar like a starfish," and go on to describe with great appreciation Apollinaire's fatness, his laughter, his modesty and his incomparable gift of words.

As the group *Les Six*, with Cocteau's indefatigable aid, gained recognition, he began to write a short guide-book to the arts, and particularly to music, in the light of his present enthusiasms.

C

This volume, *Le Coq et l'Arlequin*, was dedicated to Georges Auric but, to quote Poulenc once more, the musical part of it was less a manifesto for *Les Six* than a eulogy of Satie's *esthétique* as compared with that of the pre-war composers, including Debussy, Ravel, Stravinsky—and of course Wagner. It also condemns the stupidity of the public.

In the preface to *Le Coq et l'Arlequin* Cocteau explained how, much as he admired Cézanne's and Picasso's harlequins, he disliked Harlequin himself with his coat of many colours and his deceitful ways, but adored the brilliant, parading bird (which said Cocteau twice over):

> *Vive le Coq! A bas l'Arlequin!*

The early part of the book consists of a number of characteristic aphorisms, the first one being: "Art is science made flesh," another: "One must be a living man and a posthumous artist," and the last: "What does the canvas on which a masterpiece is being painted think about it? 'They're dirtying me. They're misusing me. They're hiding me.' Thus man decries his free destiny."

The rest of the book consists of fragments discussing *Les Ballets Russes*, with a eulogy of Nijinsky and a description of the making of *Parade*. In another of his pronouncements Cocteau rather surprisingly extolled simplicity, naming Satie as its exponent:

> A poet always has too many words in his vocabulary, a painter too many colours on his palette, a musician too many notes on his keyboard.

*Le Coq et l'Arlequin* was published in 1918 and André Gide wrote a letter to Cocteau that was published in *La Nouvelle Revue Française*. He said that he thought Cocteau had little to gain by trying to paint in few colours, as he was at his most poetic when he let himself go. Gide's comments were on the whole unfavourable, although as usual he paid tribute to Cocteau's gifts. Cocteau surmised that Gide was jealous of his success and wrote a reply to his letter which the *N.R.F.* refused to print.

Stravinsky too was somewhat vexed at Cocteau's way of dismissing his former enthusiasms in favour of his new ones and a breach developed between him and Cocteau which took a long time to heal. Diaghilev, on the other hand, was impressed with the book and more than ever now made use of French artists and composers in his ballets.

So in a frenzy of triumph the war drew to a close. The heroes returned—among them Jean Cocteau's brother Paul, covered with decorations—but the death of another hero brought grief to the circle of friends. In February 1918 Roland Garros had made a fantastic escape from his German prison. He was received with high honours and offered a post in the Ministry of War, but he insisted on continuing his war service.

Death of Thomas

"Do what you can to stop Garros," Cocteau wrote to Misia. "Tell him that we shall need heroes just as much in peace-time."

But Garros took no heed and was shot down and killed in a battle near Vouziers in October 1918. In the cabin of his plane was found a proof copy of *Le Cap de Bonne-Espérance*.

Jean Cocteau mourned the death of Garros deeply and then on 11 November, the morning of the 1918 armistice, came another blow. Picasso and Max Jacob went together to rue d'Anjou to tell Cocteau that Guillaume Apollinaire was dangerously ill. The fat had developed round his heart and that same night he died.

The theatre of war was closed, but for Jean Cocteau the theatre of Paris was wide open.

CHAPTER V

## ON LOAN

"THERE'S a little boy with a cane here to see you, Monsieur Jean," said the valet at 10 rue d'Anjou one summer's day in 1919, and Jean Cocteau went eagerly to greet his guest.

He had met Raymond Radiguet the Sunday before, 8 June, at the gallery of Léonce Rosenberg, where a *matinée poétique* had been given in memory of Guillaume Apollinaire. Raymond Radiguet, who was then sixteen years old, had been one of the readers of Apollinaire's poems. It was an important occasion, not only for the young poets gathered in homage, but also for the musicians, for a performance was given of Apollinaire's *Le Bestiaire ou Cortège d'Orphée*, set to music by Poulenc, the first time this young composer's work had been heard in public.

Years later Cocteau wrote in *La Difficulté d'Etre*:

At my very first meeting with Raymond Radiguet I may say that I guessed his star quality. How? You may well ask. He was small, pale, short-sighted, his badly cut hair hanging round his collar and giving him side-whiskers. He puckered up his face as if in the sun. He skipped as he walked. It was as if for him the pavements were made of rubber. He pulled little pages of copy-books out of his pockets which he screwed into a ball. He smoothed them out with the palm of his hand, and hampered by one of the cigarettes he rolled himself, tried to read a very short poem. He glued it to his eye.

Jean Hugo described the sixteen-year-old poet on this occasion as wearing a big winter overcoat in spite of the sweltering heat. He had, according to another description:

The profile of a Hindu, full lips, narrow, almond-shaped eyes and strongly marked eyebrows which made him look like one of

Hugo's pipes which one day later on he smoked, observing merrily:
"I am smoking myself!"

He really did look like a little boy and from the beginning
Jean Cocteau called him *"Bébé"* or *"Monsieur Bébé"*, while
everyone else addressed him as "Radiguet". He was one of seven
children living at Saint-Maur with their parents of modest means
and background. His father, in fact, earned a precarious living,
drawing comic illustrations for newspapers. Young Raymond
had come to Paris for the first time, still wearing knickerbockers,
to sell some of his father's drawings to André Salmon for
*l'Intransigeant*. On a later visit Raymond shyly offered André
Salmon some drawings of his own, signed "Rajki", which were
published on the front page of *l'Intransigeant*. Radiguet then
confessed to Salmon that he also wrote poetry and Salmon
gave him an introduction to Max Jacob. Radiguet now asked
if he might join the staff of *l'Intransigeant* and there being no
vacancy Salmon found him a place on *l'Heure*. Radiguet therefore donned long trousers and spent most of his free time at
the Café du Croissant, much frequented by journalists. It was
here that he used often to meet Marthe, who was to become
the model for his novel *Le Diable au Corps*—all his short life he
was passionately attached to women. Within a short time he
was taken up by writers, artists and musicians and particularly
liked and respected Georges Auric, although he understood little
of music. Max Jacob had even shown his first poems to Guillaume
Apollinaire, but in view of Radiguet's extreme youth, Apollinaire
had refused to take Jacob's enthusiasm seriously.

André Breton, lately demobilised, was one of the artists greatly
taken by the young poet and they were seen everywhere together,
which may have been the reason why Radiguet did not become
a member of Cocteau's intimate circle at an earlier date. Breton
was strongly under the influence of dadaism, born the year
before in Zurich; Cocteau too participated in certain dada

manifestations and allied himself with Picabia—all of them, Radiguet too, were searching for a new form of expression; but Radiguet was to turn against the *avant-garde* while Breton would plunge into surrealism, and although the latter shared with Cocteau many revolutionary ideas, they were to remain for ever hostile to one another.

It was in 1919 too that Cocteau's volume of poems *Le Cap de Bonne-Espérance*, dedicated to Roland Garros, appeared, exquisitely printed by *Editions de la Sirène*, a firm founded by Cocteau and his friend Blaise Cendrars. Cocteau was always concerned with the actual production of his work and took great pains over its appearance, often giving a plastic form to his poems, as in his *Ode à Picasso*, written at this time. The firm also produced a small poster, with a little siren designed by Jean Hugo, for circulation among the bookshops—then an entirely new form of publicity. This was an early sign of the sense of publicity Cocteau was steadily to develop and often to use in the service of his friends. He realised, of course, that the scandals that so often greeted the first appearance of his own works, particularly in the theatre, were excellent advertisements.

Adrienne Monnier gave a lively and revealing account of Cocteau reading from this volume at her bookshop:

God knows I'm fond of Cocteau and I admire him too, now even more than ever. He is such a spoilt child! He's a poet without any doubt, more in prose than in verse in my opinion. In prose his highly individual style has an alluring false virginity, whereas in verse his tricks, reinforced by the essential trickery of verse, become maddening. For my part he gives me a migraine. I may be unfair but at the moment when one has a migraine it is difficult to be fair.

She also stressed how marvellously Cocteau read "in his famous metallic voice that acts as a megaphone", and she laughed at him for throwing himself so eagerly into the *avant-garde*, "he is never the first into the breach, but always the one to plant

the flag", and for the little tricks he played to get into the limelight. On this occasion he had said to Adrienne Monnier: "Gide
would like me to read Le Cap at rue de l'Odéon" (her bookshop). And to Gide he said: "Adrienne Monnier would like me
to read Le Cap at rue de l'Odéon in your presence. You will
come, won't you?" When they both found how they had been
tricked, Adrienne Monnier made Cocteau pay for his naughtiness
by providing the cakes for the occasion. He was indeed spoilt,
loved and laughed at.

Valentine Gross and Jean Hugo, who were to be married a few
weeks later, were also present at this reading, Jean Hugo in
uniform on leave from the Army of Occupation in Germany.
André Breton and Philippe Soupault were there too, "bristling
with hostility", and certain fashionable women acclaiming
Cocteau's genius increased Breton's fury.

"The war with the future surrealists had begun," wrote Adrienne
Monnier. "It was to be a long one."

At the end of the reading, she went on to relate, Jean Cocteau,
who would have liked to please the literary Left besides the Right,
tried to win over Breton by explaining to him at great length that
Le Cap was out of date, that it was old stuff "like Victor Hugo"
and that together they would revolutionise literature. He failed
to convince Breton, however, who remained hostile. As the
years passed the gulf between them widened.

Cocteau was also now enjoying a wide audience for his Carte
Blanche, a series of modish articles in the journal Paris-Midi, so
called, of course, because the editor gave Cocteau carte blanche
to write what he chose. His intention was to make the reader
au courant with the newest developments in the world of the arts,
for the public was unaware, he declared, of anything between
the two poles of the Académie and the Boulevard. So he wrote
happily of Dufy, Derain and Marie Laurencin, of Max Jacob
and Adrienne Monnier, of Auric and Poulenc, of Mistinguett

and Charlie Chaplin (Cocteau was in fact one of the creators of film criticism), and everyone else who was claiming his attention—including of course himself, whom he never forgot. Cocteau described at length in *Carte Blanche* the recitals of poetry and music in the small room in rue Huyghens and the Barbazange Gallery, where in spite of the discomfort—one could not sit down—lovers of the contemporary arts came to hear Pierre Bertin singing the young musicians' songs and Marcel Herrand reciting the work of the young poets. Jean Cocteau was the moving spirit of these seances and to him they owed their publicity. His taste for the sensational and for novelty led him one day to do a reading himself of the poems of that very young boy—Raymond Radiguet—some of whose work Max Jacob was having published.

It was not long before Raymond Radiguet was drawn into Jean Cocteau's circle—a very Right-bank circle what with the Daudets and the Hugos, who now lived in the Palais-Royal, where Cocteau himself would live later, Madame de Chevigné and the exquisite and brilliant young writer and diplomat Paul Morand, who was to become such a friend of Marcel Proust's. In fact Cocteau was now surrounded by wealthy and elegant people and as always he mirrored the society in which he was moving. Even Raymond Radiguet became after a while something of a dandy, affecting for the last part of his short life a well-groomed head, a bow-tie and a monocle. "Coco" Chanel, now internationally famous, was also a friend of Cocteau's, and his favourite rendezvous with his set became the bar Le Gaya in rue Duphot.

It was Darius Milhaud who said to Cocteau that they must find a bar in which they could all meet, and he led him to the tiny Le Gaya where they were received by the jovial patron. In the dimness a pianist was playing American jazz and the patron said to Cocteau: "I shall have to sack my pianist; my clients don't like him." Quickly Cocteau replied: "Keep your pianist and sack your clients." From this moment Le Gaya became the headquarters of these young people and the pianist, Jean Wiener, the first real exponent of American jazz, who was to become famous as a composer of music for films, continued to play for them. Sometimes Cocteau sat beside him and played the percussion himself. Word went round that Jean Cocteau was running the bar and his reputation for eccentricity increased; of this his enemies made great play.

Raymond Radiguet was Cocteau's constant companion now; in a way he revived the myth of Dargelos. They spent the evenings in cafés, at fairs or the circus, at the Folies Bergère or the cinema, at parties, in Le Gaya, often in the company of the Hugos, Paul Morand and Lucien Daudet. The La Bastille station, from which Radiguet had to leave for Saint-Maur, was far from the centre of Paris and Radiguet often missed the last train. Sometimes on these occasions he stayed the night at 10 rue d'Anjou, but after a while Madame Cocteau demurred. She did not approve of her son's latest infatuation—to begin with Radiguet's lack of breeding displeased her, and also whenever Jean became wholly absorbed in another person she was somewhat jealous, as this inevitably meant a lessening of his attention towards herself. Indeed when they first met, Cocteau himself had been slightly disconcerted by Radiguet's commonness, but soon this simply became an added fascination in his beloved "Monsieur Bébé". On other occasions Radiguet would sleep at some artist's among the tubes of paint and brushes, or he would go back to Saint-Maur on foot and be childishly frightened, as he walked through the dark wood, by the roaring of the lions in the zoo.

Sometimes now the Hugos invited Radiguet to stay with them; at other times he spent the nights, often with some young girl, in Montmartre or at his room in the little Hôtel Foyot on the Left Bank. Each afternoon he joined Cocteau in the rue d'Anjou where they liked to sit and talk on the small balcony—keeping late nights, neither of them ever rose early. Cocteau complained to his cousin Marianne that Radiguet made a wild disorder in his rooms and effectively stopped any work being done, but he would forgive his Monsieur Bébé anything. In any case in those first months there was little time for work; life was so delightfully distracting.

After a while, for in spite of their frivolity they were both highly creative, the urge to work returned. Indeed Cocteau was determined that Radiguet should go on writing, for he sincerely believed in his genius.

"The only honour that I claim," he was to write in his preface to his young friend's posthumous novel *Le Bal du Comte d'Orgel*, "is to have given to Raymond Radiguet during his lifetime the illustrious place accorded to him after his death."

Through the character of François in this novel Radiguet voiced his own vexation at being considered an infant prodigy. He was, naturally, always being compared with Rimbaud. "Nothing could be more untrue than to call him precocious," wrote Radiguet of François. "In fact François was just his own age, but in spite of his youth and idleness he was well thought of by men of distinction older than himself."

Radiguet was not only well thought of by his elders—he was fourteen years younger than Cocteau—but he influenced them profoundly, although he did also make use of certain of their ideas, such as fragments of *Le Coq et l'Arlequin*.

"He gave ancient formulas back their youth," wrote Cocteau. "He rubbed down banalities. He cleaned up the commonplace."

But Radiguet extolled the commonplace too, decrying the *avant-garde*—he particularly disliked the work of Alfred Jarry—reading old masterpieces and begging his friends to "write like everybody else" so that originality might come of its own accord. "He taught me not to lean on anything," Cocteau declared. Also, once Radiguet really started working, he set his friends an example of great industry—he was living against time. "I burn the candle at both ends," says the young hero of his novel *Le Diable au Corps*, "like people who are bound to die young."

In 1920, before Radiguet started to write novels, he, Cocteau and Poulenc worked together on a one-act comic-opera *Le Gendarme Incompris* which was produced the following year, and then on an opera based on *Paul et Virginie*, the popular eighteenth-century novel by Bernadin de Saint-Pierre which, according to Larousse, started *"le genre exotique"* in France. Radiguet also encouraged Cocteau to read Madame de la Fayette's *La Princesse de Clèves* and *Adolphe* by Benjamin Constant; there was no end to their enthusiasms, and even if some of them came to nothing they culminated for Cocteau in a brilliant inspiration for a new ballet.

For this, his third ballet, the chosen musician was another member of *Les Six*, Darius Milhaud, who had already composed a fantasia called *Le Boeuf sur le Toit* after a Brazilian folk-song, which he thought might serve as a gay accompaniment to one of Chaplin's films. But as soon as Cocteau heard the music he demanded it for the live theatre and began to devise a ballet-farce, inviting Raoul Dufy to do the décor and the Fratellini to take the leading parts. Now he had the joy of actually working with the clowns whom he had adored since childhood. This time there was no Diaghilev and Cocteau was not only his own author-choreographer, inventing movements true to his concept rather than rhythmically suggested by the music, but also his own director and producer. He successfully raised the backing for the show himself, starting off by an appeal to Comte Etienne de Beaumont. What more could he want?

The sub-title of Cocteau's *Le Boeuf sur le Toit* was *The Nothing-Doing Bar*; the scene showed an American bar and the characters included a Barman, several Negroes, a Décolleté Lady and a Policeman who was temporarily decapitated by a giant electric fan. Besides organising his own contribution, Cocteau was responsible for the whole of this *Premier Spectacle-Concert* at the

Comédie des Champs-Elysées in February 1920, of which *Le Boeuf* formed a part. There was also music by Poulenc, Auric and Satie, in addition to various other turns.

After the scandal of *Parade* Cocteau was nervous about the reception of *Le Boeuf sur le Toit*, but it was well attended and well received, although Gide, it is true, dismissed it as of little importance:

"An American farce by a Parisian who has never been to America."

Paul Morand, on the other hand, reviewed the Spectacle-Concert enthusiastically in *La Nouvelle Revue Française*, praising Cocteau's support of *Les Six* and mentioning Radiguet's eager participation which led to him becoming co-editor with Cocteau of *Le Coq*. The first number of this review appeared in May and three further numbers were to be published before the end of the year, containing contributions by Cocteau, Radiguet, Paul Morand and Lucien Daudet, drawings by de La Fresnaye and compositions by Satie and *Les Six*, the review thus reflecting the whole atmosphere of this circle of friends, including Max Jacob and the Hugos, who met every Saturday evening for dinner in Montmartre or la place de la Madeleine. The tone was in general one of anti-dadaism, indeed Cocteau declared himself anti all "isms", but he was none the less prepared to support any individual, except Breton, who showed talent whatever "ism" he professed.

At these dinners new ideas were discussed, new programmes prepared and new poems recited—Radiguet was at this time writing a great deal of poetry. Sometimes, instead of dining out, the friends were invited to Paul Morand's house where the parties became more conventional. These used to remind Cocteau of the gatherings at his grandfather Lecomte's—but presently they ceased.

In July of this same year 1920 *Le Boeuf*, under its sub-title of *The Nothing-Doing Bar*, was presented at the London Coliseum,

with an English cast. In the same programme, among its usual
variety of comedians and acrobats, both Grock and Ruth Draper
appeared. Cocteau and Milhaud went over to superintend the
rehearsals—the first time that Cocteau had ever been in England.
He and Milhaud were disappointed by the production and found
the orchestra defeated by the modernity of the score. Nor were
the critics enthusiastic about the show.

Cocteau and Milhaud stayed at the Carlton Hotel, whence
Cocteau despatched two postcards of bulldogs to the Hugos.
The first card ran:

My dear Hugos,
    If I had to choose a flower to symbolise England I would choose
the poppy because of its scent, its charcoal heart and its pink cheeks.
Also because it is the flower of sleep. I am so *sleepy*. Everything
passes in a dream. Firouze is only free in the evenings, he has given
me a white motor-car in which I drive around the countryside
asleep. This sense of opium (perhaps it is due to the tea) tires me and
lulls me. I haven't got in touch with anyone. I DREAM. London is a
mass of

Then came the second card:

provincial towns. The shops are not chic. *C'est trop chic, un chic pour
tous* . . . Read these few lines to our friends, this sleep of the crocodile
stops me from writing . . .
                I am busy with *le Boeuf.*

And he signed the second card "*votre Jean*" with a tiny drawing
of a heart. He saluted love even in his signature.

Back in Paris, still working in the *esprit nouveau* that had
inspired *Le Coq* and *Le Boeuf*, Cocteau began to write *Les Mariés
de la Tour Eiffel*, a *spectacle* in which a wedding-party, complete
with in-laws, a photographer and the General who, often quoted
by Cocteau, became a symbol of bourgeois stupidity, takes place
on the first platform of the Eiffel Tower, the action being mimed

and the scene described in dialogue between two actors, dressed to resemble phonographs and posted like a Greek chorus at either side of the stage.

The music consisted of separate pieces composed by five members of *Les Six* (Louis Durey having by this time given up composing). It did not prove popular, but as a record of *Les Six* it was important, as it was the only time they ever produced a work in common. For years after the production the score was believed to be lost, but shortly before Cocteau's death it was found in a Stockholm museum, to which Rolf de Maré had bequeathed it. Milhaud had it recorded and today there is a disc with both text and music which gives a fair impression of the performance in 1921. The music had been carried off to Sweden after the production by Rolf de Maré, along with the scenery and the costumes.

Rolf de Maré was a rich young man who had arrived in Paris with his ballet—the latest thing from Sweden—had roused Cocteau's enthusiasm, for the time being supplanting Diaghilev, and eagerly undertaken to present *Les Mariés*.

Everyone had set to work: Jean Hugo designing the costumes and the masks for the Swedish Ballet and Valentine Hugo taking a hand in the latters' construction. Jean Cocteau and Radiguet were also fully engaged in these preparations; this was a production created entirely among friends.

The Hugos had spent Christmas at Carqueiranne, a little village near Lavandou. On their return to Paris they talked to Radiguet of the beauty and serenity of this district and at the end of February he went off to Carqueiranne where he set to work on a number of poems. Cocteau stayed in Paris; at *mi-carême* he attended the famous Magic City *bal travesti*—with men dressed as women—in the company of the Hugos and the de Beaumonts. These *bals travestis*, to which women also went, were enthusiastically attended by what Valentine Hugo called "the nonconformists". Much as he hated being separated from

Radiguet, there was too much going on for him to join his
friend at present—these balls, a concert of Les Six, a Marie
Laurencin exhibition, and of course the preparations for Les
Mariés. It was not until the middle of March that he was able
to travel south with de la Fresnaye, who was going to Grasse,
and rejoin Raymond Radiguet. Cocteau was always glad when
his adored young friend, who was after all only seventeen, was
away from Paris, where the temptation to lead a life of dissipa-
tion was too strong for him. Cocteau found him staying in rooms
above a miserable little bistro and in his letters to Valentine
complained of the discomforts and of the baby that cried all
night. "Quelle laideur charmante!" In spite of the primitive condi-
tions, however, he stayed at the bistro for a month with Radiguet,
both of them happy and at work. For a change they would make
excursions to Lavandou and to Toulon where there were lively
bars and sailors to amuse them.

When presently they returned to Paris, Radiguet was conspicuous for his bronze complexion, in those days before tanning
was fashionable, but in fact his health was very frail. Both
Madame Cocteau and Marianne Singer were worried about the
effect his way of living would have on Jean and the latter's conduct was now causing considerable scandal. A number of his
friends, including Mauriac, would have nothing to do with him,
but Marianne was still wonderfully faithful in her visits to rue
d'Anjou—now she used to bring her little girls with her and
Francis Poulenc and Darius Milhaud would applaud their prowess
at the piano.

The creative urge continued. Radiguet began to think out his
novel Le Diable au Corps, the story of an adolescent's love-affair
with a young married woman while her husband is away at the
war. She dies bearing his child, which her husband believes to be
his own. The book is highly sensual and remarkably mature for a
boy of eighteen. Aldous Huxley gave it high praise when it
appeared later in an English translation.

But what concerned everyone most now were the rehearsals of *Les Mariés de la Tour Eiffel*. Once again Cocteau was his own choreographer, aiming at the mime being performed very slowly with the effect of a *tableau-vivant*. Radiguet too was constantly in the theatre and on the stage making suggestions. Once again it was a party. There are various versions of the text; the one that Pierre Bertin and Marcel Herrand spoke as the phonographs differs considerably from the version printed later. The predominant action of the piece is the appearance of a child with ping-pong balls, symbolising shot, who murders the marriage; *La Noce Massacrée* was its title up to the last moment, when Cocteau suddenly decided to call it *Les Mariés de la Tour Eiffel* as being more alluring and more Parisian. He kept the former title for the essay on Maurice Barrès which he was to dedicate to Radiguet. The piece was presented by Rolf de Maré with his Swedish Ballet at the Théâtre des Champs-Elysées on 18 June 1921, Radiguet's eighteenth birthday. At the first performance there was a certain amount of booing and cat-calling. Some of the critics were cutting. Cocteau did not generally read notices of his work, good or bad, but his friends, more concerned than he was himself, insisted on him reading Béraud in the *Mercure*:

> this young Cocbin, son of a moneyed father, who isn't worth a sou any more than the group that follows him . . .

At later performances, however, the public took kindly to this bizarre fantasy which Cocteau once whimsically declared, "must not be regarded as farce, even in the most elastic sense of the term, but as great and grave poetry". The real public, Cocteau wrote later, always listened to him.

In spite of these other preoccupations, Cocteau had continued to write a great deal of poetry and the volume *Vocabulaire* was published the following year by *Editions de la Sirène*. This was a kind of journal recalling his journey to Rome and Naples with

Picasso and Diaghilev in 1917 and the Paris of fairs and picture postcards.

In these poems Cocteau returned to "the rose" of Ronsard and to the French classicism which he extolled in *Le Secret Professionnel*. Some of the verses in *Vocabulaire* are almost a pastiche of Ronsard:

> La jeunesse me quitte et j'ai son coup reçu.
> Elle emporte en riant ma couronne de roses;
> Mort, à l'envers de nous vivante, tu composes
> La trame de notre tissu.

In the last poem of the collection he uses Ronsard's exact prosody:

> Courage! Ronsard te l'enseigne;
> Car, s'il est aujourd'hui vainqueur,
> La rose lui troua le coeur.
> C'est pourquoi de l'encre je saigne.

*Vocabulaire* was the last work Jean Cocteau wrote before obeying the teaching of Raymond Radiguet. He might in the future be criticised for many things, but never again for following fashion. The next volume *Plain-Chant* was a collection of love poems of a new sincerity. Here for the first time Cocteau accepted the flesh and the imperfections of man, the difficulties and imperfections of love. They were written of course about Raymond Radiguet, the one he found so hard to hold, so hard to love, but who now filled his whole life.

> Je n'aime pas dormir quand ta figure habite,
> La nuit, contre mon cou;
> Car je pense à la mort laquelle vient si vite
> Nous endormir beaucoup . . .

The long poem of which these lines form a part contain all

Cocteau's most precious themes: sleep and death, the absence of the beloved, the one body with the two heads, the angel, the sleeper betraying the one who is left awake.

Sleep, sleep the image of death, was so often now in Cocteau's mind. He made endless drawings of Radiguet asleep, in which his profile became that of Dargelos, that of the angels he would one day paint in those chapels, and that of the postage stamp he would design shortly before his death.

Meanwhile the follies continued. One evening Jacques Porel, the son of Réjane, another of Cocteau's idols, gave a party. For this occasion Radiguet wore his first dinner-jacket, subscribed for by the Hugos, Lucien Daudet and Milhaud. To amuse themselves some of the guests covered Radiguet's jacket with gold-dust. It proved quite impossible to clean off. Cocteau was furious, made a scene and left the party, alone.

Later in the summer Cocteau took Monsieur Bébé to the Hôtel Chantecler at Le Piquey in the Bassin d'Arcachon, where he had been in 1918 with some of his painter friends. Cocteau had, as always, the urge to revisit favourite haunts of the past with a new friend. The Chantecler was a little wooden building with a balcony, on the edge of a pine forest with a sandy path leading down to the sea. The provisions were brought by a horse and cart, and to get to Arcachon they had to take a boat and cross the bay. This was one of Cocteau's happiest times; he had Bébé to himself and away from Paris and its temptations. He set to work on *Le Secret Professionnel*, a thesis on poetry.

In this essay, among much else of interest, is a dissertation on angels, a forerunner of Cocteau's obsession with the angel Heurtebise.

"Poets speak often of angels," he wrote. "According to them and according to us, the angel's place is just between the human and the non-human. He is a startling young animal, charming and vigorous who passes from the visible to the invisible with the swift force of a diver and the thunder of the wings of a thousand wild pigeons. The swiftness of the radiant movement of which he is composed prevents one from seeing him."

He goes on to describe how he was told by a friend that the words "angel" and "angle" were synonymous in Hebrew, so that:

the downfall of angels could as well be translated as the downfall of angles. The sphere is composed of an accumulation of angles. Through these angles, through these points, power escapes. This is the reason for the architecture of the pyramids. The fall of angles therefore signifies: ideal sphere, disappearance of divine power, appearance of the mundane, of the human.

All these gifts do not inspire a poet but they stimulate him. Moreover, when you hear an artist or a woman spoken of as angelic, do not look for the angel of your first communion pictures.

Disinterestedness, egoism, tender pity, cruelty, tolerance, purity in debauchery, a mixture of a passion for earthly pleasures and a contempt for them, naïve amorality; make no mistake about it, these are the signs of what we call angelism and which every true poet has, whether he writes, paints, sculpts or sings. Few people realise this, for few people respond to poetry.

Up to the present Arthur Rimbaud remains the characteristic angel on earth.

In the following year Cocteau, urged by Radiguet to write novels "like everybody else", produced *Le Grand Ecart* and *Thomas l'Imposteur*. Soon too came a new production of *Parade* and the founding in January 1922 of the enormously successful bar in the rue Boissy d'Anglas—*Le Boeuf sur le Toit*.

The patron of Le Gaya Bar had asked Cocteau and Milhaud for permission to use the title of their ballet for his new bar. Before long Cocteau and his friends were the moving spirits of Le Boeuf and once again, as at Le Gaya, rumour had it that he was really its proprietor. The premises were minute with a dance floor the size of a pocket handkerchief, and there Eugene McCown, a young American painter, introduced to the circle

by the composer Virgil Thomson, played the best of trans-
atlantic jazz on the piano.

"There was very little jazz in Paris then," Virgil Thomson writes—
he himself was in his mid-twenties. "The establishment housed two
rows of tables, perhaps ten in all, with a piano and a bar at the far
end. One drank there champagne for luxury, whisky for style, or
the white wines of Alsace, home base of the host Moyses; but one
did not dine there (not yet), although after a theatre or a concert one
could have thin sandwiches or thick *foie gras en croûte*.

Against pale tan cloth walls hung two pictures by Francis Picabia,
both painted on the finest linen canvas and both of them examples
of dada art . . ."*

Before long the proprietor opened another room, smaller still,
for people who came to Le Boeuf for conversation. Musicians,
painters, writers, socialites, all spent some hours of the night
there; indeed this bar became the favourite meeting place for the
stars of what Maurice Sachs called "the decade of illusion". To
be in the swim one had to be seen there. Even Marcel Proust, on
occasion, patronised Le Boeuf. Here, night after night, Radiguet
dissipated his failing strength and Cocteau too, always in his
company, gained the reputation of a "*noctambule débauché*".

On 18 November 1922 the literary world was shaken by a
major event: the death of Marcel Proust.

During the last months of Proust's life Cocteau was constantly
in his apartment in the Boulevard Haussmann and later he
described this vividly in *La Difficulté d'Etre*: the brass bedstead
hooded with cork, a table crowded with bottles, another with
photographs of dukes and duchesses, cocottes and footmen,
device enabling him to listen in to certain theatres, a pile of
exercise books containing his work, everything covered with
dust, everything smelling of anti-asthmatic powder. Here Proust
would receive his friends:

* *Virgil Thomson* by Virgil Thomson (Alfred A. Knopf, New York, 1966, and
Weidenfeld & Nicolson, London, 1967).

lying on his bed, dressed, collared, cravatted, gloved, terrified by the fear of a scent, a breath, a window ajar, a ray of sunlight. "Dear Jean," he would ask me, "have you not been holding the hand of a lady who has touched a rose?"—"No, Marcel."—"Are you sure?" And half serious, half in jest, he would explain that the passage in *Pelléas*, where the wind has passed over the sea, was enough to give him an attack of asthma.

Each night Marcel Proust would read to them from *Du Côté de chez Swann*, starting anywhere, confusing the passage, breaking off with an exclamation, tittering at the book's foolishness.

And then one day they were all gathered about his bed once more, but Marcel Proust was dead and the little exercise books lay abandoned on the chimney-piece where they had been arranged by his faithful housekeeper, Céleste, "continuing to live, like the ticking watch on the wrist of a dead soldier".

A few days later Jean Cocteau and Raymond Radiguet together attended the funeral of Marcel Proust. Radiguet insisted on stopping at a café on the way to have a pancake, but all the same they managed to arrive at Père Lachaise before the great cortège and its hundreds of followers.

When summer came again Cocteau took Radiguet away, this time to Pramousquier in le Lavandou. Presently the Hugos and Auric came to join them; wherever Cocteau and Radiguet went the group formed again around them. Here, while Radiguet finished *Le Diable au Corps* and began *Le Bal du Comte d'Orgel*, Cocteau wrote his first play on a Greek theme—a short and rather slight adaptation of Sophocles' *Antigone*—which he spoke of as an aerial view of Greece. The play was produced in December at l'Atelier, directed by Charles Dullin, who played the part of Créon, while Cocteau himself spoke the Chorus—his first part in a play, an experience he had always wanted and thoroughly enjoyed. His voice came through a hole in the back-cloth, speaking "very quickly as if he were reading a newspaper article". This back-cloth was part of the beautiful décor Picasso, working closely with Cocteau, designed for the play, while Gabrielle Chanel dressed the characters in tunics of heavy Scottish wool, very different from the classic costumes of the usual Greek play, and Honegger contributed the twentieth-century music.

The part of Antigone was played by the Greek actress Génica Athanasiou, who did not know a word of French. Cocteau taught her the part syllable by syllable, which produced a somewhat strange diction, but her dramatic power was such that she captured the audience every night. On the evening of the public dress rehearsal, André Breton and his friends invaded the theatre and made a disturbance. Between his lines Jean Cocteau declaimed in the same dry voice: "Go away, Monsieur Breton, we will continue when you have left the theatre." This occurrence marked the beginning of the open warfare between Cocteau and the future surrealists—Antonin Artaud, who played Tirésias, was himself to become one of their leading poets. They were convinced that this play confirmed their view that Jean Cocteau was hopelessly bourgeois.

Their paths ran parallel, their conception of poetry was identical; Cocteau's theory of "clothing the night in light" was the exact doctrine of Breton and his friends; they admired the same things and Rimbaud was their god. Yet the gulf between them grew ever deeper, perhaps because Cocteau made his imprint through artistic and worldly successes, while the surrealists could only make their mark by an anarchy, often in somewhat bad taste. They interrupted Cocteau's shows in the rudest manner; it would be hard to imagine the gently nurtured Cocteau thus upsetting the shows of his worst enemies.

Early in 1923 Bernard Grasset brought out Le Diable au Corps, Radiguet, with his publisher's approval, insisting on flashy publicity as if for a beauty product. Cocteau was delighted to help in this; the novel had an immediate success and the sales were high. Cocteau was overjoyed and very proud that his protégé had become a celebrity overnight.

When spring came Jean Cocteau went to London once more, this time taking Monsieur Bébé with him—Valentine Hugo lent the latter a suitcase for the journey and received this letter from him:

> Dear Friend. We've managed everything, even in England, in spite of the dangers this expedition held out for such bad travellers as Jean and me. The suitcase has been a boon. All the same I will bring it back to you! Bridgeman is more delightful then ever and his house is charming. The day before yesterday we went to Oxford, that paradise without Eves. What a splendid town! Once again I see that what is called poetic license is the only truth. How like its poets Oxford is! It provides their stage props. The deer, Gothic and Greek, the lawns 'enamelled' with pre-Raphaelite flowers. We shall be back at the end of the week, very English; all your gin will go! No, more French than ever, as is only right! *A bientôt* dear Valentine. My most affectionate thoughts to you and to Jean.
>
> Raymond Radiguet.

The "Bridgeman" referred to in this letter is Reginald Bridgeman, who had been a Secretary for some years at the British Embassy in Paris and had an enormous affection and admiration for Jean Cocteau. Rue d'Anjou being very close to the Embassy, Bridgeman often visited both Jean and his mother, whom he found a most charming woman. He also knew Jean's brother Paul and sister Marthe. Nor were the visits one-sided, for Jean also loved to visit the Embassy and sit in Bridgeman's office, discussing life and art for as much time as the young diplomat, who was Private Secretary to the Ambassador, could spare. Cocteau lost no time in presenting Radiguet to his English friend, who was at once interested in his dear Jean's brilliant young Bébé and had now invited them both to stay at the house in Pinner, near Harrow, which he had recently inherited. Cocteau and Radiguet were both enchanted with this Edwardian villa set among trees in a large garden on the edge of a picturesque English village, and Bridgeman enjoyed taking them to Harrow, his old school, where the boys' flat-brimmed straw hats greatly amused them. Here, among a bundle of walking sticks in a shop, Cocteau found a stick with small bells round its handle like one that he had dreamt about and joyfully acquired it. It was a wonderful visit; Bridgeman had just become engaged to be married and presented the young men to his fiancée, and they showed the liveliest interest in her and in everything else they saw during their visits to London and to Oxford. Cocteau was then working at his poems for the volume *Plain-Chant* and Reginald Bridgeman enjoyed hearing him read them aloud. "What nobility and generosity of spirit!" Bridgeman now sums up the memory of his friend.

On their return to Paris at the end of April, Cocteau and Radiguet spent almost every evening with the Hugos. Georges Auric was often with them and one of their favourite pursuits was table-turning. With his death-obsession and his love of mystery, this process fascinated Cocteau and he was later to use the theme of supernatural messages for the talking horse in *Orphée*. The table spoke poems for him, as the tables in Guernsey had spoken poems for Victor Hugo, and what more auspicious sign than that he, Jean Cocteau, should relive this experience in the company of a descendant of Victor Hugo's? It was all most entertaining; and at other times these friends would forgather with Morand, Milhaud and Max Jacob at Le Boeuf or at various other bars or bistros, even where the food was inferior, or go to whatever concerts, balls or cabarets took their fancy.

The month of May was Raymond Radiguet's month indeed. On the 3rd, invited to give an address at the Collège de France, Cocteau praised him to the skies in a speech entitled *D'un ordre considéré comme une anarchie*, and on the 15th *Le Diable au Corps* was awarded the *Prix du Nouveau Monde*.

This prize had been inaugurated by a rich and cultured American, who was interested in current European literature and offered

Bernard Faÿ the sum of 7,000 francs a year to be awarded to a young French novelist. Faÿ chose the jury: first of all Cocteau, "because he knew the young better than anyone else and because he was aware of current trends, could smell out genius and detect original gifts", and with him several other literary figures including Paul Morand, Jean Giraudoux, Max Jacob and Jacques de Lacretelle of *Le Figaro*.

The prospective award was announced and Bernard Faÿ was inundated with books, manuscripts and presents. On the day the winner was to be elected the jury met at their chosen restaurant and after luncheon "Cocteau launched an attack, flinging the name of Radiguet among them like a hand-grenade". Bernard Faÿ objected that *Le Diable au Corps* would shock the Americans and was not the book to serve as a bridge between the nations at this moment when France was unpopular overseas. Most of the jury, however, did not listen to Faÿ; except for Morand and Giraudoux they voted for Radiguet—Cocteau standing proxy for Max Jacob who was not present.

The Right-wing press objected at an immoral book being acclaimed in such a manner and the Left-wing papers regretted that the prize had not gone to some book of social significance. In the United States it roused little attention and the donor wrote to Bernard Faÿ that while the novel interested him it did not conform with the object of the prize.

Cocteau had imposed Radiguet on the jury, but he had not succeeded in imposing him on America. Gertrude Stein, however, was one American who admired his work, in which she found that great thoughtfulness served a most spontaneous gift. She considered Radiguet of more importance than Cocteau whom she liked but who, she observed, talked too much to write anything that would live.

Meanwhile Cocteau's novel *Le Grand Ecart* and the poems *Plain-Chant* were being printed by Stock and *Thomas l'Imposteur* was with Gallimard; Gaston Gallimard had actually asked him for this manuscript when they met in the death-chamber of Marcel Proust, and it would be André Gide who would read the proofs of this novel and correct the punctuation. It only needed the proofs of *Le Bal du Comte d'Orgel* to arrive for Jean Cocteau and Raymond Radiguet to be free to leave Paris once more for their usual summer holiday. Radiguet was drinking more than ever and Cocteau was thankful to get him away. Once again they went to Le Piquey and this time Georges Auric went with them. He had a piano installed in the Hôtel Chantecler, on which he composed and played to the great pleasure of his friends, and he also helped Radiguet to correct his proofs. At other times the writers would sit at one end of the bistro at tables covered with American cloth, writing their poems, and this again was a happy period, in spite of Radiguet secretly obtaining great supplies of wine and spirits from the proprietress of the hotel.

Little by little that summer other friends, including the Hugos, joined them at Le Piquey. By the middle of September, when Cocteau and Radiguet accompanied the Hugos to Bordeaux on their way to Languedoc, Valentine and Radiguet were already suffering from strange internal pains. In October, when Cocteau and Radiguet returned to Paris, these pains of Radiguet's continued. Ill as he was, he left Cocteau and went off to the Hôtel Foyot with a woman whom he had met at Le Boeuf sur le Toit. Cocteau was deeply distressed and only the demands of his work kept him from breaking down.

*Le Grand Ecart* and *Thomas l'Imposteur* came out, the former to be greeted enthusiastically by the critics and the latter ignored except by the author himself, who wrote an article in *Les Nouvelles Littéraires* explaining exactly in what way this novel differed from the other. His appreciation of Picasso, dedicated to Satie, was published too by Stock. Towards the end of the essay he wrote:

It remains for us to salute Picasso's example. He teaches us not to confuse discipline and fear. It's one thing to live on a refuge and another to know how to cross the road. He shows that personality does not depend on perpetual daring, but on the freedom that daring allows.

Cocteau's long article on Barbette also now appeared in the *Nouvelle Revue Française*. He had adored this acrobat, who was also a female impersonator, ever since his boyhood. "He's an angel, a flower, a bird," he wrote to Valentine.

As the weeks passed Valentine Hugo, still in Languedoc, grew seriously ill and early in December was operated on for peritonitis from which in due course she recovered. At about the same time Radiguet's health took a turn for the worse and he was moved from the Hôtel Foyot to a clinic in the rue Piccini, where his illness was diagnosed as typhoid fever. His heart and his liver were in no condition to withstand such an illness and from the first the doctors held out very little hope of his recovery. "I always knew he was only on loan," Cocteau wrote later to Maritain, "and I should have to give him back."

In the preface to *Le Bal du Comte d'Orgel* Cocteau wrote:

These were his last words:

"Listen," he said to me on the 9th December, "listen to something terrible. In three days I am going to be shot by God's soldiers."

As, choked with tears, I remonstrated, Radiguet continued: "Your information is not as good as mine. The order has been given. I heard the order."

And again in the preface Cocteau wrote:

Raymond Radiguet was born on June 18th 1903; he died without knowing it, on December 12th 1923, after a miraculous life.

He was alone at the clinic in the early hours of the morning when he died, and although Cocteau said that he went "without knowing it", he was in fact found with an expression on his face of terror and despair.

When Cocteau was told of his death he collapsed. He stayed

in bed, almost out of his mind with grief, and presently Madame
Cocteau sent for Marianne Singer as the person most likely to be
able to give him some comfort. He did not go to the funeral, an
all-white funeral because of Raymond Radiguet's youth, which
shocked many people who felt that his death had not made his
life or *Le Diable au Corps* less scandalous. The expenses of the
funeral and of the clinic were paid jointly by Gabrielle Chanel
and Misia Sert, while other friends paid the bills at the Hôtel
Foyot and the Boeuf sur le Toit.

To add to Cocteau's misery, Radiguet's family accused him of
having contributed to his death by encouraging his debauchery.
Cocteau remained prostrate and wrote to Valentine Hugo:

I am trying for Maman's sake not to die. That's all there is to do.

And to the Abbé Mugnier, who had always been his friend
and was to show him great kindness during the loss of his faith:

... death would be better than this half-death which my sole desire
not to hurt Maman forces me to live. Friendship, heaven, are no
longer any help to me ... I am ashamed to find in myself all the dimness, all the murkiness that I detest. I suffer day and night. I shall not
write any more ...

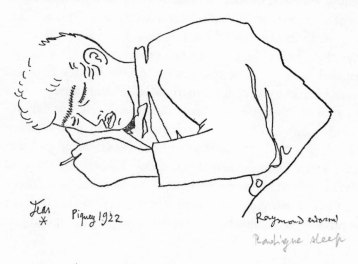

Jean
＊ Piquey 1922                    Raymond endormi
                               Raditguet sleep

## CHAPTER VI

## ANGELS OF HEAVEN AND HELL

RAYMOND RADIGUET's death after three years of passionate activity changed the whole tenor of Cocteau's existence. During this period he had not set up any new gods or taken part in any intrigues to become famous; he had swum in a steadily flowing stream of creation and devotion and his life had been in some magical way fulfilled. The loss of Radiguet chloroformed him, he said, but by this he did not mean that he was insensible to pain, but simply that he was insensible to joy. He was inconsolable and although he now constantly referred to Radiguet as his "son", his whispered nickname in Paris became "*le veuf sur le toit*". He was thirty-four and he felt that his life was over.

His friends rallied round him and early in 1924 Diaghilev carried him off to Monte-Carlo, where he was now producing ballets with a group of young artists and various members of *Les Six*. Cocteau was glad to be back with Diaghilev, after his flirtation with Rolf de Maré and the Swedish Ballet in *Les Mariés*. He took an interest in Auric's *Les Fâcheux* and Poulenc's *Les Biches*—with its delightful décor by Marie Laurencin, and wrote about these ballets in the Souvenir programmes. He was also fascinated by the young Irish dancer Anton Dolin's acrobatic gifts and began to write the scenario of a ballet for him.

In spite of these distractions, Cocteau still felt suicidal and presently Louis Laloy, the musicologist, who had been working with Georges Auric on the score of *Les Fâcheux*, introduced him to the solace of opium-smoking. Laloy himself had become addicted while studying oriental music and he did not have much difficulty in persuading Cocteau to follow his example. The latter was attracted not only by the euphoria offered by opium—he wrote later that it would be better if medical science attempted to render opium-smoking harmless instead of concentrating on improving disintoxication—but he was also attracted by the elegance of the practice. He was never an excessive smoker and he liked the chic of inviting his friends to have a pipe with him. This became an addition to his social life when he returned to rue d'Anjou, where he would receive his friends attired in black silk pyjamas, bring out his apparatus of luxurious ivory pipes from under the bed and introduce these people to his new distraction, without in any way urging it upon them. Later, in *Opium*, where he minutely analysed the effects of the drug upon him, he wrote:

> Everything that one does in life, even making love, one does in the express train rolling towards death. To smoke opium is to leave the train while it is running; it's to concern oneself with something other than life and death.

Without any doubt, opium gave him relief from his agony of mind, but it also began to upset his health which had been for many years extremely good. Neither his grief, however, nor his attempt to escape from it, could keep him out of the limelight. On 2 June 1924 Etienne de Beaumont presented at one of his *Soirées de Paris* the version of *Romeo and Juliet* Cocteau had made from translations of Shakespeare some years before. This was a play, not a ballet, but Cocteau's whole approach to the production was choreographic and very successful. The music was composed by Roger Désormières, Jean Hugo designed effective costumes in black and white, great attention was given to the lighting which included vivid red footlights—"the red river" once again—and to crown everything Cocteau played Mercutio himself, a part which suited him to perfection. To be both producer and actor and admired in both rôles fulfilled another dream, but all the same he said that every night he had hoped that he really would be killed in the duel. The production was dominated by the presence of death and the climax of the *cérémonie funèbre*.

Only three weeks after this success came the presentation by
Diaghilev at the Théâtre des Champs-Elysées of Cocteau's ballet
*Le Train Bleu* which he had written for Anton Dolin. This was
the most modern of Diaghilev's productions with music by
Milhaud, choreography by Nijinsky's sister, Nijinska, décor by
Laurens and costumes including woollen bathing suits by Chanel.
It presented a beautiful spectacle—inspired by the *train bleu*
taking holiday-makers to Deauville—of a beach dotted with
bathing-huts and bright umbrellas, and admirable use was made
of Anton Dolin's acrobatic gifts. There may have been too much
athleticism and too little real dancing for this to be a first-class
ballet, but there was no doubt that here was another resounding
success for Cocteau, both in Paris and in London.

He was living two lives now: one in the world and one out
of it, and in neither did he forget Radiguet. It was at this time
that he wrote his moving preface to *Le Bal du Comte d'Orgel*
which was to bring its young writer more posthumous fame.
Radiguet was always with him and now he also had another
invisible companion, the angel Heurtebise. He had thought
about angels ever since he flew with Roland Garros and had
written about them in his poems and in *Le Secret Professionnel*,
but Heurtebise was his guardian angel, his archangel, both evil
and good, his other self—and Radiguet.

Cocteau's friendship with Picasso had continued steadily ever
since their collaboration in *Parade* and Cocteau had written his
*Ode à Picasso*, besides an essay, extolling him as poet-painter. He
often declared his own desire to produce a similar kind of art in
his own medium, and at the same time Cocteau's admirers saw
the influence of his pure and brilliant line on the Spanish master's
drawings. Picasso was now linked in a strange way with the
naming of Cocteau's new obsession. The latter was on his way,
so he tells us in *Opium*, to see Picasso in rue la Boétie, when
going up in the lift he felt that he was "growing" in order to
match something terrible that was to be eternal. A voice called

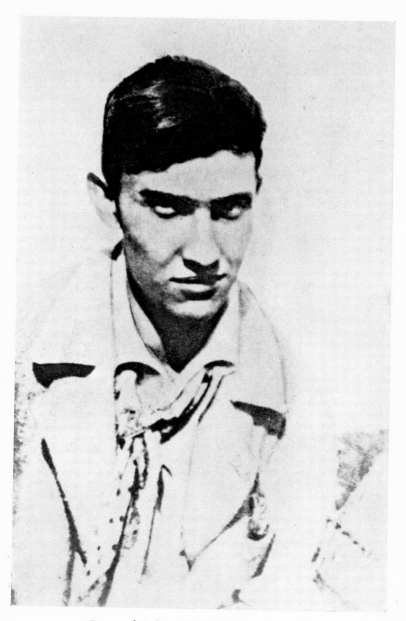
Raymond Radiguet (*Collection Bernard Grasset*)

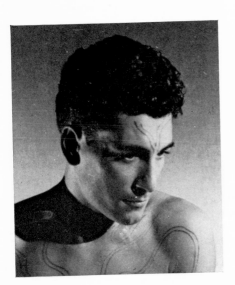
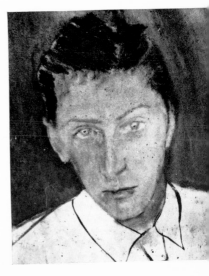

THE FRIENDS:

Roland Garros (*Private Collection*)
Jean Desbordes in sailor's uniform (*Collection Raoul Leven*)
Marcel Khill (*Private Collection*)
Jean Bourgoint, oil painting by Christian Bérard
Jean Cocteau and Al Brown (*Private Collection*)

to him: "My name is on the plaque!" A jolt awakened him and he read on the brass plate of the hand-lever: *Ascenseur Heurtebise*. He remembered how Picasso had said that everything was a miracle; it was a miracle that one did not melt in the bath like a piece of sugar. A short time afterwards the angel Heurtebise began to haunt Cocteau and he started to write the poem. At his next visit to Picasso he looked at the plaque again. It bore the name *Otis-Pifre*. "The lift had changed its trade-mark."

This was not the first time Cocteau had seen a likeness between an angel and a lift. In *Ascenseur* (*Poésies 1920*) he had already written:

> Gabriel artificiel
> en tombant du ciel
> freine un peu.

He did not finish the poem until later, when he was undergoing the first of several unsuccessful disintoxications, but it continued to live in him and he told a more detailed story of its birth in the later memoirs, *Journal d'un Inconnu*. He hoped that once he had named the angel it would leave him in peace, but the torment continued. His mother suffered in his suffering, although she said nothing; but Cocteau knew that even if his angel was behaving diabolically it *was* an angel.

The fifth verse of this long strange poem runs:

> Ange Heurtebise, mon ange gardien,
> Je te garde, je te heurte,
> Je te brise, je te change
> De gare, d'heure.
> En garde été! Je te défie,
> Si tu es un homme. Avoue,
> Mon ange de céruse, ta beauté
> Prise en photographie par une
> Explosion de magnesium.

D

When at last this poem was finished the angel ceased to haunt him. "Once he was a poem he cared very little whether I was or was not preoccupied with him." But Cocteau did not give him up. He was soon to disguise him in the play *Orphée* as the glazier in blue overalls carrying panes of glass like wings on his back. The glazier with window-panes on his back remains— occasionally to this day—one of the most picturesque sights of old Paris. With Heurtebise Cocteau aimed to be both Parisian and utterly fantastic.

Besides angels, Cocteau also had a great liking for birds, and he now brought out a volume of drawings, *Jean l'Oiseleur*. This charmer of birds was of course Cocteau and he continued to call himself by this name even later in *La Fin du Potomak*.

Succour now came from another direction. Georges Auric took Cocteau to see Jacques Maritain and his wife Raïssa at Meudon. Maritain, the philosopher, seven years older than Cocteau, was interested in contemporary poetry and admired Cocteau's work, a fact that the latter naturally found endearing. Another thing that moved him greatly, as he was shortly to write in *Lettre à Jacques Maritain*, was that the Maritains' house reminded him of his childhood.

> Yes, my dear Jacques . . . dining for the first time in your dining-room at Meudon, I breathed again the atmosphere of Maisons-Laffitte where I was born, the same chairs, *the same plates* that I used to turn about obsessively so that the blue lines would coincide with the foot of my glass.

In his hypersensitive state Cocteau found Jacques Maritain wonderfully sympathetic. Not only did he feel that the child in Maritain saw the child in himself—and although Cocteau declared that the main characteristic of childhood was the desire to escape from it, he knew very well that this he had never really succeeded in doing—he also felt that Maritain perceived his predicament.

To the ordinary spectator the tight-rope walker's gesticulations in the air are bound to appear comical. You with your intuition and your sense of pity saw at once that this behaviour was a sickening struggle, face to face with death.

The deeply religious, indeed saintly, Jacques Maritain had already declared in *Art et Scolastique* that modern art was more religious than classic art—"*l'art pour dieu*". He saw in Jean Cocteau a splendid example of his thesis—a young man whose poetry declared "*il y a des anges*", who wrote of God, of the Trinity, of Joan of Arc and explored the mysteries: "*Je taquine l'éternité*"—a young man clearly predisposed to grace. Cocteau opened the doors of literature and art wider for the Maritains, sharing with them, for instance, his admiration for Rouault's religious paintings, and Jacques Maritain took him to his heart, was quite uncritical of him and overrated his spirituality.

Cocteau had been brought up conventionally as a Catholic, but although as a child he had liked the theatricality, as he saw it, of the Church, he had never shown any tendency to become religious. His angels were not God's angels and his Christ was not so much the Son of God as the symbol of a persecuted poet. But in this moment of inner emptiness and despair he found the religious climate in which the Maritains moved very seductive. His great friend Max Jacob had already been converted to Catholicism and begged Cocteau to seek comfort in his religion.

"Go to Confession and take Communion," he exhorted him. "What?" Cocteau wrote to him. "Are you advising me to receive the Host like an aspirin tablet?" And Max Jacob replied: "The Host should be taken like an aspirin tablet."

And Cocteau did indeed confess and receive the Sacraments in the private chapel inside Maritain's house where, as a rare privilege, he was permitted to house the Consecrated Host. This was religion in luxury which strongly appealed to Cocteau, and he was further captivated by meeting at Maritain's Père Charles

Henrion, who wore on his breast the red heart surmounted by a cross of the Desert Fathers. This blazing heart seemed to Cocteau a symbol of his own agonised heart—he still at this time signed everything with a heart—and he admitted to receiving the same kind of "shock" from meeting this young priest as he had had from his first contacts with Stravinsky and Picasso. His religious fervour increased; Jacques Maritain was overjoyed and people began to speak of Cocteau's "conversion" which, he pointed out, was absurd, since he was already a Catholic.

At the same time as Cocteau was being loved and succoured by Jacques Maritain, he was being idolised by a very different kind of person, Maurice Sachs, the young grandson of the famous Madame Strauss, whose salon had been visited among many other celebrities by Marcel Proust.

In *Journal d'un Inconnu* Cocteau affirmed that he had forgotten how or where he met Maurice Sachs. In fact Sachs had been taken to rue d'Anjou a couple of years before, at the age of sixteen, by a friend who found him pinning up a portrait of Gide—his god at this time—and told him that Gide was finished. "There is no one but Cocteau," Sachs' friend assured him.

Cocteau had received them in the famous black pyjamas with a red silk scarf round his neck and led them to his rooms, where the walls were covered with portraits and photographs of himself and Radiguet. Maurice Sachs was immediately bewitched.

"The enchantment was perfect, total, spontaneous, delicious," he wrote in *Le Sabbat*. "When we left this magician I knew without any doubt that from now on I should live for him alone. I write these words all the more freely because no physical attraction came into play."

Now he covered his walls with photographs of Cocteau and said his prayers before one of these.

"It's a case of utter veneration and devotion . . ."

Seduced as he always was by admiration, Cocteau found his

new friend very charming. This young Jew was an extraordinary creature, very gifted and just beginning to write, although his books were not published until some time later. Cocteau introduced him to Max Jacob and took him to Meudon to meet Jacques Maritain, who encouraged his Catholic leanings with the same lack of judgment he had shown over Cocteau. There in August 1925, when he was nineteen, Maurice Sachs was baptised, with Cocteau as his godfather. Not long afterwards he entered a seminary, although this phase did not last long. Until then, according to Cocteau, Sachs hardly left rue d'Anjou except to visit him in the hospital where Maritain had persuaded him to take a cure. Sachs was quite amoral—he stuffed his pockets with toilet-paper to give himself the illusion of having a supply of franc notes and stole from Cocteau in order to give him presents. He went so far as to go to rue d'Anjou in Cocteau's absence, show his mother a forged letter from him and carry off a cartload of his books, drawings, letters and manuscripts, which he sold indiscriminately. Cocteau, although he was never infatuated with Sachs, forgave him everything. "I have always preferred thieves to policemen . . . he gave more than he took and he took in order to give."

Another young man of whom Cocteau was now seeing a great deal and who meant more to him than Maurice Sachs was Jean Bourgoint. He and his sister Jeanne were the real prototypes of *Les Enfants Terribles*, although several other people claimed to recognise themselves in these characters, and Jean may also have been "the new angel" referred to in the poem as replacing Heurtebise—or Radiguet:

> Un autre ange le remplace dont je
> Ne savais pas le nom hier . . .

This brother and sister were wonderfully good-looking, Jean in a very effeminate way, and he was passionately interested in the decorative arts, such as embroidery and fashion design.

The two of them smoked opium together and lived in their mother's house in Paris in the same fantastic disorder as *les enfants terribles*, which quite defeated the unfortunate woman. Jeanne had even married and brought her husband to live with the family, but after a few months she and Jean had got rid of the intruder.

Cocteau had first met Jean Bourgoint at Le Boeuf with Christian Bérard and had been delighted by his beauty, elegance and wit; he was a brilliant talker. Liking as Cocteau always did to bring his favourites together, he introduced Bourgoint, as he had Maurice Sachs, to Jacques Maritain. Once again there was a conversion. Jean Bourgoint had never been baptised and now he too was christened in the chapel at Meudon with Jean Cocteau as his godfather. In 1924 Cocteau drew a portrait of his godson, dedicated to "Jean, soldier of Christ". His conversion did not, however, change his life of debauchery, although twenty years later he actually entered a Trappist monastery.

During this period Cocteau joined Henri Massis, Jacques and Raïssa Maritain, Père Henrion and other friends in founding *Le Roseau d'Or*, with the aim of publishing the work of Jacques Maritain's young followers and proving that modern art was not irreligious. Massis was firmly allied with the extreme Right, the movement known as *Action Française*, and Maritain also was in sympathy with this. *Le Roseau d'Or* was therefore regarded by some people as a die-hard Catholic review and Cocteau's liaison with it doubled the hatred of the surrealists for him. They were all strongly Left; they had already put Cocteau *"dans le même sac"* as Paul Claudel, and added to this was their contempt for him because they considered he had "arrived" as a result of the wealth of the Beaumonts and the rich *bourgeoisie*. Certain surrealists had even been known to telephone to Madame Cocteau and say insulting things about her son. Cocteau had now to give up one of his favourite dreams—that of pleasing the surrealists and being recognised by them, but this did not stop him from saying to

Jean Hugo: "It says in the Gospel that one should love one's enemies more than one's friends. I do love them."

The appearance of *Le Roseau d'Or* and the publication shortly afterwards of Cocteau's *Lettre à Jacques Maritain* and his reply to it, had two notable effects. It made religion a talking-point among artists and writers, and several of the young men drawn to Cocteau's court at rue d'Anjou felt also drawn towards God as a new piece of chic, which finally estranged Cocteau from the surrealists who could stomach neither his link with *Action Française* nor this fashionable piety.

In the *maison de santé*, where Cocteau underwent the first of his unsuccessful cures, he did a great many drawings and wrote the first of the poems for his new volume, *Opéra*. In the spring of 1925, at the suggestion of Christian Bérard, he went to stay at the Hôtel Welcome in Villefranche which was soon to become a centre of literary and artistic activity.

Cocteau adored everything about this little Mediterranean town: the life of the sailors and the fishermen, the tourists and the natives and the company of fellow artists. High on his list was Christian Bérard, the artist whom everyone called Bébé, and who had a white poodle as his constant companion. His approach to art was at this time frivolous—he was turning out innumerable small drawings—and it was Cocteau's influence and admiration of his talent that led him to the theatre and greater things. Isadora Duncan was another artist who "haunted" Villefranche and whom Cocteau drew, and about whose dancing he wrote with admiration. There was also the young painter Francis Rose, whose seventeenth birthday party at the Hôtel Welcome Cocteau amusingly describes in *La Difficulté d'Etre*.

Jean and Jeanne Bourgoint had also been invited by Cocteau and Bérard to join them at the Welcome, so they were a large and merry party. Stravinsky was living not far away; the breach between him and Cocteau was now healed and they greatly

enjoyed one another's company. The endless activities of the
days distracted Cocteau and the silence of the nights soothed him.
After this visit he returned constantly to Villefranche and did
much work there. He had the urge to rove now and was never
again to be so constantly at rue d'Anjou with his mother. He
continued writing his *Opéra* poems, which became more erotic
and less religious, and once again his mind turned towards
Greece. He started to work on his play *Orphée*, which is full of
originality and no mere adaptation, like *Antigone*, of a classical
myth, and in which Heurtebise comes to life again more poetic-
ally than ever, as the Parisian glazier. He also worked on the
libretto for *Oedipus Rex*, much of which Stravinsky, before
writing the score, had translated into Latin. Erik Satie had
recently died, leaving piles of his friends' letters all unopened, and
although this was not actually a tragedy for Cocteau it was a
further grief, and he was glad to be working again with
Stravinsky. He speaks of walking back from visiting him, his
ears still deaf to anything but the music of *Oedipus Rex* "*dorée,
frisée, bouclée, annelée*" like the head of Zeus.

Another thing that supported him in these years of bereave-
ment was his correspondence with Max Jacob, a most faithful
friend who wrote him long and deeply affectionate letters about
many things that interested them both—the hatred raging
between themselves and André Breton, the treatment of Joan
of Arc by Bernard Shaw, the brilliance of Maurice Sachs, of
Radiguet's *Le Bal du Comte d'Orgel*. Meeting seldom now as Max
Jacob lived in the Loiret, in their letters they carried on a non-
stop conversation.

Back in Paris in 1926 *Orphée* was produced at the Théâtre des
Arts, Georges Pitoëff playing Orpheus, Ludmilla Eurydice and
Cocteau's young friend, Marcel Herrand, Heurtebise. Once
again Jean Hugo designed the fine sets and Chanel the beautiful
costumes, while Pitoëff directed the play and Cocteau, as always,
occupied himself with every detail of the production. When

*Orphée* was revived the following year Cocteau played Heurtebise himself.

As a sign of his gratitude to Valentine Hugo for the help she had given her husband in making the décor for *Orphée*, Cocteau presented her with a pair of antique vases. Having, however, been seduced meanwhile by the surrealists, Valentine refused to be present at the play and lost no time in selling Cocteau's gift. She remained faithful to the surrealists and particularly to the poet Paul Eluard. Soon she and Jean Hugo were to separate and she and Cocteau cease to be friends.

In this recreation of the Greek myth in modern dress, dissolving mirrors became the gates between this world and the other—"mirrors are the doors through which Death comes and goes . . . With these gloves [Death's] you'll pass through mirrors as through water."

It is all there in *Orphée*—Cocteau's fascination with mirrors, his obsession with Death, his desire to take his own life. When at the end of the play, the Commissioner of Police questions the bust of Orphée, he gives his birthplace as Maisons-Laffitte, spells out his name Jean Cocteau and states that he lives at 10 rue d'Anjou. The whole imagery of the play is self-revealing and autobiographical in a light-hearted way. Orphée's prayer in the final scene—in heaven with Eurydice and Heurtebise—runs:

O God, we thank thee . . . for having sent Heurtebise to us, and we are guilty of not recognising him as our Guardian Angel. We thank thee for having saved Eurydice because, through love, she killed the devil in the shape of a horse, and in doing so she died. We thank thee for having saved me because I adored poetry, and thou art poetry.

*Orphée* has grown in reputation throughout the years. On its first appearance it was only moderately well received and this more on account of the respect in which the Pitoëffs were held than on account of the text. Nor did Cocteau derive much lasting comfort from this catharsis. In spite of Jacques Maritain's

protestations—he was still trying hard to save his friend's soul—
Cocteau continued to smoke opium and to give way to despair.
With *Antigone* and *Orphée*, in which he had tried to exorcise his
angels, he had exhausted his inspiration and except for a few
poems he wrote nothing more for some time. He tried instead
to distract himself by making *poésie-plastique* or *poèmes-objets*
out of pipe-cleaners, hairpins, matches, pieces of fabric and the
like. Among these were figures of Orphée, Heurtebise, Romeo
—a Woman constructed from lumps of sugar and the surrealist
(in spite of the fact that the surrealists did not accept him) *"Mains
et Pieds de plâtre attaquant les hommes au bord de la mer"*. Before
long an exhibition of these strange objects was held in Paris and
Cocteau wrote in the catalogue:

> As I have no desire to write, I have to occupy my hands, to play
> with everything lying about in a hotel bedroom. But poets cannot
> play. Death and mystery at once enter into the game.

Most of these objects, being so fragile, were destroyed, but
Charles de Noailles bought a head made of pipe-cleaners which
he kept in a glass case and which was later used in the film *Le
Sang d'un Poète*.

All Jean Cocteau's life, however, fate would have another
angel lying in wait for him. This time it was Jean Desbordes.

This young man from the Vosges was just twenty years old.
He was a Protestant and had lived all his life in the country,
seeing nobody but his mother and sisters, reading little and
covering pages with indecipherable handwriting. Cocteau's
novel *Le Grand Ecart* fell into this solitude—a visitor leaving it
behind—and the book turned the young man's head. He at once
wrote to Cocteau declaring that his life was in his hands and
Cocteau replied begging him to subdue his fever.

"As well suggest sol-fa to a nightingale."

The same summer Jean Desbordes was called up for his
military service and he and Cocteau met for the first time. He

was attached to the Admiralty in Paris. "He therefore wore the most charming uniform in the world while escaping the proper function of this charm, for our sailor never went to sea."

One day in the September of this year Maurice Martin du Gard, the editor of *Les Nouvelles Littéraires*, met Cocteau in a garage. He was buying a Citroën and was annoyed because they would not deliver it on the same day. It was Cocteau's first car.

"It is Desbordes who will drive it," he explained, "because I can't go out on the road all alone. I always see enormous women in front of me, lifting their great arms in their white dresses, and I should be terrified of running over them." Then he changed the subject and said: "Claudel confuses me with the surrealists."

He then told Martin du Gard that Maritain had refused to publish Desbordes' scripts in the *Roseau d'Or* and finally he recounted the harsh words that he, Cocteau, had said to Maritain, meaning them not as a gibe but very seriously:

You will be a true Catholic the day they no longer allow you to have the Consecrated Host in your house.

Once his military service was over, Desbordes remained in Paris, supported by Cocteau, Chanel and others of Cocteau's circle. For a while Cocteau and Desbordes were guests together in Chanel's elegant house and Desbordes stayed on. Cocteau took him to Le Boeuf and introduced him as he had Radiguet to the hectic life of Paris. Nor were Cocteau's relations with Desbordes any more tranquil than those with Radiguet had been, for although he did not drink, in other ways this young angel did not behave any better than his predecessor, so once again there were constant scenes and constant reconciliations.

Desbordes had brought Cocteau an illegible manuscript and the latter had at once recognised him as another genius and resolved to help him to find himself without losing his freshness.

Once again he wrote the preface for a young writer's début, defending him from the charge of being an infant prodigy and comparing him with his predecessor. "Radiguet's genius looked like a high degree of talent. It was in this way that he misled the public. Jean Desbordes' genius looks like nothing but genius."

The beauty of Desbordes' book *J'Adore*, a collection of short pieces lyrically extolling love, lies in its youthful candour. Cocteau induced him to remove certain passages that would be too shocking for the reader, and then persuaded Grasset to publish the book. Desbordes certainly did not lose his freshness. He loved the earth, the sky, the sun, God, people, plants, animals —"love is the glorious and supple force that goes out from us in every direction, and the difference between one love and another is simply in the object loved." Or again: "To love love is to love God and savour His serenity on a shoulder," and: "Love is royal. It reigns over the Versailles of the heart."

Several of the little essays that make up *J'Adore* are fervent appreciations of Cocteau, who "walked a little way above the ground", and of his work, especially *Orphée* and *Antigone*, which in the year after Cocteau's meeting with Jean Desbordes was turned into an opera by Arthur Honegger and also produced again as a play. In 1927 Stravinsky also conducted the first performance of *Oedipus Rex* at the Théâtre Sarah-Bernhardt and Rilke died while he was translating *Orphée* into German.

This time Cocteau did not try to impose his young friend on his mother and at this period he scarcely saw his cousin Marianne. He took an apartment near the Place de la Madeleine where Jean Desbordes could visit him and at other times they stayed together at Toulon, where they both much enjoyed the company of the sailors and Cocteau found others with whom to smoke opium. As Cocteau was to recount in *Le Livre Blanc*, on one occasion they met a young sailor in a bar, who had just come out of prison. His chest was tattooed with the words *"Pas de Chance"*, and Cocteau and Desbordes were enchanted by him and adopted him as their bosom companion for the summer, after which naturally the friendship ended because of the difference in their backgrounds. Cocteau saw in Pas-de-Chance a vague reincarnation of Dargelos, "*Dargelos en marin*", and in Jean Desbordes a definite reincarnation of Raymond Radiguet.

"Raymond has come back in another being," he wrote to one of his friends, "and he often reveals himself to me."

Just as he had once drawn Raymond Radiguet sleeping, he now made drawings of Jean Desbordes asleep, which he published under the title *Vingt-cing dessins d'un dormeur*, writing in the preface:

These are not exactly portraits of Jean Desbordes, but rather of the friendship I have for him and of my sincere admiration.

*J'Adore* was published in 1928 and all the Catholic critics, with the notable exception of Max Jacob and Pierre Reverdy, denounced it. Max Jacob, who knew and liked Desbordes, wrote a review, praising the book, for *Les Nouvelles Littéraires*. Unfortunately this was replaced by a less favourable notice expressing the view that only time would show whether Desbordes was a good writer. Cocteau, who was determined that *J'Adore* should have as great a success as *Le Diable au Corps*, was furious and complained to Martin du Gard.

Cocteau spared no pains to help his protégé. He arranged to have a window of the big bookshop, Flammarion, given up to the book. There was a large photograph of the author in naval uniform and posters signed by Cocteau:

"Jean Desbordes' book is a revelation."
"Young man do not kill yourself before you have read *J'Adore*."

Jacques Maritain was naturally deeply shocked by the book

and wrote a severe review which ended Cocteau's close friendship with him. Desbordes had already written in *J'Adore* that he did not want Jacques Maritain's God "shut up in a church"; now Cocteau, strongly influenced by Desbordes' hatred of dogma and his own more pagan religion wrote: "Let Maritain return to his Christian philosophy, and I will return to poetry."

As a mark of this change and of his renunciation of the sacred heart, symbolised by the red heart worn by Père Charles Henrion, which had so much impressed him, Jean Cocteau now gave up putting a tiny heart beside his signature and for the rest of his life put a star instead—a star, he said, suggested by the scar on Apollinaire's forehead.

Père Henrion continued to see an intuitive mysticism in the poems of Jean Cocteau, recalling the great saints of the Catholic Church. He sincerely believed him to have the gift of grace and invited him and Jean Hugo to visit him in the desert. Jean Hugo went; Jean Cocteau did not.

Cocteau's erotic book *Le Livre Blanc* now appeared in a small edition, bearing neither the name of the author nor of the publisher, who was in fact Maurice Sachs. The drawings and preface, acknowledged to be by Cocteau, were only added to later editions, so Cocteau's hope that his mother would never hear of this book or connect it with himself may well have been realised; but in the literary world its origin was well known.

As for the book itself, here once again is the theme of Dargelos which was to appear so dramatically during the coming months in the novel *Les Enfants Terribles* and the film *Le Sang d'un Poète*. Here too is the mirror once more—the mirror that separates the two boys and is their sole means of communication, and here is yet another version of *Le Grand Ecart*. In fact the book is a set of variations on Jean Cocteau's most obsessive theme, but it is not—he makes this clear himself—an autobiography, although it contains autobiographical material, as for instance a description of the Pas-de-Chance encounter, which like so many of Jean Cocteau's adventures could only end in nothingness.

No, I thought, we don't belong to the same species. It is all very well to rouse feelings in a flower, a tree, a beast. Impossible to live with them.

André Gide was lent *Le Livre Blanc* by a friend while awaiting the copy that Cocteau had promised him, and wrote:

What vain turmoil in the dramas he relates! How stiff his style! How self-conscious his poses! What artifice! . . . All the same some of the obscenities are described in the most charming manner. What shocks one, and greatly, are the pseudo-religious sophisms.

Besides these recurring themes and memories there are passages of pure imagination in *Le Livre Blanc*, but the most revealing part of the book is contained in these few words describing the writer's temperament:

Heart and senses are so mingled in me that I find it hard to use any of them without the rest being involved.

During all this period Cocteau had continued to smoke opium which now seriously affected his health. For this reason, and because he was just as much opposed to becoming the slave of opium as the slave of any literary or moral doctrine, he consented to take another cure. Had not Père Charles Henrion himself exhorted him: "*Restez libre!*" Towards the end of 1928 therefore he went into a clinic at Saint-Cloud, where he remained for several months, visited continually by his friends and particularly by Christian Bérard and Jean Desbordes. It was now that he wrote *Opium*, illustrated it with strongly surrealist drawings and dedicated it to Jean Desbordes "who has by nature that profound lightness which opium imitates a little".

"There are spots even on the sun," Cocteau, with characteristic magnanimity wrote in the dedication. "There are none on your heart. Each day you grant me this spectacle; your surprise at learning of the existence of evil."

*Opium*★ is a diary of Cocteau's disintoxication and a collection of notes and anecdotes to which he added freely in proof the following year. It is, as Margaret Crosland and Sinclair Road point out in the interesting preface to their translation of *Opium*, about Cocteau and only incidentally describes the delights of the addicted and the miseries of the cured. He did not discover a great deal that was new, but although Thomas de Quincey came to much the same conclusions a hundred years earlier, he did not express them so succinctly. De Quincey took, for instance, several pages to explain that the effects of alcohol were different from those of opium and several more to suggest that medicine should learn how to make opium harmless rather than how to cure the harm it did. Cocteau uses few words to express the same opinions. To quote his translators:

> The value of Cocteau's remarks about opium lies obviously in the way he makes them, in that sad and splendid aphoristic turn of phrase that marks everything he writes . . .
> *Opium* is not easy reading, for it was not easy writing. If Cocteau had merely been making descriptive notes of how he felt from day to day it would still have required a considerable effort to write them; but along with physical change he was attempting to describe what can only be called spiritual adaptation. Elusive, subtle, changing from hour to hour, his thoughts needed clarifying, and this could only be done by writing them down . . . Cocteau's journal is often staccato, obscure and without any apparent continuity. And yet, because it is written by Cocteau, it has the deeply-hidden but satisfying unity of a strange poetry . . .
> The Cocteau-enthusiast will be delighted to hear so many favourite stories again and to recognise that unmistakable voice saying quite seriously, "I detest originality. I avoid it as much as possible."

★ Translated by Margaret Crosland and Sinclair Road (Peter Owen, 1957).

So, during this agonising period of "weaning", Cocteau continued to write some of his best work. During his visits to the Clinic, Christian Bérard, who was a wonderful teller of tales, in order to distract the invalid talked to him about the lives of Jean and Jeanne Bourgoint, the brother and sister who had already so greatly fascinated Cocteau. These tales reawoke his memories of that other "perfect couple", whom he had met long ago in Mürren and described in *Le Grand Ecart*, and inspired him in the last weeks at Saint-Cloud, to write the novel *Les Enfants Terribles*. This was written, according to the additions to *Opium*, under the influence of *Make Believe* from *Show Boat*. "Those who like this book should buy the record and read the book while playing it."

Cocteau did not have to invent the extraordinary room in which the brother and sister, whose age he puts back to adolescence, enact their lives in a strange world of their own making, without any need of money or contacts with the outside world, the room was that of the Bourgoints themselves and the invalid mother was theirs too. So was the accommodating doctor and the sister's marriage. Where fiction entered the plot was in Cocteau making Elizabeth's husband Michael an American and giving him a tragic death—strangled by his scarf caught in the wheel of his car. But even this terrible event was not pure invention, for Isadora Duncan had died the year before in Nice, strangled by "the long red scarf that hated her", and this tragedy had bitten deep into Cocteau's imagination. He was to use the same theme again when describing the death of Jocaste in *La Machine Infernale*.

At the beginning of the book Cocteau reconstructed the Cité Monthiers and brought Dargelos of the noble knees and the sinister magic to life again. Although he appears so briefly in the story, his influence is underlined by the young girl, Agathe's, likeness to him. But it was not only of Dargelos surely that Cocteau was writing here, but of himself—identifying himself with Dargelos-Agathe and entering the being of the brother-sister, recreating the dream that had haunted him since adolescence. In *Opium* Cocteau explains how "after the gift of the final pages"—that is to say his revelation of the way *Les Enfants Terribles* must end—the vision of Dargelos, the dark angel, inspired its beginning.

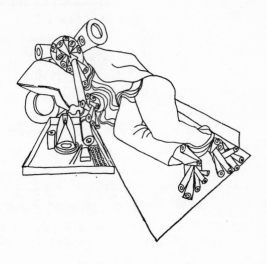

## CHAPTER VII

## LOOPING THE LOOP

WHEN Jean Cocteau emerged from Saint-Cloud in April 1929, he stayed for some months in an hotel in rue Bonaparte, the only occasion that he lived on the Left Bank. Spring time, well again and work in hand, he expected any room in any hotel to be a delight after the clinic; but he had forgotten, as he wrote in the additions to *Opium*, that without the drug to fill even a strange room with memories, a "sinister" place remained just this. As always his friends gathered about him, and as always, ill or melancholy as he might feel, he was unfailingly entertaining; the sinister room rang with laughter and he was often to be seen at Le Boeuf and other favourite rendezvous.

Jean Desbordes was working in an art gallery close by and writing his second novel *Les Tragédiens*, a graphic description of a very strange boyhood, which was affectionately dedicated to his mother and must have surprised her. The book has as preface a characteristic verse of Cocteau's:

> Reviens, mon chéri, mon bel ange!
> Aie pitié de ma douleur!
> Mais l'enfant reste sourd et mange
> La bonne soupe des voleurs.

Cocteau's relationship with Jean Desbordes was quite different from that with Raymond Radiguet. He never ceased to proclaim how much he had learnt from his former angel and that the only influence he had exerted over him was in inducing enough self-discipline for Radiguet to be able to express and record his genius. With Jean Desbordes Cocteau revealed the young man's nature and talent to himself and he did not learn from him—he

simply refreshed himself at this fount of youthful innocence.
Desbordes' eulogy of love in *J'Adore* had in it an element of
anarchy that appealed particularly to Cocteau at this moment
after his experience with Jacques Maritain and his attempt to
become a good Catholic. He felt now that for a poet to subscribe
to any ideology was dangerous and he welcomed the freedom of
his pagan young angel. It was brave of him, as Joseph Kessel
pointed out in his review in *La Nouvelle Revue Française*, to stake
his reputation a second time by launching a young writer, but
once more, in spite of the scandal over *J'Adore*, he was victorious.
*Les Tragédiens* deservedly succeeded and Jean Desbordes set to
work on a play, *L'Age Ingrat*, later published as *La Mue*, which
again concerned a mother and son—a mother too fond of her
son and a son who tragically breaks away.

Cocteau meanwhile was turning to something quite new—the
one-act play *La Voix Humaine*, a telephone monologue inspired
by Cocteau accidentally overhearing part of a telephone conversation. The sorrowful tones of the speaker, broken by seem-
ingly endless silences, gripped his imagination anew, for he had
already written a poem about this apparatus that Proust calls
"*la voix sans visage*" ten years before:

> le téléphone
> raccroché
> laisse l'aventure détruite.

*La Voix Humaine* has a slightly peevish preface explaining that
the author had been accused of too much elaboration in his
plays and had therefore devised this one of the utmost simplicity—
"one act, one room, one character, love and that most banal prop
of modern plays, the telephone". Further, he said, he was accused
of demanding from his actors an obedience limiting their talent
and putting himself in the limelight, so this time he had written
nothing but "*un prétexte pour une actrice*", in which she would
have two parts to play, one when she was speaking and the other

when, by interpreting the silence, she portrayed the character of her unseen, unheard partner in the "monologue-dialogue". The interpretation of this quite ordinary woman, whose only characteristic was love, must be left, Cocteau said, to the actress alone, but in the preface, besides minutely describing the décor of dishevelled bed, white covers and trailing telephone, he did in fact tell the actress exactly how to play the part—as if losing her life's blood, so that the end comes with the telephone dropped like a stone in a veritable pool of blood.

Jean Cocteau knew very well what it was like to have a broken heart and in *La Voix Humaine*, he quietly portrays despair. He had promised the piece to Ludmilla Pitoëff, but as he put it to Maurice Martin du Gard, "the Pitoëffs would follow it with *je ne sais quoi*", so he took it to the Comédie-Française, reading it himself to the *Comité de Lecture*. Everyone asked why the exotic Jean Cocteau was offering a play to the staid Comédie-Française instead of to one of the small experimental theatres. He explained that the whole position of the theatre had now changed; the Boulevard—or popular theatre—was given over to the so-called *avant-garde*, and the public expected to find in it modern notions, while the old *avant-garde* theatre had been superseded by the cinema. In fact the Comédie-Française, "a theatre like another, better kept than another and with a golden frame that suited it", was exactly the one Jean Cocteau wanted for his entry into the commercial theatre. The play was warmly accepted by Les Sociétaires; the young, vital, popular Berthe Bovy was engaged for the part and Christian Bérard set to work on the décor. He had, thanks to Cocteau, been permanently engaged by the Comédie-Française and was doing admirable work for them. He now designed a little white boxed-in set for Berthe Bovy because she was so tiny.

For the public dress rehearsal in February 1930 Cocteau asked for no less than two thousand seats for his friends and it was finally arranged that there should be a special "intimate" rehearsal

for his guests. Berthe Bovy had begun her act when suddenly—
Jean Hugo and Maurice Martin du Gard both remember this—a
shout came from the circle: "This is obscene!" and then:
"Enough of this! It's to Desbordes you're telephoning!" Other
people shouted back and the row became such that the curtain
had to be lowered and the auditorium lighted. The film-director,
Eisenstein, had received two tickets from Cocteau and had
brought the arch-surrealist Paul Eluard with him, and it was the
latter who was hurling the insults. A supporter of Cocteau
having burnt Eluard's neck with a cigarette, a fight was about
to begin; Cocteau arrived just in time to stop it, peace was
restored, the curtain was raised and Berthe Bovy went on with
her act. The scandal ended after the show in the Administrator's
office, where Eluard had to explain his conduct in front of
Cocteau. The latter appears to have behaved with the greatest
restraint and this episode did not prevent him from becoming a
friend of Eluard's at a later date.

This production of La Voix Humaine at the Comédie-Française
established Cocteau as a respected playwright. Another new
feature of his career was the making of his first records for
Columbia. He chose poems from Opéra that he considered of hard
enough texture to be read aloud without facial expression or
gesture in his cold, rather nasal, very carrying voice. About this
time too, at the suggestion of Charles de Noailles, he attempted
to make an animated film cartoon, but the difficulties of production proved too great.

In the winter of 1930-1 Cocteau moved back again to
the Right Bank, taking an apartment at 7 rue Vignon near the
Madeleine in the same building as Jean Hugo, although the
latter was seldom in residence as he now lived mainly at the Mas
de Fourques near Nîmes. For the first time Cocteau moved all
his possessions from Madame Cocteau's apartment in rue
d'Anjou, and established a home of his own. He was now forty
and some of the exuberance and much of his folly had evaporated,

but as always his inventive mind was turning to new things: from the simple realistic monologue of *La Voix Humaine* that had exasperated the surrealists, to his own audacious expression of surrealism (however much he might deny the name) in the film *Le Sang d'un Poète*.

Cocteau had already made a 16 mm. amateur film which, following Chaplin's *His New Profession* or *His Favourite Pastime*, known in Paris as *Charlot fait du Cinéma*, he called *Jean Cocteau tait du Cinéma*. Nobody appears to have seen this film, but André Fraigneau remembers that Cocteau, bent on producing a plastic line for his actors, draped them in wet sheets. Although the experiment proved abortive—the film is entirely lost— Cocteau's interest in the cinema did not flag. He went to many films, adored Charlie Chaplin and Buster Keaton and was particularly interested in *Un Chien Andalou* by Luis Buñuel whom until then he had not known. Hollywood, Cocteau said, was becoming a *garage de luxe* and its films more and more like beautiful designs for motor cars, but *Un Chien Andalou* was the very stuff of free poetry. In this appreciation Cocteau showed how much in sympathy with the surrealists he really was—the antagonism had arisen chiefly through the personal antipathy of Cocteau and André Breton—Cocteau had in fact preceded him both with his first plastic objects and with the illustrations to *Opium*. Now Cocteau was fired to make an ambitious film himself, but for this he needed a patron. He approached Charles de Noailles with the result that the Vicomte gave him and Luis Buñuel each a large sum of money to make a film, the outcome being *L'Age d'Or*, which Buñuel made with Salvador Dali, and *Le Sang d'un Poète*, which Cocteau made entirely by himself.

> All poetry is a coat of arms.
> It has to be deciphered,

run the opening lines of the projected text, and the film "this bunch of allegories", as Cocteau calls it, is surprisingly enough dedicated "to the memory of Pisanello, of Paolo Uccello, of Piero della Francesca, of Andrea del Castagna, painters of coats-of-arms and enigmas".

Georges Auric wrote the music and for the actors Cocteau chose amateurs, many of them his friends, including Jean Desbordes for the Louis XV "*camarade*" and the Noailles as extras, the beautiful Lee Miller, whom he had met at Man Ray's, as the Statue, a handsome young Brazilian to play the part of the Poet and the most appropriate-looking of the technicians to play a glowering Dargelos—in a magical Cité Monthiers constructed in the film studio. The Dargelos myth still haunted Cocteau and he had recently paid a nostalgic visit to this region of his childhood.

Cocteau did not work to a scenario and the film had no dialogue. He invented each scene as it progressed, a medley of poetic ideas, of figures and of objects—the classical head made of pipe-cleaners, for instance, and wings in the form of a bee for the back of the negro angel. Cocteau created the ideas and made the objects, rejoicing as always in his skill as an artisan, and the whole film is a reflection of his inner being. Everything seen in Le Sang d'un Poète was within Cocteau—he wrote that to make it he had plunged as deeply within himself as explorers plunge to reach the bed of the sea. In this expression of his essence the mirror plays a large part, but it is no longer enough for the poet to mirror the world around him or to be seen in one, ("looking-glasses should reflect longer," he neatly observed, "before projecting their images")—the time has come now for the poet to go into or through the mirror—naturally Cocteau knew and loved the works of Lewis Carroll. And so Cocteau himself plunged into the looking-glass of his subconscious and achieved complete introversion, while in the film he replaced the glass with a vat of water into which the actors dived.

Some of the images in Le Sang d'un Poète are strangely cruel— the little girl, flying like a miserable Peter Pan from the chimney-piece and sticking in a corner of the ceiling like a fly to avoid the

vicious governess with a whip, the body of the schoolboy killed
by the snowball lying under the table where the Poet, engaged in
a game of cards with the Statue, plucks an ace from the dead boy's
heart—which is later retrieved by the dark angel. "Without the ace
of hearts," the Statue who is Death observes, "you are a lost soul."

How that snowball obsessed Cocteau! In the beautiful scene
where the Cité Monthiers lies under the snow, empty except for
the small dark body of the young victim, he recites to music his
poem, *Le Camarade*, with the closing lines:

> Ainsi partent souvent du collège
> Ces coups de poing qui font cracher le sang,
> Ces coups de poing durs des boules de neige,
> Que donne la beauté, vite, au coeur, en passant.

When for the second time in the film, the poet shoots himself
and dies on the snow-covered table, his face a trellis-work of
blood, a bizarre audience ranged about the set in theatre boxes
watches and applauds his death, and so horrified were some of
Cocteau's friends to find that they had applauded this macabre
spectacle that they rebelled and the scene had to be re-shot with
other actors. Cocteau then invited Barbette, still a favourite, to
play the part of a *femme du monde*.

He was pleased and excited by the result of this film and also
by Buñuel's *L'Age d'Or* which he called "*le premier chef-d'oeuvre
antiplastique*". It was clear now that the breach between Cocteau
and the surrealists, in spite of the continuing animosity of André
Breton, had narrowed.

Picasso too was closer to the surrealists now—they had in fact
always admired him, for he had early put into practice what they
later developed as a theory. Cocteau's admiration for Picasso
never wavered and to this he had added a veneration for Chirico.
He wrote about these painters in a random collection of notes
scribbled on every conceivable kind of material, which was
published by Bernard Grasset with an appreciative preface under

the title *Essai de Critique Indirecte*, the extraordinary script being later sold to an American collector.

Cocteau described himself at the beginning of this fascinating book as driven from his home—the apartment in rue Vignon— "by the dust, the memories, the photographs, the letters, the fetishes of every kind". He might have added by the ghosts, for it is this apartment that he describes in *La Difficulté d'Etre* as the most haunted of all his homes. Probably, he continued in *Essai de Critique Indirecte*, he would never really live anywhere again, but on the chimneypiece "*de cet endroit-là*", wherever it was that he would continue to exist and "*de faire amitié*", more difficult than making love, he wished to lay his reflections on Chirico and Picasso. Indeed there are reflections on many other artists too in this book: Stravinsky, who from a growing tree had become "a tree that tries to speak and speaks", Picasso the sword-swallower, Miró who influenced Felix the Cat, Barbette who always fired Cocteau's imagination. Once again too he considers his difficulties with Maritain and meditates upon "*le mystère laïc*" of Chirico and "*le mystère religieux*" of Maritain. How far the author of this indirect criticism had developed from the *Prince frivole* of earlier days!

In the summer of 1931 Cocteau once more went to Toulon. He and Christian Bérard had for some years given up Villefranche in favour of Toulon; they stayed at the Hôtel de la Rade, where Cocteau's room looked out over the old harbour. Gradually the hotel came almost to belong to them, for Bérard took several rooms, one of which was his studio, kept in an amazing disorder, where he worked very little, although he remained indoors all day in his flowered dressing-gown, having a great dislike of both the sea and the sun. The rest of the hotel too in these summers was largely occupied by his and Cocteau's friends, who took rooms on every floor, so that the warm nights rang with endless conversations held between one balcony and another, nobody paying any attention to what was overheard. Georges Auric, who had a

villa at Hyères, which Cocteau sometimes visited—Gide speaks
of meeting him there—was often one of the party and he,
Cocteau and Bérard went frequently to dine with Edouard and
Denise Bourdet, at La Villa Blanche, their country house close
to Toulon. Edouard, the dramatist, was about the same age as
Cocteau and belonged to the circle of Paul Morand and Jean
Giraudoux. It was also through him that Cocteau met Louis
Jouvet, and Denise Bourdet had often appeared in the cabaret
of Le Boeuf sur le Toit. These were delightful evenings; Cocteau
would bring a poem to read—although he was not writing much
at this period but spending more of his time drawing—he and
Bérard together decorated the walls of the Bourdet loggia. Bérard
would play ping-pong with whomever he could induce to join
him and Georges Auric would endlessly discuss music and the
theatre, and sometimes Cocteau and Bérard, now sporting a great
beard, would dress up in old hats and bath-robes and do dances
in the style of the Folies Bergère, their caricatures of *les dames
de casino* throwing their friends into paroxysms of laughter.

In the summer of 1931 Cocteau was once again at the hotel in
Toulon, with an Annamese boy and a small monkey as his
companions. In September he went down with typhoid fever, a
terrible reminder of Raymond Radiguet's fatal illness.

It is not very funny to get seriously ill, when 'le boy' loses his head,
the monkey tries to bite you and the hotels turn you out.

He was moved to a clinic where the doctor, Jean Desbordes
and the Bourdets became, he says, his guardian angels. His illness
was pretty severe; Edouard Bourdet, whose play *La Prisonnière*
Cocteau was reading—being unable to see it on the stage until
its revival—visited him every day, and he and the monkey spent
his convalescence at La Villa Blanche, where Denise cared for
him tenderly and once more, in spite of his weakness, his gaiety
kept everyone in a constant state of mirth.

By the time winter came he was well enough to return to

Paris and in January 1932 *Le Sang d'un Poète* was shown for the first time at Le Vieux Colombier. Cocteau gave a great reception to which "everyone" came, including Gide, who had been sitting in a neighbouring café writing up his journal while waiting for the film, which was not shown until ten o'clock. The critics on the whole found the film morbid and sadistic and accused Cocteau of imitating Buñuel and the surrealists—as a matter of fact to this day the Buñuel and Cocteau films are frequently confused with one another. The critics also declared that *Le Sang d'un Poète* consisted of a medley of images rather than of ideas and implied that these images were such that they could only have been devised by a homosexual. The film had been made on 16 mm. for Charles de Noailles and was therefore not circulated commercially in France, but Charlie Chaplin saw and admired it and arranged for it to be shown in the United States, where it has since been seen many times, as also in England. In France it has remained a film for the innumerable small film-clubs and in the provinces it has continued to meet with hostility.

Cocteau's thoughts now turned towards Greece again. He had originally meant to write "a sort of tragi-comic prologue to *Oedipus Rex*" for the *avant-garde* theatre, but now through his friendship with Louis Jouvet he was more closely allied than before to the commercial theatre. He read his first draft of *La Machine Infernale*, his fine original version of the Oedipus story, aloud to Jouvet, who was at once eager to direct the play. Cocteau worked closely with Christian Bérard who designed the sets—the first décor he was to make for Jouvet. For Jocasta's bedroom he designed a mirror in the shape of a human figure, in which Oedipus and Jocasta dramatically observe themselves—a truly Cocteau touch.

The text is full of Cocteau's obsessions too, as for instance his theory of "folded" eternity which he was to develop later in *La Difficulté d'Etre*. Here he makes it unusually clear, illustrating his idea with the folds in the Sphinx's dress:

Press them one against the other. And now if you pierce the lot with one pin, remove the pin and smooth the stuff out so that there is no trace of the former folds, do you think that any country bumpkin would believe that those innumerable holes appearing at such distances from one another were the result of a single prick. . . ? The time of mortals is that of "folded eternity".

*La Machine Infernale* was dedicated to Marie-Laure and Charles de Noailles, and Cocteau finished it at Saint-Mandrier in 1932, although it was not published by Grasset until 1934. In the same year it was performed at the Comédie des Champs-Elysées, the last time Louis Jouvet used this theatre, as he found it uneconomical for his productions—and the only play of Cocteau's that he was ever to direct. Oedipus was played by the handsome Jean-Pierre Aumont, Cocteau himself, unseen, spoke the prologue to each act, Jouvet played the small part of the Shepherd, and the rôle of the Corinthian messenger was taken by the very young Marcel Khill, whose beauty fated him to become one of Cocteau's angels.

Cocteau explained that the *"machine infernale"* was an arm of predestination and that the fates had patiently and relentlessly plotted the course of Oedipus's doom from the very day of his birth. The gods tricked him too into believing that all his misfortunes were blessings in disguise, thereby luring him from one misadventure to the next.

Of the production Cocteau wrote in *Echo*, 11 April 1934:

Without the inventive genius of Christian Bérard, the courage of Jouvet, and the cast, it would have been impossible for me to put into production four acts in which are four distinct plays. I hope that the public will forgive us the inevitable weakness of an undertaking which consists of nothing less than fighting with ghosts.

Cocteau was aiming to avoid on the one hand detailed realism and on the other abstraction. *La Machine Infernale* has none of the fantasia of the film *Le Sang d'un Poète*, nor is it, like *Orphée* with the angel-glazier, transposed into modern times, although the language is unaffectedly modern. Like Picasso, Cocteau never repeated himself, but was always trying out new forms of expression. Its simplicity gives the play a certain classic flavour, although in spite of its irony some passages have a tenderness that is not Greek, and there are also moments of lyric poetry. At the end, which is written as pure human tragedy, Jocasta hangs herself with the red scarf, which like Isadora Duncan's scarf hated her and was always attempting to kill her—Cocteau puts the very words that he used of Isadora's death into Jocasta's mouth. After Oedipus has put out his eyes with the great golden brooch that pinned the scarf, Jocasta appears in the doorway, white and beautiful, her eyes closed and the long red scarf wound about her throat. Oedipus cries out and she tells him:

> I am dead. You are seeing me because you are blind. The others can no longer see me.

Christian Bérard had great taste and a powerful dramatic sense and he, Jouvet and Cocteau made a remarkable team. Visually *La Machine Infernale* was beautiful: there was an azure background and a small stage in the centre of the forestage draped in blue; the dominant colours of rocks and columns were white, grey and brown; the room for the wedding-night scene was draped in red; the costumes were brilliant.

On the whole the play was well received. True some of the critics accused Cocteau of imitating the appearance of the ghost in *Hamlet*, but in fact Cocteau's ghost of Laius never quite succeeds in materialising or of getting his message said—he is a clever tragi-comic invention.

*La Machine Infernale*, although it only ran for sixty-four nights, further established Cocteau as a serious playwright and brought him Marcel Khill, the youth who had played the tiny part of the Corinthian messenger. He was Arab by origin, his real name being Kélilou, and besides being a dark-skinned beauty he was an extremely agreeable young man and he appeared just at the time that Cocteau was in need of a new angel, for Jean Desbordes had somewhat faded from his life.

In 1935, after writing a little farce for Arletty, *l'Ecole des Veuves*, Cocteau became a fashionable journalist. He was commissioned to write a series of memoirs in the form of weekly articles for *Le Figaro*, which were collected as the volume *Portraits-Souvenir* and dedicated to Marcel Khill. He prefaced the book with a line from *Opéra* "*je suis un mensonge qui dit toujours la vérité*", and he explained at the beginning of the first article that his memory was not to be trusted, that he muddled dates and confused characters, thus anticipating any charge of inaccuracy that might be levelled against him.

He tremendously enjoyed writing these articles—"Poets have nothing but their intimate memories. . . . A curtain falls a curtain rises"—and in their pages his childhood and the many fascinating characters who had peopled his stage, leap vividly to life, not only in the words but in the drawings.

It was Marcel Khill who had the idea that he and Cocteau should try to go round the world in eighty days. Cocteau had loved Jules Verne ever since seeing the show with "Jéphine" at the Châtelet, and 1936 was his hero's centenary, so what better time for such an adventure? Cocteau, who had never set foot outside Europe, was enchanted by the prospect of seeing the world, and *Paris-Soir* was delighted to finance the journey—in the form of a wager such as Phileas Fogg had made, with the fee for Cocteau's articles as the stake, and Marcel Khill as the perfect Passepartout.

By the terms of the wager the travellers were not permitted to fly, except in America, but had to restrict themselves to trains and packet-boats. The whole project was deliciously romantic; Cocteau welcomed his new rôle of actor-traveller and his chance not only to prove that Jules Verne's calculations of times and distances, made in 1876, held good in 1936, but to prove that he was a visionary poet and give visible evidence that the invisible and the unreal existed. Gide had complained that Cocteau never let himself go—now he was determined to do exactly this and to dedicate the articles, which would prove his *laisser-aller*, to André Gide.

The night before Cocteau and Khill left for Rome a private showing of *Modern Times* was given for Cocteau in Paris, a most auspicious send-off, for the highlight of his journey round the world was to be his meeting with Charlie Chaplin—"*rencontre destin*".

The itinerary was carefully planned to follow that of Phileas Fogg and took the travellers to Greece, Egypt, India, where Cocteau read Kipling and found Kim and Rikki-tikki-tavi to be true characters, and so on to the Far East, only occasionally delayed by slight difficulties with authorities who could not understand the purpose of their journey. Cocteau greatly enjoyed all the places they visited and kept a detailed journal from which he created the brilliant articles for *Paris-Soir*. On 11 May he recorded:

> Two poets are following the straight line of their destinies. Suddenly these two lines cut across one another and their meeting forms a cross, or if your prefer, a star. My meeting with Charlie Chaplin remains the charming miracle of this journey.

So many people had tried to arrange a meeting between these two artists, but there was always an obstacle, until chance, "which has another name in the language of poets", threw them together on an old Japanese cargo boat, plying with its merchandise between Hong Kong and Shanghai. With Paulette Goddard and "Passepartout" they made a joyous quartet.

> I do not speak English. Chaplin does not speak French. And we talk without the slightest effort. What happens? What is this language? It is the live language, the most live language of all, that is born with

Jean Cocteau with Jean Marais and Josette Day during the production of
*Les Parents Terribles*, Théâtre du Gymnase, 1945 (*photo Roger Viollet*)

Jean Cocteau in his apartment at the Palais-Royal (*Private Collection*)

the desire to communicate at all costs, the language of mime, the language of poets, the language of the heart. Chaplin detaches each word, puts it on the table, on a pedestal, returns and moves it to the position where it will best catch the light. The words he uses with me are easy to lift from one language into the other. Sometimes the gesture precedes the word and escorts it. Before he says the word he announces it and after saying it he comments on it. No hesitation or only the sham hesitation of a juggler juggling. He doesn't ever jumble them up; one can follow them in the air.

So, joyfully, Cocteau wrote in the Chinese seas, two-thirds of the way through his travel journal. He found two characters in Chaplin: the child—the child who had come so exuberantly to his cabin when he heard that he was aboard, the child who at once invited them to California, the child who, after the film *Modern Times*, had sped away at a moment's notice to Honolulu with Paulette Goddard; the child, the little ragamuffin saint— and opposed to this the *impresario*, who knew the world and knew his stuff. Skilfully Cocteau pieced the two sides of Charlie together for his portrait.

Not many days of this inspiring brotherhood had passed before Chaplin asked Cocteau to let him have Passepartout to play opposite Paulette Goddard in the film he intended making in Bali. Marcel Khill was naturally delirious with joy, but he could not leave Cocteau in order to comply with Chaplin's condition— that he should learn English, in England, within the next three months. So Cocteau recorded:

The miracle, said Passepartout, without a shadow of bitterness, was that Chaplin offered me the part. The luxury is not to have been able to accept it. This has made my life magical!

From this time onwards the four travellers were inseparable. They shared the same table and in the next boat arranged to occupy a suite of cabins. At Tokyo an American lady presented Cocteau with a cricket which Passepartout christened Microbus

E

and which came out of its cage at night to sleep on top of the thermos flask and "play enchantingly on a long green guitar that formed part of its body". Microbus now shared their journey and the indefatigable Cocteau wrote a story about him "*Le Cadeau du Mikado*" to amuse Chaplin. When the quartet finally parted in San Francisco, which Cocteau found a strange "mic-mac" of bits of France, they were all broken-hearted. Cocteau and Marcel Khill continued by air to Los Angeles, the first experience of flying for both Khill and Microbus. The latter did not enjoy it and finally to ensure that he should have no further suffering, Passepartout set the little Japanese cricket free in the Californian grass on the way to Hollywood.

> A cricket is sure to have a part in Charlie's next film. Perhaps a producer will pick you up. Perhaps I shall see and hear you again on the screen. I shall recognise your antennae and particularly your voice among thousands.

Chaplin had telephoned to King Vidor and he showed the travellers over the set for his current Wild Western film and then that of the *Shanghai* film that Gary Cooper was making and which filled Cocteau with nostalgia for the true beauty and elegance of the Orient. On then, via the Grand Canyon, where Cocteau was rather ill as a result of the flight, on, flying sometimes by day and sometimes by night, still taking in, comparing and recording every detail of the journey to New York:

> "The Ambassador Hotel. From our window Madison Avenue is Venice, the Grand Canal, bordered by palaces, on which the rare Sunday cars glide like gondolas. . . . The sky-scrapers hang straight and light as curtains of tulle"—which last impression the journalists mistranslated as: "The poet feels that New York wears a woman's dress."

> "I like the hot-beds of cities," Cocteau wrote further. "The hot-beds of Paris attract a Picasso, a Stravinsky and all those who know that the flowers of art can't grow in nickel and crystal."

And so, while admiring the glitter—Radio-City and "marvel of marvels: Broadway as evening falls"—Cocteau sought the hot-beds of New York—and found them in the ghettos and in Harlem, where he was captivated by "le Swing" which he found to have replaced "le Jazz".

To his great pleasure, Cocteau met Cecil Beaton again in New York. During this visit Cocteau was interviewed and photographed by press photographers in every kind of unlikely pose. These photographs, with the one of Cocteau and Chaplin together in the boat, appear to be the only photographic records of this journey.

The last visit the travellers paid was to Coney Island, where Cocteau had wanted to go ever since seeing it as a boy in a film.

I looped the loop at Coney Island, the blessed isle of the young of the New World. In silence with a heavy heart but a light spirit I turned round and looked at Passepartout. We shook hands.

The next day they boarded the *Ile-de-France* and for a moment Cocteau, hearing French spoken, thought that he had come to understand a foreign language.

I am in bed. I am at peace. We are in France. I have looped the loop. *Je rentre chez moi.*

In this journey round the world Jean Cocteau had materialised a journey already made in imagination. It was a poetic achievement.

## CHAPTER VIII

## GALAHAD

ON their return in June 1936 Jean Cocteau, unwilling to lose his delightful travelling companion, at once invited Marcel Khill to go with him on a long visit to Jean Hugo's Mas de Fourques where he had stayed in earlier times with Jean Desbordes. Once again Cocteau enjoyed revisiting a place he had known with one loved friend in the company of another. It was a beautiful place: an avenue of fine trees led to the old mansion in a courtyard framed with barns, and round it clustered vineyards and orchards, while on the hills above stretched the bleak "*garrigue*". Here, far from Paris and the Côte d'Azur with all their distractions, Cocteau was happy with Marcel Khill, and Christian Bérard also spent some time with them at Le Mas. Here too, in a house close to that of Jean Hugo and his second wife, Cocteau found Jean Bourgoint living in retirement, and the friends made long expeditions in the *garrigue*. This was a hard stony terrain with no flowers and only small stunted trees that appealed to Cocteau, and the like of which he was later to use in his last film. On these rambles they collected praying mantises, small snakes and lizards which they used to keep in a kind of cage. Cocteau enjoyed observing the little creatures and drew them constantly, particularly the lizards which seemed to have a certain link with his own quick, neat hard style. He was drawing again now and not writing and delighting in the change from Paris, although he continued to declare that he could not live anywhere else.

One day somebody made the mistake of adding a field-mouse to the little zoo, which gnawed through the bars of the cage and let all the creatures escape. That was the end of this particular entomological enthusiasm.

When at last the friends returned to Paris, Khill was anxious that Cocteau should continue his sight-seeing in his own city. Although Le Boeuf sur le Toit had continued to be a favourite meeting place for his circle and had been followed by another successful night-club Le Grand Ecart, Cocteau had not of late taken much part in Paris night-life. Now Khill accused him of laziness and took him for a tour of "*les boîtes*", and although Cocteau found this adventure exhausting, he was impressed by the enormous vitality and talent in "the minor arts with which Paris borders her evening dress".

Cocteau described this *Promenade dans la nuit* in the first of the columns he was commissioned to write for the Left paper *Le Soir* by Louis Aragon, the first of the surrealists with whom he was reconciled and who was shortly to become famous for his poems of the Resistance. Aragon wanted articles about artists of every kind, which idea naturally appealed to Cocteau and he kept up a supply of them for several months. This first column started off with an appreciation of Suzy Solidor, whose début had been at Le Boeuf and who was now singing sailors' songs in a *boîte*, dressed half as man half as woman. Largely through Cocteau's influence, the French sailor had become a kind of trade-mark in Paris literary life and Cocteau himself wrote some *chansons parlées*, songs spoken without music, for Suzy Solidor. The artist who really captivated him now, however, was Al Brown, the negro boxer who had left the ring three years before and was conducting the orchestra at the Caprice Viennois in Montmartre, "galvanising it, dominating it with a fist of bronze". Although Al Brown was far from beautiful, he captured Cocteau's imagination, and in his last book of memoirs, *Le Cordon Ombilical*, he was to write:

> ... he is so foreign to the world of letters that he is practically a lyric creation himself. I'm speaking of the ex-featherweight world champion, Al Brown. The similarity between his methods and my own struck me so forcibly that, odd as it may seem, I resolved to

rescue him from his hell of drugs and alcohol and to prove, by putting him back in the ring, that intelligence, if an athlete uses what he has, is a weapon capable of replacing force. In short in this black there was a kind of poetry.

And so, mocked in some quarters for this new enthusiasm and defying the scepticism of the boxing profession, Cocteau took Al Brown up. He was a simple creature who loved his patron, bought him little presents and agreed to undergo a long and painful cure and training in order to return to the ring. Cocteau wrote about him in *l'Auto* and *Le Soir*, taught him a few tricks, such as to drink mineral water from a champagne bottle just before a contest, and supported him in every way.

In due course Al Brown fulfilled Cocteau's faith in him by winning eleven bouts running.

In this same year Cocteau went to stay with the conductor Igor Markevitch, Marcel Khill having drifted away with a woman friend. In the course of this visit the vision for Cocteau's play *Les Chevaliers de la Table Ronde*, which had earlier come to him in a dream, materialised. He abandoned Greece and, in spite of his professed dislike of Wagner, turned to the Arthurian legend which was, it so happened, in the air because of Joseph Bédier's recent translation of *Tristan and Isolde*. To the mediaeval mythology Cocteau added a little mythology of his own such as a flower that spoke, and his characters expressed themselves sometimes in prose, sometimes in verse. He wrote a synopsis of the play as a preface, telling of Arthur drugged by Merlin being disintoxicated by Galahad and forced to face the terrible violence of reality. To this analysis Cocteau added: "I hope very much that my observant readers will realise how completely detached from this work I am."

Not only did Cocteau write the text of *Les Chevaliers de la Table Ronde* while he was staying with Igor Markevitch, but he also designed the décor, including furniture and textiles, much of which was exhibited in Paris and at the Guggenheim Jeune Gallery in London the following year. As soon as he was back in

Paris, Cocteau showed the play to Louis Jouvet who to his disappointment did not like it, so he decided to make arrangements to have it produced at the Théâtre de l'Oeuvre.

News of this project came to the ears of Jean Marais who, at the age of twenty-four, had at last begun to realise his ambition to go on the stage by taking Charles Dullin's famous acting course. Dullin had produced *Antigone* in 1922 and Marais never ceased to have the greatest respect for him, while he, for his part, encouraged this handsome eager young man and allowed him to take the course free, in exchange for doing odd jobs and playing small parts in performances. In this way Marais managed to earn a few francs. His mother, who had early separated from her husband and brought up Jean and his brother under great difficulties, naturally wanted him to have some "serious occupation". So far, after a highly unsatisfactory childhood, being expelled from one school after another, he had earned a precarious living as assistant photographer, assistant stage-manager, painter of postcards and caddy, and had had a few parts as an extra in the films of Marcel L'Herbier. Now he was determined to become a professional actor, but he had promised Madame Marais, in good faith, to give this ambition up in a year's time if he had not by then succeeded in obtaining a leading part. At this point, when he was playing a small part in *Julius Caesar*, he heard that Jean-Pierre Aumont was to create the rôle of Galahad in *Les Chevaliers de la Table Ronde*. Marais made up his mind to ask Jean Cocteau if he might understudy Aumont, but he failed to find Cocteau's address, so he decided to leave his fate to luck. He had resolved some time before to believe in his luck—it was a comforting way of facing vicissitudes.

"I think luck likes one to like it," he wrote, "to help it and believe in it."

His faith was rewarded. Fellow students came to tell him that young actors and actresses were needed by the Théâtre Antoine for the 1937 Paris Exhibition and that Marais must leave *Julius Caesar* and try to get taken on.

I refused. They added that it was for *Oedipe-Roi* by Jean Cocteau. I agreed. After the audition Cocteau offered me the part of Oedipe.

The delighted Jean Marais was unable to accept Cocteau's offer as most of the other actors involved were his seniors, in experience at least, and he was not considered eligible for the lead. He therefore played the Chorus, standing motionless on a pedestal, and enjoyed quelling the audience, which appeared to him impervious to the beauty of the play, by the ferocity of his expression. He also played Malcolm in the short adaptation of *Macbeth* that was part of the Théâtre Antoine's programme for the Exhibition. Among Cocteau's other contributions to this were the drawings he had made at Fourques.

In spite of his earlier intentions, Marais had not dared to ask Cocteau if he might understudy Galahad, and now to his utter astonishment Cocteau offered him the part itself. From the moment Cocteau saw him Marais was his perfect Galahad, and as Jean-Pierre Aumont was occupied with a film Cocteau was able to engage his new young favourite, with whom he worked hard, determined that he should be a success. The play, however, failed. The stage of the Théâtre de l'Oeuvre was too small for it, the production not good and its reception justified Louis Jouvet's opinion.

"My success was just one of physique," Jean Marais wrote. "I did not succeed in coming to terms with the various aspects of the character Cocteau presented to me. I lacked *métier* and I complained that the production was too formal and did not do me justice. It was my fault. With that production and more *métier* I should have done better.

"The eulogies of my physique made me understand that this was something I must fight against rather than profit by. I made up my mind to work as hard as I would have to if my appearance was against me and I had to acquire enough talent to compensate for it."

And Cocteau wrote:

> I did not know him well and I directed him in a way that contra-
> dicted his nature. His physique triumphed over his weaknesses which
> were I consider my fault.

Cocteau also observed how strange it was that with this magnificent physique Jean Marais took no interest at all in athletics,
unless something of the kind was necessary for a part, when he
would take every sort of risk.

Jean Marais was living with his mother at le Vésinet near Saint-
Germain, and although Cocteau was once more seeing a certain
amount of Jean Desbordes, and although Marcel Khill from time
to time appeared again, from now on the golden-haired, blue-
eyed actor became the centre of Cocteau's life—and now he had
truly met his angel, his Galahad, for in his association with
"Jeannot", although he had been an *enfant terrible* himself,
Cocteau found a stability that had been lacking all his life.

The next thing he did with Marais was a public reading of *Les
Mariés de la Tour Eiffel* at the Mairie at Puteaux, a "red" suburb
near Paris, which at one time Cocteau would have shunned. As
they worked together he grew steadily more certain of Jeannot's
talent and seriousness. One evening he took him to the Odéon
where Yvonne de Bray was playing Catherine the Great in a
curtain-raiser, and when he found that Marais was as enthusiastic
about her as he was himself, he decided to write a play for them
to star in together which Louis Jouvet would direct. He invited
Marais to go with him to the Hôtel de la Poste at Montargis, near
Saint-Benoît, where Max Jacob lived, and set to work on *Les
Parents Terribles.*

> "It was the first time I had seen him (Cocteau) write," Jean Marais
> recorded. "He told me that a nurse had said to him: 'When you are
> writing, I wouldn't like to meet you in a dark wood.' She was right.
> I watched him over the top of my book. His face frightened me."

This time Cocteau determined to write a play that should not be a vehicle for décor—he only insisted that the doors should be solid enough to be banged—but a vehicle for human beings, and the human being most in his mind was of course Jeannot. He listened to his tales of his mother's adoration of him and of the complications and scenes arising from this, and he thought too of the difficulties he had had himself with Madame Cocteau, in spite of her reserve, when he first wanted to live a life of his own. On this foundation he worked out the theme of *Les Parents Terribles*; there was a reflection too of Jean Desbordes' play *L'Age Ingrat*, which opens with a scene of a distraught mother awaiting her son, and the ensuing wrangle. So often the mirror of Cocteau's art, despite his originality, reflected some aspect of another's work. Thus the plot of *Les Parents Terribles* developed with the adoring mother, the frustrated father living in a web of lies, the golden boy in love for the first time—with, though neither of them know it, his father's young mistress—and the climax of the mother's suicide. Although this work has the smartness of a boulevard play, what Cocteau really intended was a tragedy.

Jean and Jeannot returned to Paris in the early spring of 1938 with the finished script. A bizarre sight met their eyes, for all the buildings of the great 1937 Exhibition were being demolished and Paris looked like a city of ruins. Cocteau had always liked ruins, not so much because of their picturesqueness, but because he had a slightly morbid taste for things in a state of decay—one finds this in many of his drawings and particularly in the *Orphée* film. He could not have been better pleased when Cecil Beaton asked him to accompany him on a tour of these ruins. Cocteau described the event enthusiastically in one of his *Articles de Paris* for Aragon:

Cecil Beaton, serious, sharp-eyed, armed with his camera, climbs and leaps over obstacles. Virgil and Dante did no better on the edge of the abyss.

Cocteau's interest in Al Brown had not diminished and now that he was back in Paris he was involved in his final retraining. The boxer was accused of not fighting according to the rules and an attempt was made to stop Cocteau from sitting close to the ring, as he was said to hypnotise the boxer. In any case that spring Al Brown regained his title of World Featherweight Champion and Cocteau wrote:

Al Brown let them say, "You aren't a boxer. You're a dancer." He laughed and won.

He became the idol of sporting Paris and his sweaters, patterned across the chest and sleeves, were all the rage. But it was a short-lived victory, for he soon drifted back into "show business", first at the Cirque Medrano, where Cocteau got him an engagement, and before long he returned to Harlem, where he once more took to drugs and died.

In the autumn of that year, 1938, which saw Al Brown's triumph, came the production of *Les Parents Terribles* at the Ambassadeurs. The part of the mother was not after all played by Yvonne de Bray, for she fell ill during the rehearsals and Germaine Dermoz took her place. The girl, Madeleine, was played by Alice Cocéa who also, working closely with Cocteau, was responsible for the production. It was a great success, particularly for Jean Marais, although Cocteau was disconcerted by the laughter of the audience in what he considered tragic passages. In spite of the good notices, the play was presently banned by the Conseil Municipal of Paris, which owned Le Théâtre des Ambassadeurs and considered its theme incestuous. It moved to the Théâtre des Bouffes-Parisiens and continued to play to full houses, until Marais had an attack of otitis, and, after a dramatic performance during which the audience threw him handkerchiefs to staunch the bleeding of his nose and ears, was forced to give up the part. Without him the play was less successful.

Before the end of this year Cocteau voiced his premonitions of war in the long poem, *L'Incendie*, dedicated to Jean Marais.

Ce fut alors que l'incendie
Commença, pareil à mille anges en colère,
Ils projetaient cheveux et poings fermés en l'air,
Criant à bouche sombre (tous): L'ai-je assez dit!

He wrote this during the spring of 1939, when he and Jean Marais went off with Cocteau's friend Roger Lannes, for a motor tour of the Dordogne, after which they went down to the Bassin d'Arcachon and stayed at the Hôtel Chantecler in Le Piquey, where Cocteau had lived with Raymond Radiguet nearly twenty years before. Cocteau's intention was to write another play for Jeannot, but the sequel to *Le Potomak* insisted on being written first. So, while Jean Marais, awaiting the new play in a state of great veneration for Cocteau and, hardly daring to show him his work, occupied himself with painting landscapes, which in fact the master greatly admired, Cocteau plunged into a world of meditations and memories. As he was to observe in the preface, like *Le Potomak* in 1913, *La Fin du Potomak* in 1939 was written on the very eve of the war. In it he declared that the terrible Eugènes which he had created in the first book had now spread their malaise all over the world and Potomak had become an invisible monster. In the early pages he described "the Dictator Adolf" playing chess in Berchtesgaden, "moving the pieces with a soft hand and smiling, under his little moustache, at the terror of his adversaries", and with this sense of doom about him Cocteau roamed once more among his fantasies, his fetishes and his obsessions. With the character "Persicaire" he revisited rue Vignon, *"l'appartement des énigmes"*, exploring the mysteries of his precious objects from the Faust lithograph by Delacroix to the crystal ball from a dragon's jaws at the Imperial Palace of Peking—which Persicaire handled, said Cocteau, like Dargelos handled the famous snowball. He devoted some pages of the book

to that favourite of all his obsessions, Dargelos, the cock of the
college with his sinister magic, his dark locks and bruised and
inky knees, although in the final edition of the book he left this
passage out.

Another thing Cocteau stressed in *La Fin du Potomak*, putting
his own views into the mouth of Persicaire, was the importance
of poetry. He had by now written a great number of poems, and
almost all his work in whatsoever field was dominantly poetic.

According to him (Persicaire) poetry is the only one of man's
achievements worthy of the slightest respect. He distrusts metaphysicians, philosophers. He finds them frivolous. Their principles
are destroyed by science, and science itself becomes ridiculous.

In the last pages of *La Fin du Potomak* for the final Notes, which
Cocteau left the reader to apply to the appropriate passages
himself, he returned to the subject of Raymond Radiguet,
mourning his death and contemplating his own:

And so I come to the end. On the same table where that short-
sighted child wrote his books. And his death was approaching and
he was expecting it.

Since the day of my birth my death has been approaching. It
approaches me without any haste. Our zigzags are quite useless. It
approaches in a straight line, always cutting across them . . .

La mort aimait l'enfant qui finissait un livre
Toujours il travaillait et dormait à demi.
Depuis qu'il a cessé de vivre,
Le bonheur est mon ennemi.

Ai-je une minute à vivre?
Ce pas est-il votre pas?
Qu'importe, je laisse un livre
Que vous ne me prendrez pas.

As soon as *La Fin du Potomak* was finished Cocteau and Jean

Marais left Le Piquey and stayed for a while in the Hôtel du Parc at Versailles and here suddenly the new play took shape. Claude Mauriac, in his *Conversations avec André Gide, extraits d'un journal,* gives this description:

*Friday, 26th May 1939.* To Versailles with Roger Lannes where we were to spend the evening with Jean Cocteau who had exiled himself to work in peace . . .

On the chest-of-drawers, among the detective stories and cheap editions of Molière, the manuscript of the new *Potomak* displayed its great white sheets of paper. On the table five or six of his exercise books, familiar to me since childhood, with the design of a fire-balloon on their grey covers: this is the manuscript of his new play, *La Machine à Ecrire,* which he has just composed in five days, at a single go. "The marvellous setting of the park is the only thing that has made this miracle possible," Cocteau said. "Everything is laid out like machinery. In avenue upon avenue the wheels of this astonishing machine disclose themselves. The statues keep up their inimitable jokes. These witty words were once for all modelled in marble . . . which shows the importance of décor for the artist! It was by chance that I returned to Piquey the other day; there wasn't room anywhere else on the Bay. So I consented to stay there and a short time afterwards I knew why: the new *Potomak* imposed itself on me. Where could I speak better about Radiguet than in this very room where I had been with him? So, in spite of the cold and the discomfort, I stayed on in Le Piquey until the day when I was able to put the final full stop to the new work."

Although in the end he wrote it so quickly, Cocteau said himself that he had more trouble over the pseudo-detective tragi-comedy *La Machine à Ecrire* than over any other of his plays. The final idea for the plot came from his friend Albert Willemetz to whom he subsequently dedicated the play, but the whole idea was originally inspired by Cocteau hearing of an actual case of anonymous letters. Once more, as in *Les Parents Terribles,* he had turned to real life for his copy with perhaps a loss of poetry, for *La Machine à Ecrire,* a clever construction giving Marais the chance to play twin brothers, is the least poetic of Cocteau's works. It was, however, to be a long time before Marais was free to act. He had scarcely gone south again to Saint-Tropez with Cocteau than the expected blow fell. There was general mobilisation, war was declared; Marais was called up and Jean Cocteau went back to Paris alone.

Madame Cocteau joined her son Paul in Touraine; Marianne Singer also left Paris with her family; Jean Desbordes and Marcel Khill were mobilised and Cocteau regarded his life, alone in rue Vignon, with despair. Before long Yvonne de Bray, who shared his love for Jean Marais, took pity on Cocteau and invited him to live with her on her house-boat, a converted barge on the river at Neuilly. He was grateful but he was bored. Boredom and frustration were indeed the chief maladies of the intelligentsia and the artists at this time. Cocteau occupied himself with making more drawings of mediaeval figures from *Les Chevaliers de la Table Ronde*—whatever else was happening he always drew—and then, in order to distract both himself and Yvonne de Bray, who was still a member of Jouvet's company, he began to write a backstage comedy, *Les Monstres Sacrés*, still based on real life, hoping all the time that Jeannot would come back to play in it.

When, after some months, Cocteau left the boat, he went to live at the Hôtel Beaujolais with Christian Bérard, leaving for ever the Madeleine for the precincts of the Palais-Royal and becoming Colette's next-door neighbour. Here Jeannot from time to time turned up on leave and Coco Chanel conceived a great liking for him. When in the winter of 1939-40 he was serving in les Vosges and it was terribly cold, she sent him a magnificent pair of gloves—couturier's gloves. Jeannot wrote and thanked her but explained that he could not wear them as nobody else had gloves. Whereupon Chanel sent gloves for the entire company.

In February 1940 *Les Monstres Sacrés* was produced at the Théâtre Michel with Yvonne de Bray. It was dedicated to Jean Marais, but he was of course not there to play in it. Christian

Bérard designed the sets and Cocteau, faithful to an old obsession, wrote in the foreword: "The red of the villa de Chatou is the red of the theatre." The title revived the nickname Cocteau had early given to prima donnas and theatrical stars, and the plot in which a young actress, a *"mythomane"*, suddenly declares to the leading lady that her husband is in love with her and wishes to leave his famous wife, is simply an excuse to describe the theatre *milieu* that Cocteau knew so well.

"It is a light piece," he wrote, "in which tears and cries are controlled. . . . It is a dream—a dream shared by the audience and the author."

Cocteau now set to work on *Le Bel Indifférent*, a one-act piece for the music-hall artist Edith Piaf, whom in his articles for *Le Soir*, he called a genius. Like *La Voix Humaine*, *Le Bel Indifférent* is a monologue, but in this piece the man is on the stage—a silent figure in the hotel bedroom. When *Les Monstres Sacrés* moved to the Théâtre des Bouffes-Parisiens, *Le Bel Indifférent* was played as a curtain-raiser and the whole show was a success.

Meanwhile the shadows darkened. News came that Marcel

Khill had been killed at the front. The terrible prophecy of
*L'Incendie* was proving all too true:

> Et dire que l'épouvantable roue
> Continue à tourner. La loterie
> De chair humaine, au lieu que rie
> La berge verte ointe de bonne boue.

## CHAPTER IX

## L'INCENDIE

IN spite of the absence of Jean Marais at the front and the impending sense of doom permeating *La Fin du Potomak*, it was not until June 1940, when the German armies set foot on the soil of France once more, and many people fled, that Jean Cocteau was deeply affected by the war. Each day became more nerve-racking and more tragic. Nobody knew where Jeannot was and with an unreasoning hope that one day he might appear, Cocteau stayed on in Paris. He had recently bought an apartment in the rue Montpensier in the Palais-Royal, but had not yet moved into it, when a friend in the Cabinet telephoned to tell him that the Germans were coming and he must leave at once. There was no particular reason for Cocteau to leave, but he did as he was bidden. The publisher of Charles Trenet's songs offered him a lift in his car and the Raoul Bretons—Madame Breton was known for her elegance as "the little Marquise"—invited him to Perpignan.

Years later, in a broadcast interview with André Fraigneau, Jean Cocteau described the exodus:

> These friends had piled up the car with trunks and furs and had said to me: "Come to Perpignan because we have a big house there; you shall have two rooms."
>
> And then on the way, the house grew smaller. It became a flat. And the longer the route grew, the shorter the flat became. In the end there was only one room for the four of them. So they deposited me chez Dr Nicolau.

As a matter of fact the Bretons had simply said: "Come to Perpignan." Cocteau had doubtless imagined that they were inviting him to a château, whereas in fact they were only offering friendly help in getting him out of Paris.

Worn out, the travellers arrived one morning in that blazing June at the house of Pierre Nicolau, the surgeon. Cocteau was wearing over his other clothes the garment that had become his uniform—a bathrobe of white towelling—a phenomenon that the children of the family found most impressive.

Cocteau knew Dr Nicolau quite well; the two men had met in Paris and were on intimate enough terms to *tutoyer* one another. The surgeon was a lover of the arts and had been for a long time a friend of Maillol, Dufy and other well-known artists. He was a wealthy man and had filled his house with pictures and *objets d'art*, and there with his wife, his three children, one of the grand-mothers and a host of servants, he lived a well-ordered and luxurious family life.

Cocteau was welcomed by the whole family with affection and veneration and given a room with two beds on the first floor—he was by no means the first artist for whom Dr Nicolau had found a refuge. And it was there, in this gracious house that recalled that of his Lecomte grandfather, that Jean Cocteau listened in tears to Maréchal Pétain's announcement of the fall of France. His tears were not only those of any Frenchman weeping for the capitulation, but those too of one who saw his personal present and future collapsing before his eyes, one who was not to know for weeks if his life had any meaning left. He had worked hard to create a private universe, and here he was reduced to tears like everybody else, submerged in the general catastrophe. This was one of the most poignant experiences of his life.

During the following weeks Cocteau was ill and stayed in bed for much of the time, incapable of writing—scarcely even able to draw. His conversation ranged round three subjects: the lack of news of Jeannot and the terrible fear that he might be dead, his uncertainty whether under the German occupation he would be able to work freely, and his obsession with the actress Nathalie Paley whom he called the Princess. He told his hosts that she was the only woman he had ever loved, that she had been carrying his child and had put an end to the pregnancy, after which he had never wanted to see her again. How much of this tale is true will perhaps never be known. It may have been a fantasy, born of a thwarted desire to achieve physical creation, or Cocteau may simply have been seeking to present himself in a better light to this family which, although open-minded about the arts, was morally conventional. Perhaps too Cocteau talked about Nathalie Paley in order to dull the anguish that gripped him when he thought about Jeannot, and the frustration that he felt and often wrote about at being cheated by nature of a son, may have become linked with this sudden new frustration at being dethroned as Prince of Paris. To this day, Jacques Nicolau, the elder son of the doctor, who was only sixteen when Cocteau went to stay with them, is speculating about this. What he remembers clearly is that during these weeks Cocteau was smoking very heavily. Jacques and his brother used to bicycle round the neighbouring villages buying up all the packets of Balto that they could find for their guest.

Among Cocteau's luggage were several jam-jars of crude opium and an ivory pipe. Although he implied that he had given up smoking opium after the disintoxication of 1931, it is clear that he had never renounced this practice. He had smoked with Christian Bérard, but there had not been a trace of the drug's influence in any of the many works he had produced since writing *Opium*. Clearly he was the master now and not the slave. It was not long before the Nicolaus realised that their guest had this habit, for an aroma of opium sometimes permeated the house. True to his principles, however, Cocteau did not preach what he practised, and although Jacques tried a pipe once—presumably without his parents' knowledge—he never repeated the experiment.

Cocteau had also brought with him a little ball of ambergris that he rolled incessantly in the palms of his hands; he smelt its perfume; he explored its contours. Ambergris is known to be

curiously sensitive to hygrometric changes, and when the ball
crackled, Cocteau took to his bed and was ill, attributing his
illness to the witchery of the little ball.

He took an interest in the young Jacques, an image of the son
he craved, and encouraged him to read great novels such as: *La
Princesse de Clèves, Le Rouge et le Noir, Le Grand Meaulnes* and
*Le Diable au Corps*. He himself was devouring endless detective
novels and would continue so to do for the rest of his life.

After several weeks of this acute anxiety, Cocteau had the
indescribable joy of seeing Jeannot arrive, bringing with him a
dog that he had found during the retreat in the forest of Com-
piègne. Marais had fled with his company before the Germans
and had been demobilised at Auch. So now Jeannot occupied the
spare bed in Cocteau's room and was adopted by the Nicolaus
as a son. The dog was named Moulouk, which Cocteau thought
meant angel in Arabic, and in his view the dog had been a guardian angel to this young soldier. His Galahad had returned and
with him happiness.

As soon as the young Jacques had taken his *baccalauréat*, they all
moved to the Nicolaus' summer home in the mountains at
Vernet-les-Bains. A few days after their arrival Cocteau shut
himself into his room and only appeared briefly for meals. The
presence of Jeannot had given him back the urge to write and
when he reappeared he had finished a new draft of *La Machine
à Ecrire*, with a setting like Vernet-les-Bains, which he proceeded
to read to his friends.

Cocteau now made a great many drawings of Jacques and his
twin sister—a subject that inevitably appealed to him, the pair,
in spite of their normality, recalling the brother and sister in *Le
Grand Ecart* and in *Les Enfants Terribles*, and all those other boy-
girl couples who haunted Cocteau's work.

It was a peaceful summer. The Occupation and the privations
it imposed were not yet felt in the free zone, and informed of his
whereabouts by some mysterious grape-vine, many of Cocteau's

friends came to visit him in his retreat. Jean Marais took to painting again, local landscapes and dead trees in the form of
human beings, while Cocteau, inspired by his Galahad, turned
out yet more romantic figures based on the knights of the
Round Table.

In September, holidays over, everyone returned to Perpignan.
Soon after this the German authorities invited residents of the
occupied zone to return to their homes. Cocteau at once decided
that he and Jeannot should go back to Paris. In spite of the
horror of the situation there was also a lure—an adventure, the
unknown.

Dr Nicolau begged Cocteau to leave behind his stock of opium
as it was too risky to enter occupied territory with the drug in his
possession. Jean Cocteau agreed and this may possibly have been
the end of his opium-smoking. An act of will perhaps succeeded
where each so-called cure had failed. He took the train at Perpignan with Jeannot and arrived in occupied Paris to start a new
life. He was determined, come what might, to be creative.

In 1941 *Les Parents Terribles* was produced for the third time,
with Yvonne de Bray for whom the part of the mother had been
written, but without Jean Marais who was playing Nero in
Racine's *Britannicus* at the Comédie-Française, of which he was
now a member. Cocteau greatly admired him in this part, indeed
later he spoke of it as his finest rôle. At the same time Marais was
busy with preparations for *La Machine à Ecrire;* not only was he
to play the twin brothers, but he was also designing the sets.

Once again *Les Parents Terribles* roused the fury of Cocteau's
enemies. The fascist *Parti Populaire Français* and the military
police joined forces against it; tear bombs were thrown among the
audience and the stage was invaded. The case against Cocteau
was twofold: he was known to have Communist friends; Picasso
for one, and Aragon, for whose paper *Le Soir* he had written so
many articles, and secondly he had proved himself immoral—the
play was again considered incestuous—and those now in authority

made a profession of morality. *Les Parents Terribles* was conse-
quently taken off.

La *Machine à Ecrire*, when it was produced at the Hébertot in
the same year, caused further trouble. "The Occupants," as
Cocteau put it to André Fraigneau, "found the play scandalous
because they were so much concerned for France." The man who
launched the attack, not only on the play but very meanly on the
cast, was Alain Laubreaux, the collaborationist journalist. At an
enormous risk to himself and to Cocteau, Jean Marais repaid
Laubreaux for his treachery first by spitting in his face, when they
found themselves beside him in a restaurant, and then by seizing
his walking-stick, as the journalist was about to attack him in the
street and beating him with his fists. Pelting rain helped Marais
and Cocteau to get away without being arrested and the play
was not taken off.

Hating the "Occupants" as he did, Cocteau nevertheless had
deep and warm ties with Germany—not with the Germany of
Hitler, but with the country of which Victor Hugo had sung,
that of such varying geniuses as Goethe and Nietzsche, and in
whose language Rilke too had written, the Germany of the great
musicians, the country of metaphysicians, the country that had
produced his beloved nurse, Jéphine, on account of whom he
knew the language so well. And in Paris now there were official
artists and intellectuals in high places, Germans whom Cocteau
knew and respected.

There was Arno Breker, the sculptor, for instance, whom he
had met through Picasso and who made the bronze head of
Cocteau that now stands in the chapel at Milly-la-Forêt. He was
an official artist of the German government, and Ernst Jünger,
the writer, although he was a Francophile and no Nazi, was a
high-ranking officer in that army. He had known Paris well
before the war and he too used to visit Picasso, although it was at
a luncheon party at Paul Morand's that Jünger now met Cocteau
again.

"Sympathetic and at the same time tormented," he wrote of him, "like a man living in a private hell, but in comfort."

When the liberation came, Ernst Jünger was one of the people who defied Hitler's orders to destroy Paris, and after the war his books were refused publication in Germany.

Marcel Jouhandeau, the writer, already a good friend of Cocteau's, also consorted with these German intellectuals, as did Sacha Guitry and Paul Morand. They often dined openly with Ernst Jünger and other friends at the restaurant Calvet, and Cocteau even went as far as to write a series of poems in German.

He also continued his journalism by writing a series of articles for *Comœdia*. He composed these, he said, to escape from a nightmare and from the insults of the journalists of *Je suis Partout*, but of his choice of material he wrote:

> It is my love for actors, singers, dancers, mimers, that encouraged me to begin the following week a series of portraits under the title *Le Foyer des Artistes*.

In these spirited articles, which continued for many months, he wrote of Arletty, Maurice Chevalier, Marguerite Jamois, Charles Trenet, Yvonne de Bray, Jean-Louis Barrault, Raimu and others, showing not only great affection for these artists but great perception of their talents.

It was strange to find Cocteau in Paris in this month of August 1941, but he was certainly fully occupied, not only with his work, but also with the move into his apartment in the Palais-Royal, this "*coin*" of which he was so fond. With Madame Cocteau failing and in a Home and Marianne Singer always away, most of Cocteau's ties with his early life, except those of vivid memories, were severed.

"I rented this tiny cave, wedged between the Palais-Royal Theatre and the block of houses ending in the Comédie-Française," he wrote later in *La Difficulté d'Etre*, "in 1940, when the German army was marching on Paris . . ."

"From this bed of sorry state," he continued when he was staying in bed, ill, "I gaze upon my room, a narrow cabin opening on to the arcade of the Palais-Royal, framed by the sound of footsteps . . ."

And then he spoke of what remained of his old possessions:

The most engaging bits of such wreckage, thrown up on this little red beach, is without doubt the Gustave Doré group of which the Charles de Noailles gave me a plaster cast from which I had a bronze made. . . . This group is on a column standing between the so-called *castor* window and a tall piece of slate that can be moved aside and that conceals a small room which is too cold to be used in winter. It was there that I wrote *Renaud et Armide*, away from everything, set free from telephone and doorbells, in the summer of 1941, on an architect's table above which one sees saved from my room in the Rue Vignon where it adorned the wall-paper, Christian Bérard's large drawing in charcoal and red chalk representing the meeting of Oedipus and the Sphinx.

The slate door and several others in the hall enable me to jot down in chalk addresses and work to be done, for I have a memory like a sieve. Visitors of a romantic disposition think they are looking at hieroglyphics, rather than at an aid to memory which I sponge out every week.

On the right of my bed are two heads, one Roman, in marble, of a faun (this belonged to my Lecomte grandfather), the other of Antinoüs, under a glass dome, a painted terracotta . . . A third head adorns that of my bed; the terracotta of Raymond Radiguet, done by Lipchitz, in the year of his death.

Cocteau then gives "a list of the pictures hanging on the walls above the flood of disorder", a motley collection including the early portrait of himself by Picasso.

"There" [the Palais-Royal], he continues, "I know everyone, their habits, their cats, their dogs. There I walk among the smiles and the news we get from one another. There I eat in those little cellars to which one descends by four steps. There I meet my friends and the ghost of Giraudoux, who came from elsewhere but was one of us. From my window I gossip with Colette, as she walks across the garden with her cane, her silken cravat, her flat felt hat, her fine eyes, her bare feet, her sandals."

Marais moved into this apartment with Cocteau and Colette was delighted with them both. In her book *Le Fanal Bleu*, so named because this was what her neighbours called "this lantern of mine, burning blue day and night between the pair of red curtains", she wrote of them both appreciatively and of "the dog Moulouk, who owed allegiance to one person only, to Jean Marais", "Jean Marais, nicknamed Jeannot, with his crest of hair and his irreproachably irregular features . . .", Jeannot who, as a born actor, could change his size to suit a part. "The hardest thing for Jean Marais, if he is to play Chéri, will be to make a temporary surrender of his natural innocence." And she described Jean Cocteau, with his long legs folded so that he could perch on her "raft", his long elegant fingers shading his face that the rays of her blue lantern turned green.

Here then in the Palais-Royal, where he felt so much at home, undaunted by the scandals caused by his former plays, Cocteau began to write *Renaud et Armide* for the Comédie-Française, Marie Bell and naturally for Jeannot, although he did not in fact play in it. And to add to the pleasure of working again for the theatre, besides the company of Jeannot he once more had that of Bébé Bérard, for the latter came back from the unoccupied zone, all the way from Marseilles, to design the décor and the costumes for the play.

"*La tragédie est-elle morte? Alors, vive la tragédie!*" Cocteau's preface to *Renaud et Armide* begins and it goes on to explain that for years he had cherished a dream of writing a tragedy in verse. Perhaps for the moment his mirror gave him the image of a new Racine.

What he achieved was a spoken opera, a quartet, an allegoric

love-story—he said himself that it was his passion for love-stories
that inspired him to write it. The theme, as described to André
Fraigneau, was "the loneliness of beings who sense one another
when they do not see and who, when they do see one another,
fail to achieve a union". In short Cocteau was once more writing
about the impossibility of love. Renaud, the conquering king, falls
in love with the invisible enchantress, and she with his visible male
beauty. He adores her mystery, and when she sheds this and is
visible, his love for her dies. In fury she binds him with spells,
only to find that she has made of him nothing but a demented
prisoner. Her only way to win back his love is to give him the
ring that he demands—Orphée's ring, "the golden ring that
mirrors . . ." But if she does this she knows that at his first kiss she
will die—and so this simple tragedy ends.

Before the production of this play, however, Cocteau was
involved in a matter very far removed from fantasy. By 1942
Jean Genet, then in his mid-thirties, had been in prison for some
years pending his trial for robbery and other criminal offences.
In prison he had begun to write poetry and autobiographies of a
poetic satanism, which were secretly circulated and gave him a
reputation surpassing that of Rimbaud with André Gide, Jean-
Paul Sartre and a number of other writers. When Cocteau heard
that Genet's case was coming up in the Cour de Justice and
included a charge of immoral writing, he joined Gide and others
in courageously defending him in the name of poetry.

"Jean Genet," Cocteau wrote, in *La Difficulté d'Etre*, "who must
surely be regarded as a moralist one day, paradoxical as this
may seem, since we are in the habit of confusing the moralist with
the moraliser, a few weeks ago said these poignant words to me:
'To watch our heroes live and to pity them is not enough. We must
take their sins upon ourselves and suffer the consequences.'" And
in the footnote Cocteau added: "In order to 'place' Jean Genet in
the eyes of the Court of Justice I told this Court that I considered
him to be one of France's great writers. One can guess how the
newspapers under the Occupation gloated over the whole business.

But a Paris Court is always afraid of repeating some famous blunder, of condemning Baudelaire. I saved Genet. And I do not withdraw any of my evidence."

Poetry triumphed. Genet was released and was now often to be found staying with Cocteau at the Palais-Royal and later at Milly-la-Forêt. Thanks to him he was able to go on writing, to have his works published and to become before long a famous playwright. Sartre saw in Genet a confirmation of his philosophic theories and because of this a sympathy grew between Sartre and Cocteau, while Genet, for his part, had a great admiration for Cocteau, both for the man and for his work. He found him gracious, compassionate and essentially Greek.

"Thus his work appears as a light, airborne civilisation," Genet wrote, in a Belgian magazine, "suspended from the heart of our own. To which is added the figure of the poet himself, thin, knotted and silvered like the olive trees."

In 1943 *Renaud et Armide* was at last presented at the Comédie-Française, produced by the author with Marie Bell playing Armide, but with Maurice Escande as Renaud. Jean Marais had left the Comédie-Française for a part in a film, just when he was needed to play Hyppolite in a revival of Marie Bell's *Phèdre*. When, because the film had not materialised, he presented himself once more at the theatre, he was not engaged, the Administrator telling him that the Comédie-Française "was not a revolving door".

In spite of this disappointment Cocteau was proud of *Renaud et Armide*, his first major work to be shown at the Comédie-Française, which gave him an official position and allayed any suspicions the Germans may have had. He was now remarkably unaffected by the Occupation; he neither lost nor gained by it, he took no part in politics and immersed himself in work and, as always, in his friends.

It was during this year 1943 that Madame Cocteau died.

"My mother's death dealt gently with me," Cocteau wrote. "She had no 'second' childhood. She returned to her own, saw me in mine, thought I was at school, talked to me in detail about Maisons-Laffitte and was not troubled. Death had only to smile at her and take her hand."★

Cocteau made a drawing of his mother on her death-bed as he had done of several of his friends.

I was left alone in their rooms for a long time. I looked at them very closely in order to follow their lines. I touched them, I admired them. For death takes trouble with her statues. She smoothes away their wrinkles . . . I felt that we were quite close, like the two sides of a coin which cannot know each other, but are only separated from each other by the thickness of the metal.

An old friend Cocteau now saw again was Maurice Sachs. He telephoned saying that he was at the Hôtel de Castille and very unhappy and he begged Cocteau to visit him. The latter found him in bed and very pale and Sachs apologised for the insulting things he had sometimes said and written about Cocteau, although he had written eulogies too. Cocteau readily forgave him, just as he had forgiven his earlier misdemeanours and remembered him for his intelligence and charm. "I have always preferred thieves to policemen."

Not long afterwards Maurice Sachs went voluntarily to work in Germany where he died.

One somewhat unexpected thing Cocteau did in this crowded year was to write a preface for a collection of El Greco reproductions entitled *Le Mythe du Greco*, his critical essay being chiefly concerned with the *Martyrdom of Saint Maurice*, a picture that José-Maria Sert owned and which Cocteau therefore knew well. And in the mirror of El Greco and his work he clearly saw himself.

Of late his mind had been chiefly turning in the direction of the

★ *The Difficulty of Being.*

cinema in which art alone or rather in which "vehicle", for this was how he described writing, drawing, making films, it was possible to attract the wide public he now desired. He had the year before worked with Marcel Carné on a picture to be called *Juliette ou la Clé des Songes*. This film had not in fact materialised, but it whetted Cocteau's appetite and he became passionately interested in the cinema. Also in 1943 he wrote the scenario for *L'Eternel Retour* and the moment he had it safely down on paper he agreed—in order to gain experience in this medium—to work on the dialogue and play a small part in Serge de Poligny's film *Le Baron Fantôme*.

"It was very complicated," he told André Fraigneau, "because one had to leave at five in the morning for the Saint-Maurice studio. One had to walk a long way in the cold after leaving the métro, and it was a real apprenticeship that I was serving.

I wanted to learn, and one can only learn on the spot. Well, in *Le Baron Fantôme* I learnt. To begin with I was very scared when I was playing. I had four words to say and I who always demand that actors should be prompt and word-perfect—well I can tell you they would have laughed, because I made a mess of it; they had to start it over again twenty times. After this I served my apprenticeship with the directors."

It was not only with the directors but with the technicians that Cocteau served as the artisan he always rejoiced to be. He had a finger in every pie. More even than when he was working in the theatre, he found his inner loneliness assuaged by working with other people—that loneliness to escape which, he said, he engaged in endless talk.

Like Carné's *Les Visiteurs du Soir* and other films of this epoch, *L'Eternel Retour*, which Cocteau now made with Jean Delannoy, drew its theme from mythology, ignoring present reality and taking no risks; for Cocteau it was a continuation of his preoccupation with the knights of the Round Table, but now his Galahad had become Tristan with Madeleine Sologne for his

Isolde and Moulouk for his dog. True to himself, in this film too, made ten years after *Le Sang d'un Poète*, Cocteau revived one of his life-long fetishes. "The highest poetic moment of this film," he wrote later, "is the scene in the garage where a brother and a sister are living like those in *Les Enfants Terribles*." And once again in *Renaud et Armide*, as in some region of Cocteau's own soul, love could not find an earthly consummation, but led inevitably to death, while yet another of his fetishes appeared— the scarf flying as a banner from the lovers' boat. "The title, *L'Eternel Retour*, is borrowed," Cocteau said, "from Nietzsche, and suggests that old myths may be reborn without their heroes knowing it."

At first the Germans were dubious about allowing this film to be made—the theme was Wagnerian, although Georges Auric was composing the music, and they did not see what right the French had to make use of Wagner. In the end they gave their consent, although the film could not be shot, as was wished, in Brittany. The producers had to content themselves with Nice and the Lake of Geneva. The same point—that the theme was Wagnerian—told against the film later in a different way, several critics both in France and in England taking the view that it was Nazi propaganda, presumably because of the blonde hair of the protagonists, Madeleine Sologne had had to bleach hers to match Jean Marais' gold. It was a relief for her to have the distraction of this film at such a time, for her husband was Jewish and in hiding, and Jean Cocteau certainly did what he could to be of help to them both.

Despite any shadow cast by the critics *L'Eternel Retour*, which was shown in Paris in 1944, was a tremendous success. Cocteau had managed to show the public the mixture of dreams and reality, of natural and supernatural that was the essence of his poetry. It was one's duty, he told Fraigneau, not to obey a public that did not know its own mind, but to lead it and trick it into swallowing the show.

Jean Cocteau and Colette in a box at the theatre (*Collection O.R.T.F.*)

Jean Cocteau and Christian Bérard during the filming of *La Voix Humaine*, 1947 (*photo Serge Lido*)

Afterwards they digest it. If they don't eliminate it instantly, the beneficial poison enters into the organism. Little by little, the sickness of stupidity begins to be mitigated, and, in some rare cases, even cured.

Jean Marais was now the rage of Paris. *L'Eternel Retour* was in modern dress and everyone started wearing Jacquard pullovers like Marais'; all the little girls hung his portrait round their necks and Madeleine Sologne's Nordic coiffure with fair hair framing her face and falling straight to her shoulders became the fashion.

A new friend had now joined the Jean-Jeannot ménage in the Palais-Royal. Marais had met Paul Morihien at a pool where the latter taught swimming. He was charming and very good-looking, so Marais led him to Cocteau who at once engaged him as a kind of manager.

In spite of this success, 1944 was a deeply tragic year for Cocteau. Max Jacob had continued to live at Saint-Benoît-sur-Loire and there Cocteau had visited him several times, sometimes alone and sometimes with Marais. But in February Max Jacob was suddenly arrested, his brother, sister and brother-in-law having already been deported to their deaths. On the way to prison Max Jacob was permitted to write a letter to Cocteau. He did not complain; it was simply a short and affectionate farewell note. Cocteau at once organised a manifesto urging his release, which was signed among others by Utrillo, Braque, Picasso, André Salmon and Sacha Guitry. His release was granted but too late. Max Jacob had died in the prison hospital, congratulating himself that he would soon be with God and apologising to his fellow Jews for their enforced view of his Christian death.

Tragedy followed tragedy. At the beginning of the war Jean Desbordes had married and soon afterwards joined the Resistance. In the summer of 1944 he was captured.

"Desbordes died shortly before the liberation in Paris," Cocteau told Fraigneau, "tortured by the Gestapo, rue de la Pompe. This child,

F

who could not bear so much as a pin-prick, died in appalling suffering without giving away the name of a single one of his comrades. One must salute him as one of the least known heroes of the Resistance."

Close to the Liberation as they now were, none of Desbordes' friends dared to give public honour to his heroic death.

These tragedies weighed heavily on Cocteau. He decided to leave Paris and distract himself by going to stay in Brittany with friends who had an old *château*, in the style, so he said, of Sarah Bernhardt's *châteaux*, with stoves that smoked and windows that rattled.

As always he found solace in work. Jeannot had demanded a play in which he should be silent during the first act, weep with joy in the second act and fall backwards down a staircase in the third, and Cocteau liked such demands. They set the machinery going, he said, and brought things out of one that one did not know were there.

So, in Brittany, he began to write *L'Aigle à deux Têtes*. In the evenings he would walk over to Pont-Aven to eat oysters. One day he went to luncheon at Madame Botrel's, an Alsatian friend who was an extremely good cook and had a delightful garden full of flowers. A fortnight later he called on her again—everyone of her camellias had disappeared and when he asked where they were, Madame Botrel told him that the ladies of Pont-Aven had taken them to put in the church in front of the statue of Joan of Arc to ask her to let the English come back to France without delay. Their prayer was swiftly answered.

In Brittany too, in these last weeks of the Occupation, Jean Cocteau added to the long poem *Léone*, which he had been inter-mittently writing during the past two years. *Léone* is an imaginary creature who haunts the poet's dreams, who visits the characters in his work—Renaud, Armide, Isolde—and the places he fre-quents, such as Brittany. She is both the bright mirror in which

Jean Cocteau contemplates himself and the dark mirror that
reflects a time when death inexplicably haunts the earth.

> Je dors et je le sais et je sais que je rêve
> Il ne tient qu'à moi seul que ce rêve s'achève
> Et que Léone enfin me quitte pour toujours.

With the end of the war Léone left Jean Cocteau, liberating
him for new exploits.

A cruel Eugene.

A cruel Eugene

## CHAPTER X

# THE PEAK

THE Liberation found Jean Cocteau back in his Palais-Royal apartment with the whole of Paris open to him, but he was not quite at ease. Some of his friends were in serious trouble as collaborationists and Cocteau felt his own position, partly because of his German friendships, to be precarious. He stressed his ties with the Left, with Aragon and the Jews, and he was delighted to be received at the British Embassy. As earlier he had flung himself into work to forget the Occupation, now he flung himself into work to distract himself from his anxiety, and the Cinema opened its arms to him.

The first commission was to write the dialogue for Robert Bresson's *Les Dames du Bois de Boulogne*. This psychological film did not accord with Cocteau's own ideas, but he liked Bresson, who remained a friend for the rest of his life, and he was enthusiastic about its star, the Spaniard Maria Casarès, who was later to play an important part in *Orphée*. He then turned to the enormous work of making the film *La Belle et la Bête*, during which time he kept a detailed journal, later published as a book.

The chief problem in making this picture was, he tells us, in addition to all the usual technical ones, that of finance in a time of stringent economy, but he adds: "Perhaps this is the way to stimulate the imagination which sleeps quietly enough in contact with wealth."

The theme was taken from the fairy-tale by Madame Leprince de Beaumont, although it is usually attributed to Perrault because, Cocteau says, it appears in the *Bibliothèque Rose*, on which all well brought up children are nurtured, in company with Charles Perrault's famous stories. And although some of his critics were to accuse him of being "too Cocteau", in fact he did not add a mite of fantasy to Madame de Beaumont's tale, which he includes at the end of the journal. And over and over again in conversation and in writing he affirmed that the most poetic, most magical moments of this film do not occur in the Beast's enchanted castle, but with Beauty's sisters in the poultry yard, just as in L'Eternel Retour they occur with the brother and sister in the garage. "Occur" is the right word, for writing of La Belle et la Bête Cocteau once again stresses that he does not intrude upon poetry. "It has to happen of its own accord. Even to whisper its name scares it away."

The production of the film was begun at the end of August 1945 in Touraine, where Cocteau miraculously discovered a house resembling that of his imagination. Walking in the region, before the house came into view, he told Fraigneau, he heard his own voice—the son of the proprietor, who exactly resembled the merchant in the story, was playing one of Cocteau's records in the garden. This later account does not quite tally with the contemporary description in the journal where Cocteau recorded that *if* he had gone there the day before he *would* have heard his own voice, but the finding of the place that he "recognised" as the setting for the film was certainly true.

The site was not far from where Cocteau's brother and sister-in-law lived, so he sometimes visited them—with members of the company and alone. La Belle et la Bête took many months to make. Cocteau was not very well much of the time; the skin ailment that was constantly to trouble him had begun and he had various other maladies, and he noted with alarm, while shaving, that his hairs had grown white. When he looked in the mirror he saw "a sad old gentleman"; he had to get used to the fact that this was himself, but he thanked God that his spirit was still young and the inspiration of the work carried him through, although sometimes doctor's orders forced him to rest. He was very sympathetic when other people were unwell, recording anxiously in his journal the riding accident of one of the actresses and Jeannot's boils which gave him agony.

Christian Bérard once more joined Cocteau to design the décor and the costumes, a wonderful combination of Vermeer with that of the original illustrations to the story by Gustave Doré, while his white poodle, Cola, joined Jean Marais, Josette Day and the rest of the cast. Meanwhile Georges Auric was faithfully composing the score; as with Bérard, Cocteau had complete confidence in Auric and never wanted to hear a note of the music until he experienced "the shock" of the whole.

Jean Marais' make-up for the Beast, devised so that he should not have to wear a mask, but have his own fair features transformed into the tragic fur face of the Beast, was an agonising affair, the covering of his whole face and hands with gum and hair taking sometimes as much as five hours for Cocteau to accomplish, and causing both of them much pain. According to Fraigneau, Laurence Olivier once told Cocteau that he would never have stood such torment, and Cocteau agreed that to persist in that metamorphosis from a human being to an animal one would have to have a passion for one's métier plus the intense love Marais had for his dog. It was not only his remarkable make-up that transformed him into the Beast, but the terrible inner process he went through in his dressing-room—such as caused Dr Jekyll to become Mr Hyde. As for Josette Day, one may well quote Colette on the occasion of a visit from her:

... the young woman who, as recompense for having her face laid bare from ear to tip of nose, from chin to forehead, every line removed from her cheeks and thus rendered glossy as a wet-glazed jar, had suddenly become beautiful enough to play Beauty herself.

Altogether this was a time of immense labour, immense fatigue and great satisfaction, culminating for Cocteau in feeling that he really had succeeded in making a dream come true.

Meanwhile, in Paris, Paul Morihien, the young man Jean

Marais had met at a swimming pool and who was still more or less Cocteau's manager had, under the latter's patronage, opened a bookshop in the Palais-Royal. "*Paul-le-libraire*" Colette used to call him, saying that this was easier to pronounce than the name "Morihien"; and now, in company with Cocteau and Jeannot, he was very much one of the Palais-Royal family—although Jean Marais with his great charm and gentleness remained Colette's favourite. Her servant, Pauline, and Cocteau's Madeleine, whom he called his *gouvernante*, "*les deux servantes au grand coeur*", almost as well-known characters as Marcel Proust's Céleste, were also important members of this "family" which called the Palais-Royal its village.

Madeleine was a great lover of cats and had persuaded Cocteau to have three Siamese. In the mornings she would put a pile of white paper at one end of the kitchen table, which also held the telephone, and there Cocteau would sit doing his correspondence —he always answered letters from strangers—while at the other end she prepared food for her master and the cats. Cocteau soon came to share her love of cats and supported quite a number of feline societies.

Another well-known member of the "family" was Colette's third husband, "le bon Maurice Goudeket", who had been at the Condorcet with Cocteau and who had always been, the latter said, "the tamer of his wife's wild beasts and of the enchanting wild beast that she was herself". The Palais-Royal friends met frequently at the restaurant Grand Véfour in their village, where Colette and Cocteau had their chairs marked with bronze name-plates. When she grew too lame to walk they carried her to her place in a chair. It was during this period that Cocteau painted his splendid portrait of her. He always adored her although he was slightly envious of her novels being best-sellers.

Colette now spent a great deal of time in bed and Cocteau, Marais and Morihien were her constant visitors. In *Le Fanal Bleu* she described how taken aback she and Cocteau both were by having to speak into a microphone when they did a first broadcast together from her room, and on a later occasion how Cocteau called on her in the middle of the morning—she would not have been surprised had it been the middle of the night—because there was a strike in the film studio and he did not know what to do with himself. "They have taken away my poison," he told her.

Cocteau decorated the walls of Morihien's bookshop, hung up his drawings and spent most of his time there, writing things for Morihien to publish. Just as people had been sure that Cocteau was the real owner of the Gaya Bar and Le Boeuf sur le Toit, so now, with a little more justification, they believed him to be the proprietor of the bookshop. Presently, as Paul Morihien knew nothing about books, Cocteau brought Raoul Leven in to help him, although the imprint on the books remained Morihien's. Leven was a middle-aged Jew, a great friend of Cocteau's, who had known both Raymond Radiguet and Jean Desbordes and had been a member of the Stock publishing house, so he was well-equipped to work in the bookshop and to help Morihien as Cocteau's co-manager.

The first work of Cocteau's that he published was the long poem *La Crucifixion* that Cocteau wrote between 1945 and 1946. This choice of subject was not a sign of a new "conversion" or of a further religious phase; for Cocteau now the Christian image of Christ on the Cross was essentially an artist's symbol of the sufferings of Man and the lone agony of the Poet. *La Crucifixion* is a highly visual poem which also has great tonal quality, and its lay-out is designed to make an agreeable pattern on the page:

> Sérénissime. L'écusson
> des meurtres.
> Les animaux
> agenouillés qui pleurent. Les clefs au nombre
> de sept. La roue
> triangulaire des miracles.
> La main

qui n'en est pas une. L'oeil
qui n'en est pas un.
L'écoeurement mortel
du rêve. La simple
difficulté d'être. La bohémienne
endormie. La tour
du jeu d'échecs. Son fou
libre.

Although so happily established in the little apartment in the Palais-Royal, which he always retained, Cocteau and Jean Marais now realised another of their dreams—a home in the country —by buying part of an old house at Milly-la-Forêt, a lovely hamlet not far from Fontainebleau, which was fast becoming fashionable—Christian Dior among others having taken a house in the district. There was a large salon on the ground floor opening into the garden, where Cocteau housed his treasures, including Bérard's designs of Oedipus and the Sphinx, and a big kitchen which was occupied by the caretakers and the telephone. On the first floor was a small room where for the first time Cocteau collected something of a library and next door to this were their bedrooms. Cocteau's contained a narrow, red-covered canopied bed, beside which stood a photograph on a reading-desk of a group of schoolboys including himself and Dargelos, and on the wall opposite Marais painted a bright landscape. The room also contained a small bureau on which stood the crystal ball, another of Cocteau's fetishes.

It was a time of feverish activity, for besides the move, the going backwards and forwards constantly to Paris—Cocteau now had a car which the gardener drove—and receiving their circle (Genet, Bérard, Morihien and many theatrical friends) at Milly, there was much new work on hand. Cocteau worked chiefly in the spacious salon, furnished largely with things he had inherited from Monsieur Lecomte. He was intent now on his beautiful "*mimodrame*", *Le Jeune Homme et la Mort*, for which

Roland Petit did the choreography and Wakhevitch the décor, while Madame Karinska and Christian Bérard designed the costumes. In this work Cocteau was trying, he said, to make use in dance, as he already had in films, of "accidental synchronisation". To this end the dancers practised to jazz rhythms, particularly *Sentimental Journey*, which were replaced at the performance by Bach's *Passacaglia*. This was putting into practice one of Cocteau's favourite dogmas—the cult of imperfection; perfect symmetry, perfect balance, perfect harmony of any kind, he maintained, engendered inertia.

The theme of this *mimodrame* could not have been nearer or dearer to Cocteau's heart—the young man, the desperate young artist in his lonely room, the young woman who taunts him and leads him to the gallows, and who returns in the guise of Death to lead him away across the roof-tops.

*Le Jeune Homme et la Mort* opened as the third item in a ballet programme at the Théâtre des Champs-Elysées in June 1946 and received a great ovation, partly because of Jean Babilée's brilliant performance. The audience seemed to Cocteau to come out of a hypnotic trance. In *La Difficulté d'Etre*, the first thing that he wrote at Milly-la-Forêt and which was published by Paul Morihien in 1947, he says:

> This evening they are taking me from my country retreat to the wings from which I shall watch the second performance . . .
> I have just come back from the Champs-Elysées Theatre. Our ballet was given the same reception. Perhaps our dancers had less fire, but they performed their dances with a great precision. In any case, whatever goes amiss, the beauty of the performance leaps the footlights, and the general atmosphere is an image of me, of my table, of my myths, an involuntary paraphrase of *Le Sang d'un Poète*.

*Le Jeune Homme et la Mort* was later produced in New York and in London with equal success. By this time, working on in the same feverish manner, Cocteau had finished *L'Aigle à deux*

*Têtes*. The theme of this play, designed for Edwige Feuillère and Jean Marais was suggested, apart from Jeannot's demands, by the assassination of Elisabeth of Austria and the mystery attaching to the death of Ludwig II of Bavaria. Perhaps at this moment Cocteau saw a slight reflection of Victor Hugo in his mirror, and the result was a tragic Ruritanian story, telling as ever of love bringing death in its wake. The same team united again for the production: Christian Bérard designing the royal costumes, Georges Auric composing the royal hymn and Jean Cocteau himself directing the play for the Théâtre Hébertot. It was first produced in Brussels, whither Cocteau and Marais had already gone for a revival of *Renaud et Armide*, and then moved to Lyons before opening in Paris in November 1946, its success being chiefly due to the performances of the stars. Ronald Duncan made an adaptation of the play in English which was also very successful at the Lyric Theatre, Hammersmith, in the autumn of 1946 with Eileen Herlie and James Donald.

This was a full year indeed for Jean Cocteau. *La Belle et la Bête* had been shown in October at the Cannes Festival and had won prizes for its production and its music; now in December the film was awarded the important Prix Louis Delluc.

Nor was this an eventful period for Cocteau's work alone, for now on to his private stage there stepped an altogether new player.

Edouard Dermit, who was twenty-two years old and came of a Jugoslav mining family, was working in a mine in Lorraine, where his sisters too worked in the office. His hobby was to paint —his constant pleading had induced his mother to give him a box of water-colours, but the idea of ever painting in oils was an unattainable dream. Young Dermit's great desire was to leave the mine and to find work in Paris, whither he repaired whenever he could snatch a few days' leave. There he frequented the Left Bank cafés, and through a friend who owned a small picture gallery in Saint-Germain-des-Prés, he met Raoul Leven, Cocteau's friend who was working in Paul Morihien's bookshop. Leven, who was always in the cafés and knew everybody, was at once interested in the handsome young miner and determined to help him. Denise Bourdet gave this description of Edouard Dermit in a newspaper article, calling him by the nickname that every-one used:

> Doudou, with that blue gaze and that white smile in his bronzed face, seldom takes part in the conversation. He is a taciturn creature and it is not easy to drag him out of his silences. He is quite used to our discussing him in his presence as if he were another person. And perhaps it is another, in fact, who listens to us, a Dermit only just returned from the depths of the earth with his miner's lamp still strapped to his forehead, whom the sunlight isolates and dazzles.

It was not surprising that Raoul Leven should decide to intro-duce Dermit to Jean Cocteau and even less surprising that Cocteau should at once engage him as his chauffeur. So, in 1947, Doudou joined the Milly-la-Forêt household, drove Cocteau's car and took his meals with the caretakers in the kitchen. Before long he graduated to the salon, and before long again he became the new angel, partly because Cocteau was captivated by his beauty and partly as a slight revenge for Jean Marais' attachment to Paul Morihien. The rise of Edouard Dermit was swift indeed; soon he had become not only the new angel, but the last angel, Jean Cocteau adopting him as his son and heir. He would have liked the adoption to be legal and Dermit to have taken his name, but this proved impossible. He therefore made him legally his heir and introduced him everywhere as "my adopted son". For the rest of Cocteau's life he and Marais remained close friends, but the reign of Jeannot was over and the reign of Doudou had begun.

In May of this year a film of *La Voix Humaine* was made in Paris by Roberto Rossellini who had liked the play and suggested making a film of it for Anna Magnani. Cocteau was enchanted to have such a director and such an actress, indeed Italy's foremost *monstre sacré*. The faithful Christian Bérard gave his assistance with the décor and Rossellini suddenly decided that the white poodle should play an important part in the film. Cocteau therefore made certain alterations to the text to suit the introduction of Cola. The film, mainly because of its brevity, was not commercially circulated and so received little attention.

Now came *Ruy Blas*, Cocteau's adaptation of Victor Hugo's play, again written for Jean Marais, to give him a different kind of part, and published by Paul Morihien.

"With *Ruy Blas*," Cocteau told Fraigneau, "it was a matter of making a 'Western', a cloak-and-dagger film," and the direction of this, not being essentially his kind of work, he entrusted to Pierre Billon. Georges Auric as usual composed the music and once more Wakhevitch designed the décor, while Cocteau himself assisted the director, although, as he explained to Fraigneau, he could not change the rhythm.

For a film of any kind is always the portrait of its director. In *Ruy Blas*, largely misunderstood by the famous *élite* and greatly liked by the general public, it is the charm and mischievousness of Billon that we expressed.

During the making of this film Cocteau was once more impressed by the subtlety and comprehension of the technicians who were constantly being asked to do the impossible—and doing it. Thanks to them and to Wakhevitch Cocteau was able to realise another of his dreams—that of hanging objects in space with nothing to support them.

The popularity of this picture with the general public was not surprising considering its nature and the fact that, to the stardom of Jean Marais was added the beauty and talent of the young Danielle Darrieux. *Ruy Blas* had a certain affinity with *L'Aigle à deux Têtes* and now Cocteau began to make a film of this play with his familiar team, Christian Bérard, Wakhevitch and

Georges Auric, and a cast headed by Jean Marais, Edwige Feuillère and Yvonne de Bray.

It was made in the Alps near Grenoble. Cocteau with his taste for intimate theatre—this was why he liked 16 mm. films—was strongly opposed to the many exterior scenes which he felt destroyed the film's intensity, but the backers insisted on these.

"The fault Bérard and I shared," Cocteau explained to Fraigneau when discussing the likeness of Elisabeth of Austria and his Queen, "was to be too true without the least historic truth, for example we have been criticised . . . for our Queen's copper bed, so different from the sumptuous beds in *The Love Parade* [an American film], whereas our bed is actually that of Queen Victoria in her youth."

*L'Aigle à deux Têtes* was shown in London before it appeared in Paris and Jean Cocteau went over with Jean Marais for the opening. Cocteau felt "in all the pores of my skin" a certain unease among the audience, consisting largely of royalty and ambassadors, and found this reaction more exciting than enthusiasm.

He was now able to turn from the exteriors of *L'Aigle à deux Têtes* to the intimacy of *Les Parents Terribles*, made in the spirit, Cocteau said, of a 16 mm. film, in which form some young friends had actually started it, although it was continued as a 35 mm. picture. Cocteau considered this film, with its intense enclosed atmosphere, one of his greatest achievements, perhaps his masterpiece. Although he repudiated the term "realistic", saying that he had never known a family such as he portrayed, he also declared that the film showed "those stormy passages that haunted my childhood and are the only roads of families which always stay at home".

In the making of *Les Parents Terribles* he found himself able to mingle intimately with his cast—Jean Marais, Yvonne de Bray, Josette Day, Marcel André and Gabrielle Dorziat—with the happiest results, and critics and public alike greeted the film with enthusiasm.

In this great stream of creation pouring from his mind and from his hands—he was always the artisan and never stopped making drawings as a relaxation from other work—whatever Jean Cocteau is portraying he gives us a portrait of himself. Everything is an indirect autobiography: in every film, play, poem or picture one gets a well-known or a new and startling vision of the poet.

As a change from making his own films during 1948 Cocteau also wrote and spoke a commentary for *Les Noces de Sable*, a film by André Swoboda, based on an Arabian legend strongly resembling that of Tristan and Isolde. Its theme therefore of love and lovers' death was familiar and dear to Cocteau, but he also specially liked the beauty of the Moroccan actors who mimed the scenes, and their slow rhythm which so well accorded with his own. The result was a deeply poetic film.

Cocteau then agreed to write a commentary for *La Légende de Sainte Ursule*, a film by Luciano Emmer, who drew his inspiration from the Carpaccios in Venice. In telling this legend Cocteau succeeded in using almost all his favourite themes: the supernatural, the dream, death, angels. But this angel differs from the earlier ones:

It is another kind of angel with other wings and another sound and this other angel is called love.

As a respite from all this work on films Cocteau now made his first cartoon for a tapestry, commissioned by Gobelins. Cocteau chose as his subject Judith and Holofernes and turned the great attic at Milly-la-Forêt into a studio, on the floor of which he drew his cartoon in pastels on black paper. The tapestry was then made in the Aubusson studio.

"What encouraged me to do this tapestry," Cocteau wrote in the *Démarche d'un Poète*, "is the problem that tapestry imposes on painting, a tapestry made from a painting being nothing but a painting translated into a language of wool, while a real tapestry needs to be prepared in such a way as to become what it ought to be, instead of abandoning its prerogatives in changing its idiom."

In December Jean Cocteau left for America, this time by air and alone, the first visit since the one with Marcel Khill during their journey round the world. His main object was to be present at the opening of the film *L'Aigle à deux Têtes* in New York. The play had already been presented there, but had not been particularly well received by the critics. They liked the film better although not as much as *La Belle et la Bête*.

There were also a number of other Cocteau events and he was cordially acclaimed and thoroughly enjoyed his twenty days in the States. While in New York he visited Jacques Maritain who had been living there since the beginning of the war. He had never lost his deep affection for Jean Cocteau and to this the latter gratefully responded. He also saw Monroe Wheeler, Director of the Museum of Modern Art, whom he had known in Villefranche in the twenties, and he went to a performance of Tennessee Williams's *A Streetcar Named Desire* which he admired and later adapted from the French translation.

In the aeroplane on the way home he wrote a *Letter to the Americans* which summed up his impressions of the country:

In New York everything is a paradox. They want the new and they want nothing to change.

The New York public is the best in the world. But the producer despises this public. He considers it incapable of understanding "high" works and therefore feels himself compelled to present it with "low" ones.

In the film of *L'Aigle à deux Têtes* the American spectators were, Cocteau said, remembering him as the author of *Le Sang d'un Poète* and looking for a mystery that was not there.

In general, contrasting the spirit of the new world with that of the old, Cocteau saw that there was still in France "a disorder that

allows for birth and for surprise". "It would be a weakness in us
to envy and to imitate nations of discipline and order. Our
strength would be to admit our indiscipline and disorder and draw
our qualities from them."

Cocteau returned to Paris early in 1949 to face yet another
tragedy, the death of Christian Bérard. On 20 February 1949, at
the beginning of *Maalesh, a Theatrical Tour of the Middle East,*★
he wrote:

"Dear God, I thank you for having lent me my lady mother," such
were the words of Saint Louis at the death-bed of Blanche of
Castille.

On my journey through life I think of these words each time that
death takes one of my fellow travellers. Many go, but I remain;
they are swallowed up by the waves which devour them with heart-
less ferocity.

The last one to go, Christian Bérard, leaves me with a feeling of
emptiness like seasickness, an unbearable sickness of the soul.

He lived his life with so deep an intensity and in the midst of such
disorder—a disorder which grew with the increasing momentum
of his work—that we thought we saw in his Olympian figure one of
the immortals come to life again.

There had never been anyone with whom Cocteau had worked
in such complete harmony:

As I saw each fresh work of art by Bérard, I felt more and more that
I had adopted his personality to the point of fearing to speak of him
lest I should seem to speak of myself.

The stroke that caused Christian Bérard's death came in the
theatre while he was putting the finishing touches to his set for
Molière's *Fourberies de Scapin*, and before many days had passed
he was laid beside Raymond Radiguet in the Père Lachaise cemetery. In the last few weeks of his life he had been living with
Cocteau at Milly in particularly mild and pleasant weather,
re-doing the décor and costumes for *La Machine Infernale*, which

★ Translated by Mary C. Hoeck (Peter Owen, 1956).

was going with Cocteau to Egypt and making the sketches and maquettes for his next film.

... I can see Bérard again, at Milly, in the room where I was writing the film *Orphée*, struggling to clothe, to draw, to give substance to the being of Death. These were his last fashion drawings. He said: "Death must be the most elegant woman in the world, because she is concerned with nothing but herself."

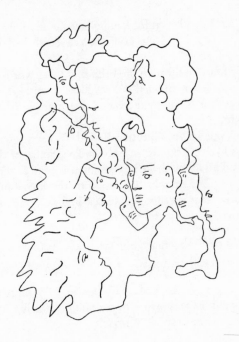

## CHAPTER XI

# ORPHÉE

THE death of Bébé Bérard affected Jean Cocteau all the more sharply because of his own ill-health. It was a relief to him to have the distraction of a tour to the Middle East, but during the whole journey he was unwell.

On 6 May 1949 he boarded the aeroplane with twenty-two actors and actresses, among them Jean Marais, Yvonne de Bray, Gabrielle Dorziat and Edouard Dermit. Dermit was not really an actor, but everyone accepted him because he was charming and because he was Jean Cocteau's adopted son. About Yvonne de Bray Cocteau was lyrical. In his journal of the tour, *Maalesh*, she has now become for him a true *monstre sacré*. This day to day record makes fascinating reading, reflecting in the many facets of its mirror the people and the places, not only those present, but also Bérard, Picasso, Genet—any person, any place that the author has in mind. Any subjects too—for instance he takes this opportunity to defend "so-called decadence".

They went first to Cairo, then to Alexandria and back to Cairo again, where besides Racine, they gave performances of Sartre, Anouilh and Feydeau, as well as three of Cocteau's plays: *La Machine Infernale, Les Monstres Sacrés* and *Les Parents Terribles*, in which, in spite of being now somewhat old for the part, Jean Marais played the son very successfully, a success due to the enormous amount of work he had put into the art of acting over the years which, coupled with Cocteau's excellent influence on his métier, had given him perfect technique.

At each one of the performances Cocteau was acclaimed—every house was sold out—and he found himself attending receptions, giving impromptu lectures, and even decorating a wall in Les

Amitiés Françaises, a building recently opened by the French Ambassador as a centre of culture. In spite of these preoccupations and of his physical and mental miseries, Cocteau found time and strength to take an endless interest in every member of the company and every aspect of his surroundings.

> As I have no sense of time, I felt it was 1936 again and that poor Passepartout [Marcel Khill] was still with me when we were doing the world tour. All at once, on opening our shutters to let in the moonlight, we had found ourselves face to face with the Pyramids. They were very near, like three ghosts, like three great actresses in the garden.*

He did a great deal of sight-seeing and turned his sharp mind on the ancient civilisations, which seemed to him to refute the creative individualism he so strongly believed in.

> It seems as if the dictatorial system which the Pharoahs instituted in Egypt managed at last to copy and to embody (to impose by strategy) a collective working system like that of the ants, termites or bees. . . . At every step individualistic disorder such as ours is refuted.... Poor Egypt !... Perhaps the best régime for her was that of the Pharoahs, rather like the present Russian régime. Otherwise she may dissolve, or crumble away into her damp heat and her dust.†

When, the following year, *Maalesh* was published, such passages displeased the Egyptian government, particularly as they had done Cocteau the honour of showing him the treasures of the Cairo museum, and the bookshops were even ordered to burn their copies.

The company proceeded next by sea to Beirut, Istanbul and Ankara, Cocteau becoming all the time more ill and more dejected. To his bronchitis was added an attack of boils for which the ship's doctor gave him injections of penicillin, although this

* From *Maalesh*.        † Ibid.

did not prevent him from enjoying the Greek fish with honey and "delicious resinous wine".

He could not sleep and lay, between three-hourly injections, for which he had to wake the doctor, thinking about old age and wondering if his indifference to it would last and praying that he would not get a boil on his nose.

As long as I can avoid that I shall not make a fuss about anything else. What an odd type of poet and what an odd type of hero! It is important that I should go on, go on as if the plays, receptions, visits to the Embassies were what I really cared about. Never let my friends think that I am tired. Never appear different from others. Act as those do who believe in what they do—and to crown all, believe in it myself.*

As they came into Istanbul through the Bosporos, Cocteau spotted the house where Pierre Loti lived and also the one to which Anna de Noailles had been taken when she was a little girl.

Far from France we are moved by such things. In Paris which respects no one, they would be made fun of. Pierre Loti and Anna de Noailles have been thrown on the scrap-heap. It's a great mistake. The Turks remember them.†

In Istanbul the company played in more primitive circum-stances, but still they triumphed and Cocteau continued to give many addresses. Speaking to the Philharmonic Society "I let myself go, carried away by memories of my childhood and youth." He spoke ardently of Debussy, Satie, Stravinsky and *Les Six*, of Apollinaire, Max Jacob, Reverdy, Cendrars . . .

I no longer saw the audience. It seemed to me that I was talking to myself about this marvellous generation of musicians and writers of which they have not the faintest idea in Istanbul. . . . I turned this way and that, in an almost hypnotic condition as I tried—like a medium at a Spiritualist séance—to make the dead live again.‡

* Ibid.       † Ibid.       ‡ Ibid.

Never did Cocteau forget any artist who had made a deep impression on his life.

Thence to Ankara and back to Istanbul where Cocteau, Yvonne de Bray, Jean Marais and Edouard Dermit took leave of the rest of the company which was returning to Paris.

Tomorrow we go to Athens, the city where the gods stroll along the streets like pigeons.*

And so once more, this Greek, Jean Cocteau, set foot in his own country.

The same emotion as in 1936—that of facing the irreparable.

The previous day I had been crushed under pillars and domes. And now, this evening, sunlight and the Acropolis and the ruins drew me upwards, made me feel light and winged. I was no longer in the least tired. And I asked myself:—why has the world lost grace? Why have those secrets which give light to our hearts been lost altogether? Why have we lost the secret of winging marble? Why are we, who perpetuate secrets, invisible? Why must our signs be hidden?

The Acropolis! I am back again on it. How lucky I am not to be an intellectual! How lucky I am to be a ridiculous creature on this strange platform, this aerodrome, this landing-place for the gods.†

To Corinth then, where Cocteau specially liked the goats with their black masks and the goatherds with their crooks ending in snakes, and finally:

We are leaving Greece feeling very sad. She received us better than if we had been kings—as old friends, very old friends.

We should have given the plays in Athens and Rome. It is a pity that our company ended its tour in Turkey, for we shall never be able to get such a company together again.‡

* Ibid.        † Ibid.        ‡ Ibid.

And so in May they boarded their aeroplane.

The pilot points out to us our obelisk, our minaret, our Acropolis—
the Eiffel Tower.*

Cocteau expected, he said, to find Paris engaged in political
discussions, but in fact he found it discussing a newly discovered
manuscript of Rimbaud's. He himself found this laboured and
soulless and so did his old enemy André Breton, but Cocteau
was delighted that Paris could suddenly become excited about
Rimbaud. "This is the city that I love," he declared, and then the
whole thing turned out to be a hoax. The manuscript was not by
Rimbaud at all, and Cocteau had been tricked with the rest.

A great deal of work was awaiting him. First and foremost the
preparations for the film *Orphée* and the forming of a company
to produce it. Financially, it was dependent on a limited loan to
Cocteau from the Crédit National, but the cast gracefully agreed
to delayed and hypothetical payment. Next there were the
preparations for the *Festival du Film maudit* which was to take
place in Biarritz in May. The idea of this festival was Cocteau's;
he wanted to present certain masterpieces that had not had a
commercial success, "because they deserved a bigger success than
this"—that was the meaning of the word "*maudit*". It was an
aristocratic enterprise, in the Greek sense of the word: ἄριστοι.

Meanwhile he was putting the final touches to his adaptation
of *A Streetcar Named Desire* from the translation by Paule de
Beaumont. The addition of Cocteau's now illustrious name
assured in advance a success for the young American writer's
play when it was produced at the Théâtre de l'Athénée in
October 1949.

Even this was not all that Jean Cocteau, in spite of his precarious
health, was engaged in, for he was working with Jean-Pierre
Melville on the adaptation of *Les Enfants Terribles* for the latter's
film.

* Ibid.

"I had always refused all requests," he told Fraigneau in *Entretiens autour du Cinématographe*, "but I accepted Melville's because his style of production would, I thought, lend the film that air of improvisation of a 16 mm. picture of which I have already spoken."

And now, while Cocteau spent his time between Paris and Milly, his company was strenuously preparing to make the *Orphée* film, while yet another campaign was drawing to its close: the long effort of his friends to get the *légion d'honneur* for its author. The prestige journey to the Middle East had helped the cause and on 3 September 1949 his nomination was announced. "*Jean Cocteau chevalier de la légion d'honneur*" the headlines declared to Cocteau's great satisfaction, for the names of the other distinguished recipients only appeared in the text. He had always craved public honours and had grieved at not being accorded them sooner, thinking with envy of other artists and particularly of Gide. But so many damaging rumours had always surrounded Jean Cocteau's name that it had taken his admirers a long time to win the ear of the authorities. Lately, because of his fame and his friendship with Jean Marais, although this had been less close since the coming of Edouard Dermit, Cocteau had been the constant butt of the *chansonniers* (the popular cabaret satirists of the day's affairs and personalities) and it may have been to avoid their further shafts that the award was not marked by any public ceremony.

In November Jean Cocteau, once more the sole master of his work, began to film *Orphée*, again speaking a few lines in it himself as "the author". The film was partly made in the ruins of the old Saint-Cyr barracks, near Versailles, destroyed during the war, although to achieve certain dream effects parts of these arcades had to be reconstructed in the studio, while the strange city, in which the Princess roams, was made up of various streets in Paris. The loss of Bérard not only once more broke Cocteau's heart, but it made him work doubly hard. There was nobody now with whom he could discuss the "zone" he wanted to create for the other side of the mirror, and which he and Bérard had agreed was to be non-lyrical and unDante-esque.

In this film Cocteau was again, as in *Le jeune Homme et la Mort*, aiming at "accidental synchronism", and to this end he made serious cuts in Auric's score, introducing into it music by Gluck without asking Auric's approval.

Cocteau always delighted in any happy effects that accident brought into a work, and here at Saint-Cyr he found the night silence shattered by the constant passing of trains. Try as they would they could not finish shooting a scene before another train arrived. But when Cocteau saw these scenes, accompanied by distant whistlings and sounds of a near-by factory, he found that these noises made a mysterious background for the dialogue that must on no account be lost.

Jean Marais played the name part with Marie Déa opposite him as Eurydice and Dermit, working for the first time under Cocteau's direction, played Cégeste, the young poet put up by the *avant-garde* in opposition to Orphée, the official poet at the height of his fame. Maria Casarès, whom Cocteau had admired in *Les Dames du Bois de Boulogne*, took the important part of *la Princesse*, as elegant as Christian Bérard had desired, although she was "no more Death", Cocteau declared, in his description of the characters, "than an air-hostess is an angel. She *is* the death of Orphée, just as she elects to be the death of Cégeste and of Eurydice. She is one of the many functionaries of Death." And Cocteau continued with the poignant line: "Each one of us contains his death which directs him from the time of his birth."

As for Heurtebise, in the film he is no longer the angel with window-panes for wings, as in the play of a quarter of a century ago, although a glazier does briefly cross Orphée's path, one newly dead and still carrying his wares. Heurtebise is no longer the angel of whom Cocteau had so often written, but he is still very important as the newly-dead youth who serves the Princess as her chauffeur. Quite apart from this change the film was in no way a screen adaptation of the play. Certainly it is still a paraphrase of the ancient Greek myth, "timeless, since time is a human invention", a meditation on the mysteries of death and a reaffirmation of the tragedy of love; but more than all else the film recreates the poetic theme of *Le Sang d'un Poète*.

"I am letting you in to the secret of all secrets," Heurtebise tells Orphée as they approach the mirror [the one in the play was a tank of water, but this one was made of 400 kilograms of quicksilver] "mirrors are the gates through which death comes and goes. Moreover, if you observe your whole life in a mirror you will see death at work as you see bees behind the glass in a hive."

In this film Cocteau was able to indulge his obsession with mirrors to the full. Hating what he called "picturesque tricks, which spoilt the poetry of a picture", he greatly enjoyed both the real mirrors and the ingenious semblance of mirrors: frames, framing a void, the construction of twin rooms and twin objects, which if you were quick enough you could see not to be perfectly inverted, Maria Casarès playing back to back with her double, Jean Marais disappearing through a void, which in the next shot was filled with a mirror—all these devices Cocteau found fascinating.

The film opens in a provincial town, at the Café des Poètes, a rendezvous for writers like the Café de Flore in Saint-Germain-des-Prés, from which Orphée witnesses the death of Cégeste, mown down by mysterious motor-cyclists. The Princess insists on Orphée going with her as a witness in the great black Rolls Royce to which she has had Cégeste carried. But, breaking the rules of her kingdom, she falls in love with Orphée, and so later appears with him before a tribunal of the dead, while Heurtebise appears for a similar offence in respect of Eurydice. Meanwhile, after witnessing many strange things, Orphée returns to his wife, Eurydice, in the Rolls driven by Heurtebise. At her suggestion the car is put in their garage and, despite her protestations and the warnings of Heurtebise, Orphée spends all his time in the

Rolls, listening to messages from the unknown transmitted by its radio, while every night the Princess, Orphée's death, visits him as he sleeps.

These radio messages are sent by Cégeste from "the other world". He uses a line from Apollinaire—"*l'oiseau chante avec ses doigts*" among many incomprehensible numbers. Orphée gives these messages to a review and is accused of plagiarism—of imitating Cégeste's poems.

Then Eurydice too dies and the Greek myth dominates. Heurtebise leads Orphée through the mirror and across a no-man's-land of ruins to the zone of the dead where they come before the tribunal which gives Eurydice back to Orphée on condition that he never looks at her face. But once again Orphée installs himself in the Rolls Royce to get Cégeste's messages, and in the driving-mirror his eyes meet those of Eurydice. She disappears.

"It was fate," Heurtebise tells Orphée and he replies: "It had to be. It had to be, Heurtebise. I have had enough of half-measures and compromises. One does not compromise, Heurtebise. One must have drama. One must go on to the bitter end."

Youths and girls, supporters of Cégeste, break into the court-yard and attack Orphée who in the midst of the fracas accidentally kills himself with his own revolver. Thus he rejoins the Princess and it seems that their impossible love, more moving than Eurydice's love for Orphée, will triumph. But "the death of a poet must be sacrificed to make him immortal", and so the Princess, aided by Heurtebise and Cégeste, send Orphée back to Eurydice. "They had to be put back in their dirty water," says Heurtebise, reviewing the result of their work, and in the foreword Cocteau explains that his words do not imply their earthly love, but simply their being "on the earth".

So, at last, Cocteau brought this great work to a close, abandoning Cégeste and the Princess to their no-man's land, from which he would retrieve them ten years later in *Le Testament d'Orphée*. He had been involved in the film body and soul, with his nerves stretched almost to breaking point. True it had been an enthralling time, but it was also a painful one, and not only because of the loss of Christian Bérard. Jeannot was hurt at being supplanted by Doudou, and this caused quarrels between Jean Marais and Cocteau. Is it too fanciful to see the underlying theme of this film as the contest between Cégeste-Dermit and Orphée-Marais? Had not Cocteau written: "All masterpieces are achieved through hidden motives."? By the time the film was finished, Jeannot had left the Palais-Royal and Milly for ever and gone to live on the barge he had bought from Yvonne de Bray. Cocteau was alone with Edouard Dermit.*

His desire to turn him into a second Marais was still paramount and together he and Melville decided to give him the leading part, Paul, in the film *Les Enfants Terribles*. Under Melville's direction, he made an excellent Paul with Nicole Stephane, an old friend of Francine Weisweiller's, playing opposite him as Elizabeth.

The film of *Les Enfants Terribles* was made very quickly. It was shot in Melville's apartment—a dingy one that, to his wife's distress, he had rented for this purpose—in railway carriages and at Montmorency where the great "Sea of Sand" served marvellously as the snow. The only studio they used was the stage of the Pigalle Theatre with its apparatus of lifts, and the music was provided by a Bach transcription of a work by Vivaldi—this time Cocteau did not use Georges Auric at all. After the film appeared people used to ask in the record shops, not for Vivaldi, who got the film "credit", but for "the music of *Les Enfants Terribles*".

The whole production was therefore somewhat amateurish, thus achieving the 16 mm. atmosphere Cocteau wanted. Although he was still occupied with *Orphée*, he busied himself as usual with

* Edouard Dermit is now married and still lives in the Palais-Royal apartment and at the house in Milly-la-Forêt.

the décor and the details of *Les Enfants Terribles*, sometimes even taking Melville's place, besides speaking the commentary throughout the film.

By Easter 1950 this picture of Cocteau's best-known novel appeared in the Paris cinemas.

" 'Not a gaiter button is missing,' one critic declares . . ." wrote Cocteau. "Well, but the work is mine. So why should there be a gaiter button missing? My job is to see that they are all found where they should be."

Melville had given the parts of Dargelos and Agathe to the same young actress. True, Cocteau himself had written in the book of the strange likeness between these two characters, but Melville carried the boy-girl obsession too far:

For Dargelos is so male a character, with a prestige so dependent on him being a young boy proud of his manly attributes, that an actress, however talented, could not succeed in making him convincing.

The critics were harsher; more in condemnation of Cocteau than of Melville. They were shocked by this world of tragic innocence and suspicious of its morals. Cocteau's admirers, however, and young people particularly, paid no attention to the press, and the film was a success.

Almost at the same time *Orphée*, which was not shown in Paris until September, won its first fame at the Festival in Cannes. Within the year it was to receive the International Critics Prize at the Venice Festival, the *avant-garde* award of the Normandie Oscar, be acclaimed in London, have a further triumph in Cannes in 1951 and yet another in Belgium.

With *Orphée* Cocteau had reached a more serious public and also pleased the general public which he had wooed with *La Belle et la Bête*. He loved this general recognition, even though it meant having to sue a glazier—some trick this perhaps of the

angel Heurtebise—for calling himself Jean Cocteau and imitating
his signature on his carts.

Another result of his fame was an invitation in the summer of
1950 to spend a week with Dermit at the residence of Madame
Francine Weisweiller, the Villa Santo-Sospir, near the lighthouse
of Saint-Jean-Cap-Ferrat. Madame Weisweiller was in her mid-
thirties and the wife of the immensely wealthy banker, Alec
Weisweiller, but the couple seldom lived together, and she
often found herself bored, alone with her small daughter in her
husband's vast and luxurious mansions. To relieve her tedium,
she invited Jean Cocteau and his friend to visit her, an impulse
that had lasting results for them all.

The Villa Santo-Sospir was only a short way from Villefranche,
where Cocteau had spent some of the pleasantest times of his
youth and he was delighted to be in the same region again with
Doudou. The Villa also greatly pleased him; it was a light modern
building, yet the architecture held something of the magic of a
château, with its luxurious salons opening on to a terrace overlooking the sea, and a row of rooms and studios clinging to the
slope beneath.

His friendship with Francine Weisweiller grew quickly,
although on the face of it they had not much in common. The
warmth of her personality, however, and her enthusiasm about all
that concerned her eminent guest, soon bridged this gap and she
invited Cocteau to choose a room and a studio and to stay on with
Dermit at the Villa Santo-Sospir. He chose a little bedroom at the
end of a passage, with another adjoining for Doudou, and a
many-windowed studio opening on the sea. And here he
remained for the rest of the summer.

He paid one visit to Paris for the presentation at the Opéra of the
ballet *Phèdre*, with décor, costumes and production by Cocteau,
choreography by Serge Lifar and music that won much acclaim
by Georges Auric. It was he who had asked Cocteau to suggest
a subject for a ballet and the latter had replied that it was always

an actress's highest ambition to play Phèdre, so why not *Phèdre* for a ballet? Failing Greta Garbo, whom he thought of as the perfect Phèdre, Cocteau invited Toumanova to dance the part.

By the end of September Cocteau had finished writing his book on Jean Marais, deeply appreciative of the character of his Galahad, and had begun to decorate the white walls of the Villa Santo-Sospir. Francine Weisweiller gave him *carte blanche* just as, long ago, Denise and Edouard Bourdet had done when they invited Cocteau to paint the loggia of their Villa Blanche at Toulon.

Cocteau took several years over his work for the Villa Santo-Sospir—to produce the two profiles of Oedipus for the portico, the mosaics for the entrance, a copy of the Judith and Holofernes tapestry for one of the salons—but during this first summer the frescoes on the walls were nearly finished. He worked in bare feet, ground his own colours, rediscovered the secret of mixing his paints with milk so dear to the Italians, and produced on these walls the first of the iridescent effects that were later to become famous in the chapels that he decorated. Here, once more, were many of his favourite obsessions: profiles of young men, still recalling Raymond Radiguet, a hunter with a falcon on his wrist wearing a black turban like a Pisanello, fishermen with their nets, *Niçoises* in local costume, angels with red wings and curly hair, and in his own room a harlequin-clad satyr after Picasso, presently to be illuminated by the nightlight in a broken vase given to him by his illustrious friend. Picasso lived not far away and their friendship, although not now so close as in youth, was warmly renewed.

For a change from all this painting, Cocteau would write, for a change from writing draw, and for a change from the house be driven around the countryside in one of his hostess's cars or his own old Citroën. He was at home; he was free to invite his friends and he was happy. All the same this friendship was deplored by many people and Francine Weisweiller has been

much maligned and held responsible for the hunger for fame that
dominated Cocteau's last years. It is easy to understand how
welcome her generous friendship was to him. He was sixty-one
and ever since the war had, in spite of ill-health, carried out an
immense and exhausting programme of work. As far back as
1927 he had dreamt of having a house in the Villefranche Bay;
now he had a home in this favourite corner of the coast with
the sea and the sunshine that he adored. Luxury had always
appealed to him and now it was his.

Not surprisingly Cocteau temporarily abandoned Milly-la-
Forêt for this glamorous abode, nor did his friendship with
Francine slacken when they all returned to Paris in September.
She invited Jean and Doudou to have most of their meals at her
house and the Palais-Royal apartment was, in its turn, deserted,

At the Académie Française: Jean Cocteau, Francine Weisweiller and Jean Marais, 20 October 1955 (*A.D.P.*)

A fresco by Jean Cocteau on the wall of the drawing-room at Santo-Sospir, 1952 (*Les Reporters Asso-ciés*)

except at night and in the morning when at about ten o'clock Cocteau would still receive a queue of visitors in the kitchen and the little red bedroom, always wearing a dressing-gown of white towelling. For the rest of the time he was at Francine Weisweiller's apartment and would say to his friends: "*Chez moi, Place des Etats-Unis.*" For his part he took Madame Weisweiller everywhere, to studios, rehearsals, parties and on every possible journey. Indeed they became so inseparable that an English newspaper actually printed a photograph of them entitled: "Mr and Mrs Jean Cocteau."

Edouard Dermit approved highly of this friendship. Not only did he derive many benefits from it, but he found in it the chance to regain a little liberty for himself. Like Radiguet and others in Cocteau's succession of angels, Dermit had come to need some privacy. Cocteau was, as always, gentle, considerate and courteous, but to live so close to him was difficult for any young man who wanted to step outside the frame of the mirror and be more than a reflection.

## CHAPTER XII

# THE BALANCE SHEET

DURING the winter of 1950–1 at Milly, Cocteau recorded the series of fourteen radio conversations: *"Entretiens avec André Fraigneau"*, in which he recounted many things about his life and his work. He did this with much charm and with a modesty that led him to speak as if his audience had never heard of him before. These broadcasts were a great success and are considered by the Radio Française among their triumphs. They shed a radiance on his work in the eyes of a public which had so far known little of Cocteau beyond his plays and his films. This public summing-up of his life was at the same time a private summing-up, a balance-sheet.

Hearing Cocteau during one of these conversations say "time is a phenomenon of perspective", René Bertrand, the amateur scientist, sought a meeting with him, and from this meeting evolved Cocteau's lasting interest in scientific and parascientific research. He dedicated the *Journal d'un Inconnu* to Bertrand, explaining that he had written it while thinking of the latter's recently published book *l'Univers cette Unité*, "optimistic pessimism, because you study our poor world while spraying your vines". *Le Journal d'un Inconnu* is a sequel to *La Difficulté d'Etre*, in which Cocteau wrote down many of the ideas people were always asking him why he only talked about. It contains poignant passages:

> The journey that we make between life and death would be intolerable to me without the encounters of friendship.
> Love is still in the fringe of orders given to us by nature. . . . But perfect friendship is a creation of man. His greatest.

When André Fraigneau asked Cocteau why after the play he

had returned again to the theme of Orphée for the film, the latter gave this characteristic reply:

> My moral stance being that of a man limping with one foot in life and the other in death, it was natural that I should fix upon a myth in which life and death confront one another.

This balance-sheet of the film-maker ends after Fraigneau's final question: "What are you working at now?"

> Nothing. Perhaps I have come to the end. Perhaps I have wound off the skein. Perhaps it is a pause. I must wait. I could write plays, books and films. But I won't let myself. There are too many plays, books, films. To start work I should have to receive the command. This command comes from myself, a self of which I know neither the ability nor the mechanics. The me that is talking to you is only the vehicle. As I have been ill, it is possible that the vehicle for the moment displeases this unknown me.

He would have liked to make a film of Racine's *Britannicus* and so preserve for ever Jean Marais as Nero, which he still believed to be his finest rôle. He talked about this at the dinner of the *Prix des Critiques*, but the film was never made. Marais was no longer in the centre of Cocteau's universe and the days of their great collaborations were over, a tragedy for them both.

Early in the New Year Cocteau had a triumphant visit to Hamburg, whither he went with Francine Weisweiller and Edouard Dermit to lecture on the play *Orphée* which was being performed there. He was given an official reception with a motor-cycle escort, such as is accorded to heads of states, or in *Orphée* to the newly dead. He was very happy to be so warmly received in Germany, for which country he still retained an affection and where he was at home in the language. He and his companions went on to Munich where he opened an exhibition of his drawings and cartoons for tapestries.

The preceding year Jean Cocteau had refused a Chair at the

*Académie Goncourt*, of which Colette was a member, probably because he was hoping that he would one day have a chair at the *Académie Française*, these two honours being incompatible. Now, in April 1951, he agreed to preside at the important *Syndicat des auteurs et compositeurs de musique*.

When summer came, he again went with Dermit to Santo-Sospir where the first thing he did was to write a commentary for *Le Rossignol de l'Empereur de Chine*, a film by the Czech, Trnka, based on Hans Andersen's fairy-tale, and then, having once more become an habitué of Nice, where naturally Madame Weisweiller enjoyed considerable prestige, he arranged an exhibition of his recent crayon and pastel drawings. He never stopped drawing at Santo-Sospir and with this exhibition his pictures began to make money.

This summer too—in order to please not only himself but his hostess—in the course of a few days Cocteau made a little holiday picture of the Villa Santo-Sospir on the best 16 mm. colour film on the market. In this film Cocteau was seen in the garden in gay mood and here too were the studios and the walls of the Villa that he had decorated. This film has seldom been shown and Madame Weisweiller has withdrawn it from circulation.

To add to the pleasures of this summer, Cocteau and Dermit spent many hours aboard their hostess's beautiful little yacht named Orphée II in honour of Cocteau. The command to write a play had been given again and it was partly in the yacht and partly at the Villa that he wrote *Bacchus*, dedicated "To Francine, who thinks with her heart."

> "*Bacchus* is a play about hard goodness as opposed to soft goodness," he wrote in the Preface. "This was the theme, never understood, of *La Lettre à Maritain*: 'to render to God the intelligence that has been paid to the Devil. . . .'"

And in *Journal d'un Inconnu*, which he was still in the process of writing, he observed:

I wanted to write this *Bacchus* for a long time. It presented itself in the form of a play, a film or a book. I returned to the idea of the play, judging that the theatre would best suit the story.

Indeed *Bacchus* has a brilliant plot for a tragedy and sparkles with polemics. It is set in a small German town in 1523 on the day when the Cardinal arrives to purify the province of Luther's teaching, which coincides with the election by the people of the Bacchus, the Carnival King who will reign with absolute power over the town for a week during the grape-harvest. The chosen candidate—and there is great competition over this—is the beautiful youth Hans, one of Cocteau's most interesting creations. Having lost his wits as the result of being subjected to a man-hunt, he has subsequently pretended still to be the village idiot in order to escape torture. It is as God's fool that he is elected to be "the Bacchus", but it is as an intellectual and subversive heretic that he wields his power and earns the hatred of those who have elected him. They plan to burn him, but the Cardinal, a noble character who recognises the heretic's purity, offers him the refuge of a monastery if he will sign a form of abjuration. In spite of the pleas of the young girl whom the Bacchus loves and is loved by, he refuses and dies, with the arrow of one of his own guard through his heart. The play in its economic intensity is reminiscent of Sartre's *Le Diable et le Bon Dieu*, written shortly before *Bacchus*, and has echoes too of Camus and Montherlant, but Hans is also another Antigone and a Joan of Arc—Cocteau's own saints—and he put into him much of himself and specially much of that self that had sought intellectual integrity after his so-called conversion by Maritain. According to Cocteau: "The play pleads no causes. It simply shows the terrible solitude of young people who are only concerned with their own ideas and refuse the directions of any doctrine whatsoever."

These were delightful weeks, the days spent writing and drawing and the evenings, when there was not a dinner party at Santo-Sospir, spent with Picasso, with Stravinsky or other friends, among whom were now numbered the Aga Khan and the Begum. Jean Cocteau was himself an honoured member of the society of the Côte d'Azur and there were few brilliant events that he did not grace with his presence. On the rare occasions when he neither went out nor received friends, after the late dinner at Santo-Sospir he would retire to his room and draw far into the night or write scraps of poetry on the pages of a great sketch-book, or a page or two of *Le Passé Défini*, the journal he had begun the year before and continued to keep until his death, and which has not yet been published—the title implying that "every word is in its place". In addition to this enormous activity, he now arranged a large exhibition of his graphic work for Berlin.

As he wrote *Bacchus*, Cocteau sent off the scenes for his secretary in Paris to type—he never in his life touched a typewriter. By the end of the summer it was finished and he was impatient for its production. He sent it to the Théâtre National Populaire, hoping that Gérard Philipe would play the name-part. When the play was refused, Cocteau used all his powers of persuasion on Jean-Louis Barrault. By the end of November *Bacchus* was in production at the Théâtre Marigny, the Right-bank theatre of the Madeleine Renaud–Jean-Louis Barrault Company. The part of the Bacchus was played by the young actor Jean Desailly and Barrault played the Cardinal and also helped Cocteau generally with the production, although it was under the latter's direction and it was he who had designed the décor and costumes, "inspired by Holbein, Cranach, Dürer and the Naples tapestries".

After scarcely a month of rehearsals, on 20 December 1951, the curtain rose for the first performance of *Bacchus* before a distinguished audience. As the last curtain fell and the applause began, François Mauriac left the theatre, making no secret of his indignation. Having always been a fervent Catholic, it was natural that *Bacchus* should offend him.

On 29 December in *Le Figaro Littéraire* Mauriac published a long *Lettre à Jean Cocteau*.

My dear Cocteau,

Don't believe the newspapers: I wasn't furious the other night when I left the Marigny. I wasn't in a rage. I was just sad that the whole auditorium, packed by all Paris, had been able to listen without protest to that comedian disguised as a bishop, who used the words of the *Pater* to make the audience laugh . . .

In actual fact Jean Desailly is your spokesman. Don't try to deny it: it is you who is speaking when he speaks. At times Desailly sheds his part and becomes Jean Cocteau about town: he gives a performance of the Cocteau Number. *Bacchus* shows us Cocteau in the light of Sartre, this same Cocteau whom we knew in 1910, suffused by the last glow of Rostand; but this dance was already ending, his eye fixed on Anna de Noailles, his *Danse de Sophocle*. Already Diaghilev, Satie, Picasso, Gide, Apollinaire, Max Jacob, other great planets, were attracting this sly satellite into their orbit . . .

"*La femme-tronc*" you are very pleased to have found this word to describe Holy Church. Pretty piece of spittle. Ah! That was matter for a good belly-laugh and in fact all Paris has had a belly-laugh about it. . . . Say what one may, this Jean, only he could find such words! . . . And yet, the priest who one day at that little house in Meudon raised his hand above you, saying those words that absolved you, asking nothing of you in return but a little repentance and a beginning of love; and the saint [Père Charles Henrion] who gave you the living bread to eat, the living Christ, nor did he require from you either silver or gold . . .

Cocteau soon replied to this letter in *France-Soir*, the paper with the largest circulation, parodying Zola's famous "*J'accuse*".

I accuse you of having invented a play by me to your own ends, in an endeavour to ruin my work and this *Bacchus* that the public likes . . . I accuse you if you are a good Catholic of being a bad Christian and of beating purity, always difficult to recognise, with the big stick of traditional purity.

I accuse you of being uneducated, for all the subversive lines in my dialogue are historical. Among others "the devil is pure because he can only do evil" is from Jacques Maritain. The passage against the

Bible is from the Archevêque Electeur de Mayenne. *"La femme-tronc"* was a commonplace of Calvinistic reform . . .

I accuse you, as you keep telling me that you are an "old" child, of having kept nothing of childhood but its cunning cruelty . . .

I accuse you of only seeing the ignoble in our world and of restricting nobleness to another world that evades us because its code is impenetrable.

At our time of life one can no longer be beautiful, but one can have a beautiful soul. I accuse you of not having looked after your soul . . .

I accuse you of only following one tradition of France. That of killing her poets.
    adieu

                        Jean Cocteau.

The "Bacchus affair" split Paris into two camps. Mauriac's attack on Cocteau, implying that all writers were irreligious and immoral, particularly Colette, caused Mauriac to be covered with ridicule from one side, and even stronger suspicion to fall on Cocteau from the other. The press took sides too and Cocteau, as always, enjoyed the publicity. One day, laughing, he said: "I would prefer not to go to Paradise for fear of finding myself face to face with Mauriac." Cocteau too had the last word with an article in *Arts: "Qu'on se taise une fois pour toutes"*, in which he insisted that far from being an insult to the Church and deserving Mauriac's censure, *Bacchus* was a play to the glory of the Church. "*Bacchus* has succeeded. The incident is closed."

In spite of all the publicity, *Bacchus* did not have the success foretold for it. It soon came off and Cocteau was saddened by the whole affair. Mauriac had alienated a section of the bourgeois and Catholic public and Cocteau was conscious of being among enemies. Recalling all this later he said to a friend: "One must let a work do what it wants to. I forced Barrault to put on *Bacchus*. No good came to me of it."

In Düsseldorf, on the other hand, whither Cocteau went in October 1952 to be present at the first night, *Bacchus* had a spectacular success. Cocteau was given an ovation and the performance ended with thirty-eight curtain calls. And in 1954 it was presented in an English translation by Mary C. Hoeck at the Playhouse Theatre in Salisbury.

In 1952 François Mauriac re-read his letter to Cocteau in *Le Figaro* and wrote:

> I hope that what will endure of this letter is the testimony in support of the Church and not the personal attack on Cocteau. I certainly had the right to express the pain that I felt at Marigny, but perhaps not to touch publicly on the religious life of the author, on his conversion, on his friendships.

To distract him from the after-effects of the *Bacchus* affair, Cocteau had an important exhibition of his work to arrange for Munich in January 1952, which was afterwards shown both at Hamburg and in Berlin. After this, although it was mid-winter, he returned to Santo-Sospir, where he finished the *Journal d'un Inconnu*, adding among other things a chapter on François Mauriac, his son Claude, who had written the book *Jean Cocteau ou la vérité du mensonge*, denigrating Cocteau, and on Maurice Sachs and the surrealists. He then set to work on the masks for *Oedipus Rex*, Stravinsky's oratorio for which Cocteau had written the original libretto so long ago, and which he was to present this summer at the Théâtre des Champs-Elysées, with the composer conducting, as part of the International Exhibition of Arts. This production was nostalgic for Cocteau, reminding him of Villefranche and that poignant period of his youth, and it became, to quote his own words: "A ceremony for the festival of our reunion, Stravinsky's and mine, after so many years passed far away from one another."

Cocteau's work for *Oedipus Rex*, he explained in the Postscriptum to *Journal d'un Inconnu*, had not been easy. "I had to

avoid killing the ear by the eye. I had to be violent, paying regard
to the monstrosity of the myth." He decided not to distract
Stravinsky's oratorio by any actions or dances, but simply to have
a series of seven *tableaux vivants*, the masked figures appearing
while he recited the speeches on a platform above the orchestra.
He said that although he was not directly influenced by the
Japanese Noh plays, he did remember the example these gave of
economy of gesture and elusive power. A woman, who was an
expert in the making of masks, had come from Paris to help him.
These masks were specially designed to be seen from beneath
—ears, noses and mouths made of cork and wire, hair of raffia
and eyes stuck on at the ends of cornets and sticks, as in the *Opium*
drawings, the whole contraptions sometimes bristling with ping-
pong balls painted red. The curtain too was in the style of the
*Opium* illustrations, being an enlargement of Cocteau's painting
*Le Carrefour des deux Routes*, all of which added to the macabre
violence of the drama.

On the first night of *Oedipus Rex* at the Théâtre des Champs-
Elysées on 14 May 1952, such violent hostility was shown by the
audience that the curtain had to be lowered before peace was
restored, and the row and the insults hurled at Cocteau were cut
out of the recording of the performance for radio before it could
be broadcast. Cocteau, however, heard Stravinsky say, "you have
made me a royal present", so although he was exhausted with
overwork and saddened by this further show of public hostility,
he was not too cast down, and Francine Weisweiller at once
carried him off with Dermit on a visit to Greece and the islands.

This journey too Cocteau described in the Post-scriptum to the
*Journal d'un Inconnu*, calling it a journey "to verify the *Oedipus
Rex* scenes", and heading it with a quotation from Max Jacob:
"The traveller falls dead, struck down by the picturesque."
Greece, Cocteau felt, was so much "an idea" that one hardly
believed that it existed even when one was there, and he relaxed
during this pleasant journey in a haze of ideas.

On their return after two weeks to Santo-Sospir, Cocteau was busy with the new illustrated edition of *Opéra* and in editing *Le Chiffre Sept* for his friend Pierre Seghers, who in 1945 had published the first study of Cocteau's work by Roger Lannes and who had now brought this long poem out of the shades by offering to publish it. It is a difficult work—"one must be a poet to read poetry" Cocteau had written in *Secrets de Beauté*, and in this poem the reader needs to have a clue to the hieroglyphics he uses. He now proceeded to develop a surrealist way of writing that he had already begun to use in *Musée Secret* in *Opéra*, for his collection of prose poems *Appogiatures*. This was a resolve to describe with geometric exactitude and an approach excluding all fantasy, phenomena usually arising from freaks of the imagination. It was published in 1953 by *Editions du Rocher*, who were now to become Cocteau's publishers, under the direction of Francine Weisweiller's brother, Gérard Worms, and were to republish all the books previously brought out by Paul Morihien, who was no longer a publisher.

Cocteau now had a legal case on his hands, an action brought against him by Darantière, the publisher of *Reines de la France*, a series of texts Cocteau had written for his de luxe publication of Christian Bérard's prints and of which, in a characteristically unthinking way, he had later given the rights to Bernard Grasset. In the end he won the case and Grasset's current edition remained in circulation.

The end of 1952 was darkened by the death of Paul Eluard with whom Cocteau had been on warm terms for many years, as indeed with all his former enemy surrealists except André Breton. Cocteau made several drawings of Eluard on his death-bed in Paris, attended his funeral and wrote a fine poem:

> La mort jalouse ceux qui vivent
> Et connaissant par quels chemins
> Tu nous rafraîchissais d'eaux vives
> Elle a même volé tes mains.

This poem, and others in the same style as *Plain-Chant* that he wrote during the next two years, were included in Jean Cocteau's last volume of poems *Clair-Obscur*, published by *Editions du Rocher* in 1956.

All this subjective work, and the constant comings and goings between the Palais-Royal, Milly-la-Forêt and Santo-Sospir did not keep Cocteau from his beloved theatre. During his visit to Munich the director of the Gartner Theatre had asked him for a ballet and he had written *La Dame à la Licorne*. He spent the winter designing the décor and the costumes—the ballet being inspired by the fifteenth-century tapestries in the Cluny museum—while Jacques Chailley, Professor of Musicology at the Sorbonne, arranged sixteenth-century music for the work. *La Dame à la Licorne*, with *Le Jeune Homme et la Mort* is the peak of Cocteau's poetic art in the medium of ballet; it is in fact a poem and not far removed in feeling from such *poèmes étalés* as *Le Chiffre Sept*. The theme could not be more characteristic of Cocteau: the lady falls in love with a knight from another world and suddenly sees in the mirror, not her own face but his—she has become the one she loves and thus condemned herself to witness the death of the unicorn. She has married death, the death of the unicorn and her own death—during her agony a banner descends from above proclaiming: "*à mon seul désir*".

Early in May 1953 Cocteau went to Munich to give the finishing touches to the décor, the costumes and to the choreography of Heinz Rosen. He was present at the first night and the ballet was enthusiastically received. A little later a friend presented Cocteau with a strange horn. He put it in the salon at Milly and would tell his visitors, half seriously, that this was the horn of a unicorn.

Jean Cocteau now enjoyed Paris less. He found his visits necessary but exhausting. He spent the whole summer of 1953 at Santo-Sospir, finishing *Appogiatures*, continuing *Clair-Obscur*, editing *Démarche d'un Poète* for a Munich publisher and making illustrations for it. This volume, containing nothing new except some interesting reflections on painting, consists of a series of meditations on his life and his graphic art. It was only published in Germany and remains the sole volume containing fine coloured reproductions of his work.

Cocteau now often saw Picasso at his home in Vallauris and went with him to the bullfights at Nîmes and Arles, where Picasso introduced to him two young devotees of the ring: the youthful writer Jean-Marie Magnan and Lucien Clergue who had been photographing the Camargue and the gipsies. Cocteau now had a growing desire to visit Spain, but first of all he had to go to Rome to see the great Picasso exhibition. The organisers asked him to pay a tribute to the master.

"Forgive me if I address you on my feet and grope my way," he began, "but I think it would be indecent to seat oneself at a table to talk about a man who lives on his feet, works on his feet and is seldom to be found in a sitting position."

He continued with a graceful discourse, running back over the years since he first met Picasso in 1916 and by each observation subtly stressing the genius of the artist whom he called a great poet. And not only did he salute his genius but his character:

The legend of Picasso the egoist is completely false. One would know him little if one did not know that he has always helped his friends in their bad times and without the slightest show.

As I have known him, so will he remain until his death, if death dares to interrupt him.

Frederick Nietzsche spoke of men-mothers . . . One could say this was a prophetic portrait of Picasso . . ., he is at one and the same time a man and a woman; an extraordinary *ménage*. I don't think in any *ménage* so many dishes have been broken.

In case you have only seen pictures of Picasso, I would like to describe him to you. He is very small with charming feet and hands and terrible gimlet eyes that pierce the exterior and the interior. Intelligence spurts out of him like water from a watering-can. One may get cold under this douche, but it always does one good.

In November, with the excuse of the first production in Madrid of *Le Bel Indifférent*, the little piece he had written for Edith Piaf, Cocteau left by car for Spain with Madame Weisweiller, Edouard Dermit and the chauffeur. At Barcelona Cocteau admired the church with Gaudi's "boughs of metal in the modern style"; in Madrid he visited the Prado to see the works of Goya and El Greco, and went to the bullfights which inspired him to write about them. He was delighted when Picasso's sister presented him with a miniature bullring that he took back with him as a precious possession.

In Madrid their pleasant journey was interrupted for several days by Cocteau having gastric trouble that was not dangerous, but which the French press made the most of. The papers took the opportunity to announce that Jean Cocteau had presented himself as a candidate to the Académie Française. Cocteau read the papers in Madrid and sent telegrams denying this, and the journey continued to Toledo and to Andalusia, where he saw for himself the gipsies whom Lorca had celebrated:

> . . . mysterious people who seem to spit flowers of fire and stamp to put them out.

What had begun as a holiday trip developed into a passionate quest with Cocteau transformed into the mirror of Spain, although the spirit of Spain never penetrated deeply into his consciousness. They returned to France via Malaga, Granada and Seville, and Cocteau at once began his drawings of gipsies and toreros, to write his Spanish poems and to muster his material for *Notes sur un premier voyage en Espagne*.

As nothing urgent called him back to Paris, December and January found him living at Santo-Sospir. He was to be seen

now going about, always bare-headed and in a duffel coat—
before this became normal wear in France—with a scarf embroi-
dered in many colours and his flat watch with a diamond at its
centre, the gift of Francine Weisweiller, hanging from his neck
on a long gold chain and carried in his trouser pocket—trousers
of the finest corduroy.

In February, the fashionable month for winter sports, he went
to Kitzbühl with Francine Weisweiller and Dermit, now wearing
a pale beige fur-lined and fur-collared overcoat. As always, he
wrote many letters here, now in an unusual sepia ink that he had
recently discovered. Here too, while Dermit skied and slept,
Cocteau wrote the last poems for the volume *Clair-Obscur*,
poems about Spain and many honouring other artists such as:
"*Hommage au Greco*", *à Velasquez, à Goya, à Picasso, à Gongora,
à Rilke, à Lewis Carroll.*

They returned to the Côte d'Azur in March for Cocteau to
preside at the International Cinema Festival in Cannes, organised
by Philippe Erlanger, the official of the *Ministre des Affaires
Etrangères* in charge of cultural matters. He and Cocteau had
known one another for a long time and were the best of friends.
Installed with his companions at the Carlton Hotel, Cocteau
proved an exemplary president, scrupulously attending each
showing of a film and every gala.

After a few weeks' rest at Santo-Sospir and the final preparation
of the *Clair-Obscur* scripts for publication by *Editions du Rocher*—
the later poems owing more to Gongora and Mallarmé than to
Ronsard—the three travellers set off once more for Spain,
Cocteau and Francine Weisweiller in lively conversation about
everything they saw and Dermit as always silent. This time they
went to Seville to see the Holy Week Feria, and here they
attended a bullfight during which Domas Gomez dedicated his
bull to Cocteau, and he made notes on his knee which developed
into *La Corrida du Ier mai.*

On 10 June 1954, during a brief visit to Paris in stifling weather,

Cocteau was leaving his publisher's office with Jouhandeau when he was suddenly seized with severe pains in his chest. Jouhandeau took him home to the Palais-Royal, where for four hours he was racked with pain. An eminent heart specialist diagnosed myocarditis, and for several days Cocteau lay in bed, cared for by Madeleine and Dermit, and unable to receive a single visitor. The little apartment, usually so full of people when Cocteau was at home, was empty and silent. In *Clair-Obscur*, now at the printers, he had recently written:

> De grâce épargnez-moi les éloges funèbres
> De louer mes amis qui devinrent célèbres
>     Leur cortège m'a précédé.
> Proche est le temps de suivre et qu'un autre me loue
> Puisque le cornet noir encore un peu secoue
>     Les quatre faces de mon dé.

Death, however, which he had invoked so often, was not ready yet for their appointment. For all his maladies Jean Cocteau had a strong constitution and he gradually recovered from this ordeal. Visitors were admitted again; Francine Weisweiller came every day and Jean Marais and Jouhandeau were often with him, besides Maurice Goudeket who brought troubling news of Colette's failing health. François Mauriac sent him his last novel *L'Agneau* with the inscription "your enemy who loves you", to which Cocteau, to seal the reconciliation, responded: "Do you remember how we constantly shared the same cubicle in the Musée Grévin?"

As soon as he was allowed to make the journey, Cocteau went to Santo-Sospir for a long convalescence. He was not permitted to write, but he was able to draw and to paint, and the specialist also recommended him to drink whisky, which now became a daily habit, and which he always vowed had saved his life.

And so gradually Jean Cocteau recovered, but during the night of 3 August 1954 Colette died. Fearing the effect this news would have on Cocteau, Francine Weisweiller kept it from him for twenty-four hours, but when at last she told him of Colette's death he simply said with great tenderness: "I am glad her sufferings are over."

The Curé de Saint-Roch, publicly supported by the Cardinal-Archibshop of Paris, refused Christian funeral rites to Colette. The newspapers took sides reminding Cocteau of the *Bacchus* dispute, although he did not take part in it. This time it was the Church who lost some of the faithful and an enormous crowd gathered to pay Colette homage as the coffin, instead of being carried into the church, lay in state under a tricolour pall in the garden of the Palais-Royal. And Madeleine called on Colette's servant Pauline saying: "I have come to weep for Monsieur Jean."

Colette was buried in the Père Lachaise cemetery and on the morning after this Cocteau was well enough to receive the journalists who called at the Villa Santo-Sospir. Soon afterward he wrote:

> At Père Lachaise it is not a matter of funeral pomp, but simply of gardeners digging, of a passage from one realm to another, of earth and flesh collaborating.

In spite of the specialist's injunctions Cocteau soon started to work again on his *corrida* notes. He also made some fine pastel drawings and several oil paintings, among which were four panels entitled *Astrologue*, "which anticipated," he wrote, "the aeronautic discoveries. Their true theme is no other than parity—this phenomenon of paramount importance in what concerns *dégravitation*". One panel was called *Une main gauche est-elle adroite*, a play of words suggested by the fact that in a mirror the viewer sees his face and his hands inverted. Cocteau was to return to this theme in *Paraprosodies*:

> Gauche était la main droite et ses doigts maladroits
> Tournaient à gauche alors qu'il fallait prendre à droite.

If *Les Astrologues* reflects his preoccupation with the para-scientific, another canvas of this period, an enormous one, *The Oedipus Complex* or *Oedipus and his Daughters*, evolving directly from the *Oedipus Rex* masks, has nothing enigmatic about it. It is one of Cocteau's best paintings and he refused ever to part with it and used it in his last film *Le Testament d'Orphée*.

When Cocteau returned to Paris at the beginning of October, the Palais-Royal without Colette was not the same, nor, after the first warning of death's approach, was he the same himself. Still looking rather young for his age—his hair at sixty-three was scarcely grey at all—and still a sparkling conversationalist, he was determined to live and he let himself be drawn more and more into society to distract him from a heavy sense of loneliness. Having sometimes, through the strange alchemy of his work, seemed like a man without a shadow; now, in the mirror slightly tarnished with age, he was becoming the shadow without the man.

## CHAPTER XIII

# THE ACADEMICIAN

On 11 January 1955 Jean Cocteau became a member of the *Académie Royale de Langue et de Littérature Française de Belgique*. The Chair to which he was elected had once been held by the Comtesse de Noailles and was now left vacant by the death of Colette. At the same election the Princess Bibesco, a close friend of Cocteau's, was also accorded a Chair. This was Jean Cocteau's first academic honour—and it had come from abroad.

Meanwhile, on 8 January, all the morning papers had announced that Jean Cocteau had presented his candidature to the Académie Française. This was a bid for the Chair left vacant by the death of Jérôme Tharaud, for which the historian Jérôme Carcopino, as well as the former rector of the University of Paris, and a little known poet were all competing.

For two months now Cocteau had been living with this project in mind; he had forgathered with the élite who had an influence on the Academy; he was often seen in public with his sister, la Comtesse de la Chapelle, and Francine Weisweiller gave frequent dinner parties and receptions for him in the Place des Etats-Unis. His old friends André Maurois and his wife Simone were often present and they were the first to be told of his candidature, Madame Weisweiller counting on the Jewish and pro-Jewish milieu to weigh against Jérôme Carcopino, who had been a Minister in the Pétain government. Also to be found at these reunions were Jacques de Lacretelle of *Le Figaro*, thirty years earlier one of the jury which awarded Raymond Radiguet the *Prix du Nouveau Monde*, Professor Henri Mondor, a Mallarmé specialist and a Professor of Medecine at the University of Paris, representing the sciences, Pierre Benoît representing the smart literary world, Philippe Erlanger, the Ministries and Embassies, the whole social pattern of these receptions being a network of alliances and diplomacy. There was nothing to fear from François Mauriac since the reconciliation of the summer, and Cocteau sent Paul Claudel, at his château de Brangues, a careful letter to remind him how they used to meet at the house of Madame Alphonse Daudet.

Dear and magnificent friend, I have sent Georges Lecomte [the Permanent Secretary of the Académie] the fateful letter. I obey my heart in letting you know. Your faithful Jean Cocteau.

The reply was brief and written on Cocteau's own letter:

Of course, dear Cocteau, you will have my vote. P. Claudel.

But Claudel's death prevented him from fulfilling his promise. A strange change was now taking place in Cocteau's outlook. Having always liked young people—he had often written of their happy influence on him—he gradually turned against youth.

I find as I meet my contemporaries," he told Denise Bourdet, "that old people are exquisite. They are no longer holding on to anything, so they have their hands open. Youth full of asperity has its fists closed. . . . I am not lenient towards my own youth so I do not see why I should be so towards that of others."

This change of view was largely due to Cocteau discovering in, for example, the newspaper article about his candidature, that he was now considered an old man. Although he still felt essentially young, his approach to the Académie had alienated a certain youthful section of his public—he had become for them "an official". In a radio interview in January he tried to justify his position and once more to Denise Bourdet he complained:

A young poet from Carcassonne has written to me: "You are going in the future to see a fine world and to listen glassy-eyed to jazz."

He forgets that I was the first to preach jazz and in this he gives an example of the giddy folly of young people: very old jazz appears to them as new.

On one hand Jean Cocteau's candidature seemed perfectly natural—he had achieved a position and he had chosen others of a similar status to back him. On the other hand, the Chair he coveted had once been Edmond Rostand's, and Cocteau had never before appeared to desire honours such as had been given to the author of *Cyrano de Bergerac*. Had he not declared to Fraigneau in 1951:

> Nietzsche wrote: "One must choose between glory and honours; if you want glory give up honours." This is because honour and honours are visible, while glory is practically invisible.

But now, in this strange insatiable state of mind that seemed a result of his serious illness and which endured until his death, Jean Cocteau coveted these two things he knew to be incompatible—glory and honour.

An exhibition of his pastels during the winter at the gallery of Lucie Weill—Cocteau now worked in a studio in the place des Etats-Unis—reinforced the Académie campaign and gave him the opportunity to receive Aragon—who never reproached him with this honours-seeking—and all Paris, at the vernissage, and also to gainsay any rumour that he had ceased to be an artist and become a man-of-letters. The exhibition was still on view when, on 4 March 1955, Jean Cocteau was elected to the Académie by eighteen votes to eleven for Jérôme Carcopino. In spite of his elation Cocteau was saddened not to have been elected unanimously. On this day, appropriately enough, he attended a cocktail party given by Amiot-Dumont for the Paris publication of Cecil Beaton's *The Glass of Fashion*, appearing in Denise Bourdet's translation as *Cinquante Ans d'Elégance et d'Art de Vivre*, at which Beaton too was present. Shortly after this Cocteau chose

his sponsors: Pierre Benoît and Jacques de Lacretelle. The following day the Communist paper, *L'Humanité*, voiced its satisfaction;
Carcopino, the former collaborationist Minister, had been
defeated and Cocteau had his place. This was also the view of
Bernard Faÿ, although he too had been a member of the Pétain
government.

> "Isn't it right," Faÿ wrote a little later, "that the civilised world
> should discover that the most civilised of its children deserved to be
> held up as a model? Ever since childhood Jean Cocteau has been
> dedicated to the Académie Française, but he chose tortuous ways to
> get there. There are worse ones . . ."

One unconventional gesture of Cocteau's was to give, at the
suggestion of Louis Aragon, an exclusive article about his election
to *L'Humanité*.

> "I have always noted that the bad path is the good one," he wrote,
> "and that the good one leads nowhere. Honours reward those that
> mock them.
> "The *Académie Française* would not have opened its doors to me
> had I been a good pupil. The prestige of the dunce inevitably has
> more appeal than the wisdom of those at the top of the class."

A few weeks later Cocteau wrote an article for *France-Soir* in
which he declared that he would like to spend his eternity with
Heraclitus and Leonardo da Vinci.

Honours brought more honours in their wake. On 20 March
Cocteau was made *"citoyen d'honneur"* of Milly-la-Forêt, and in
May the exhibition of pastels, augmented by paintings and
drawings, went to Rome, where the gallery published an elaborate
illustrated catalogue with a biography of the artist.

The ceremonial Académie attire—uniform, cape, tricorne,
sword—always costs a small fortune, but Cocteau required his to
be especially splendid. The *"habit vert"* was therefore made by
Lanvin and the sword subscribed for by the publisher Claude

Gallimard and his wife, Francine Weisweiller and other friends. Madame Weisweiller had the blade wrought by the Toledo gipsies after a design by Picasso, and the hilt was made by Cartier. This was designed by Cocteau himself, showing Orpheus's lyre, the Oedipe-Roi profile, which was also the profile of the angel and of Raymond Radiguet, the twisted cord of a theatre curtain, the star with a great diamond in its centre and a ruby at each point, the monogram "J.C." and the Palais-Royal *grille* to join the hilt to the blade. Certainly no such sword had ever been seen before.

At the beginning of the summer, when all these preparations were complete, Cocteau went to Santo-Sospir to compose his two addresses, one for the Académie Belge and the other for the Académie Française. Meanwhile visitors continued to storm the Palais-Royal, demanding to see the great man and sometimes hurling insults at Madeleine when she shouted from the window that Monsieur was away. There Madeleine stayed faithfully at her post, sending on the enormous mail each day and looking after the three Siamese cats* who, she declared, since having an Academician for their master refused to eat anything but fillets of sole.

Engaged as he was on these weighty matters, Jean Cocteau had not lost his sense of fun. He still adored laughter, and in July he was delighted to become the patron of the absurd Club des Enkakeu (*en cas que*), an association for those who treated misfortune with a certain indifference, which Cocteau called "*l'aquoibonisme*" from "*à quoi bon*"—what's the point?

As soon as the two addresses were finished he sent them off to the publishers, the one for Belgium on Colette to Grasset, and the other to Gallimard. The first of October found Cocteau in Brussels in the company of his dear friend Marthe Bibesco who gave her address on the same occasion, in the presence of Queen Elisabeth of the Belgians, Pablo Casals and other celebrities.

* At the time of writing this, Madeleine is still looking after Jean Cocteau's cats in Paris.

"This sovereign," Cocteau wrote, "who understands better than anyone else how to keep the balance between a simplicity of spirit and the demands of ceremonial . . . her modesty as a queen leading her to say: 'I am only an artist,' and her modesty as an artist to say: 'I am only a queen.'"

Cocteau said little about himself on this occasion, leaving it to the Belgian author, Fernand Desonay, to do this for him. After paying a tribute to Anna de Noailles, he launched into a eulogy of his old friend, Colette, sometimes talking intimately and not forgetting Maurice Goudeket, who was present with Colette's daughter, or Pauline, the faithful housekeeper, and sometimes speaking as an inspired critic:

Madame Colette has no need to be whitewashed, for she is white. She detests black as much as do the Impressionists, whom she resembles although she never belonged to their group and was probably quite unaware of their discoveries. She is unique. She was unique. Unique she will remain. And I want to stress this, for strangely enough it is by belonging to no school and by playing truant that she has inspired all schools.

By the end of the meeting Cocteau had made a conquest of the Queen and she had accepted his invitation to the reception at the Académie Française. A few days before this event, he sent in the final text of his discourse, but for the address the committee of censorship requested him to remove his comments on the events in Morocco during the rule of Maréchal Lyautey, himself a member of the Académie Française, and also to suppress the name of Jean Genet, for which Cocteau wickedly substituted the words: "the poet canonised by Jean-Paul Sartre."

It was in Madame Weisweiller's salon, three days before the great event that, in the presence of all those who had subscribed towards it, Pierre Benoît presented Cocteau with the Academician's sword. Cocteau replied with a short poem which was then handed over to the journalists.

The day dawned; from early morning the police closed the Place de l'Institut de France to all traffic. By 2 p.m. the crowd was dense; everyone wanted to see Jean Cocteau, Academician. There had been no less than twelve thousand applications for the seven to eight hundred places available. The *gardes républicains* formed a guard of honour, and a little before 3 p.m. Cocteau got out of the Rolls-Royce with Madame Weisweiller to be welcomed by Jean Marais who had just arrived in his sports-car— Edouard Dermit remaining modestly in the background. The journalists' cameras went into action; a few moments later Queen Elisabeth of the Belgians arrived and the *place* was crammed with famous figures of society, of literature, the arts and the theatre. Picasso was not present, although a fortnight before Cocteau had given a speech about him in Brussels, once again in the presence of the Queen, but Jean Genet, with his shaven head, was seen entering the Académie. Cocteau's sister was also present and that dear friend of his whole lifetime, his cousin Marianne Singer.

So, Cocteau in his splendour entered the Académie, flanked by his sponsors and a little disappointed to find that only about a dozen of his confrères had donned their dress uniform. He put on his spectacles—a thing that he hated to do in public—and proceeded to read his charming and often brilliant address:

Messieurs,

Rémy de Gourmont said that for Edmond Rostand luck was a form of genius. Rostand was carried to this Chair by swift fairies and in a whirl of wings that he evokes at the birth of Henri de Bornier. All the gates that close before the black warriors of literature of which Kleist remains the example, opened of their own accord before his white armour and his white plume.

When *Cyrano de Bergerac* was turning all our heads, I can imagine a young wizard of the Condorcet declaring to the boys in my class that I would one day occupy at the Académie the Chair of their idol. The old college would have collapsed under their laughter.

He went on to speak very amusingly of this "bad pupil" who had now been given an entry into the society of "brilliant pupils".

> Yes, Messieurs, I am not unlike one of those acrobats balanced on top of a pile of chairs . . . even to the traditional rolling of drums that accompanies him.

And he apologised gracefully for the constant use of the word *"je . . . je . . . je . . ."*.

Tradition ruled that he must praise his predecessor, but he spoke little of him—the first mention subtly implying that he had nothing in common with this novelist:

> You will soon see how all these meanderings are leading us in a straight line to one of the least tortuous of all figures: that of Jérôme Tharaud.

He had little to say except that he liked the name Tharaud and that he had come across a photograph of Jérôme Tharaud wearing a *bicorne* and a trench-coat over his Academician's uniform. Instead of talking about his work, he simply mentioned some of the titles of his books.

He spoke with characteristic grace of his old friends, recalling how Guillaume Apollinaire had said that the Seine flowed conserved by its books. He spoke of the absurd conformism of anti-conformist youth and recalled that Radiguet had discovered that it was not enough to defy tradition, one must also defy the *avant-garde*.

And he spoke of course a great deal about poetry—the poetry that he admired in painting, music, sport and in living itself:

> I know that poetry is indispensable but I do not know for what.

He came back to Jérôme Tharaud late in the address to explain that his only personal contact with him had been in connection with his own book *"Visites à Maurice Barrès"*, whose secretary Tharaud had been.

Finally, as he approached the end of his address, he made this heartfelt plea:

My wish is that the Académie Française will therefore protect people suspected of individualism. I dream that our gates may open for the singular that the plural persecutes. That, one day, the Institute, following the example of mediaeval churches, may become an asylum, where those guilty of the crime of innocence may find refuge.

Very often during the address the minds of the audience turned towards Jean Genet, and in his reply André Maurois smilingly echoed the new Academician:

You wish for the best to be summoned here. This is my wish too, and if you bring us a François Villon I promise to vote for him, provided he has written *Le Petit Testament*.

Following tradition, Maurois' address was a eulogy of Cocteau and he achieved a fine résumé of his work. A propos of his films he said:

Like the great English humorists, you have understood that the more fantastic the story appears, the more realistic its teller must be.

Near the end of his speech, he assured Cocteau of the respect of the Académie for the individual:

"We have elected you, not in order to change you, but to have you with us just as you are," and he added this charming anecdote:

"The parents of one of your little nieces had just given her the news that an angel had brought her a brother. 'Do you want to see your brother?' they asked her. 'No,' she said, 'I want to see the angel.' We are like your niece, Monsieur. We do not want to see another Academician. We want to see the angel Heurtebise."

The ceremony lasted for several hours, then Jean Cocteau, the Academician, left with the Queen on his arm and the guests assembled at the party given by Monsieur and Madame Alec Weisweiller in the Place des Etats-Unis, the protocol being arranged by the Prefect of Paris himself.

Absorbed by all the arrangements that were the natural outcome of such events, Cocteau stayed on in Paris. In November he made his appearance on the stage of the Théâtre Hébertot, wearing a kimono, to introduce the Kabuki ballets.

His election to the Académie had attracted a good deal of attention abroad, and his plays and novels were now being translated into many languages—English, German, Hungarian, Jugoslav, Japanese. His work was fashionable among university students and it was not long before Oxford University offered him the honorary degree of Doctor of Letters.

At the beginning of December Arthur Honegger died, the first of Les Six to leave the scene, and Cocteau gave an address at his funeral, recalling the group's history that had been so closely intertwined with his own, and at about the same time he also recorded his warm memories of Colette for the Radio Française. After this he spent some weeks of the winter at Santo-Sospir, revising certain texts that were to be republished, writing poems and a scenario for a new ballet, Le Fils de l'air, to be produced in Munich, and making drawings as a preparation for decorating La Chapelle Saint-Pierre de Villefranche-sur-Mer, which was used as a shed by the fishermen and, after years of transaction, was being put into Cocteau's hands to restore and decorate.

February found him at the rehearsals of the new production of La Machine à Ecrire at the Comédie-Française, with Robert Hirsch playing the parts of the twin brothers, and later for another revival of this play in Brussels, accompanied always by Edouard Dermit and Francine Weisweiller. As ever, in the mornings, when Cocteau was at home, the little Palais-Royal apartment seethed with callers. "Jean" had over the years lost nothing of his gentleness and his charm and received visitors, known and unknown, with great cordiality. All his life he had needed to be loved and admired—now he was enjoying a wide appreciation to the full.

The conferring of the degree at Oxford was fixed for June of this year, 1956, and soon Cocteau returned to Santo-Sospir to prepare his address and to start work on the Villefranche chapel. He had designed the tabernacle: a hanging dove as in a Greek church and the altar made from a block of limestone hewn by an Italian from a hill at La Turbie, above Nice. Cocteau in overalls, but always a dandy, supervised all the work himself; he decided to paint the façade of the chapel *trompe-l'oeil*, as indeed many of the houses in Villefranche had once been painted. In the church he had found an ancient Spanish statue of Christ covered with paint, which he had scraped down and proposed to place in the chapel, "my" chapel as he liked to call it. He enjoyed working with religious subjects, not so much as an act of faith as because they gave him such opportunities as a visual artist and as an artisan.

Cocteau's heart stood up well to all this activity and he continued to treat it with whisky and with the cocktails that he mixed himself for the friends invited to Santo-Sospir. Good cocktails could only be made, he insisted, with fresh oranges and lemons from Menton.

At the beginning of June, Jean Cocteau stayed in London for a few days with Madame Weisweiller and Dermit before going up to Oxford to receive his degree. Once again he enjoyed the ritual, the oration in Latin by the Public Orator, the procession and the special costume, and Professor Jean Seznec of All Souls College in his presentation speech at the Sheldonian Theatre observed that:

> *le docteur Cocteau* will henceforth be "*chez lui*" at Oxford and you yourselves will confirm that he wears the scarlet and black gown with the same ease as the *habit vert*.

Cocteau was to wear this gown and the tasselled mortar-board again in his last film *Le Testament d'Orphée*.

After Professor Seznec's speech Jean Cocteau delivered his own address to the audience of professors, dons and students—Madame Weisweiller and Dermit being of course present—giving it the characteristic title *La Poésie ou l'Invisibilité*.

In the course of the long speech, in which he touched on many subjects and on many people dear to him—all the great influences on his work—the title was explained:

> Is it not the long tradition of Oxford that makes possible the phenomenon of honouring not the visible but the invisible man and, guessing somehow that a man's name outruns his work, of greeting not that name, which would be only natural, as my work is little translated and almost untranslatable, but the enigma of poetry itself in my person . . .
>
> For something tells me that it is not the Jean Cocteau they talk about at random whom you are receiving at Oxford, but the humble workman who never wanted anything but to put himself at the service of the unknown force that inhabits poets . . .

Speaking of the appreciation of the French language sometimes found abroad, he made a charming reference to his old friend Reginald Bridgeman, saying that in those far off days when he was at the British Embassy in Paris, Bridgeman had shown him what the French language was like as spoken in France, before rich and uncultured people debased it. And he remembered, as in a dream, that "sunny morning of my youth when I visited your holy city". This was, of course, his trip to Oxford with Raymond Radiguet. "I wondered then: 'Shall I ever deserve to have the doors of these cloisters opened to me?'"

After the address, an elegant garden-party was held at the Maison de France, attended among other distinguished visitors by Lord Halifax, Chancellor of the University, and Jean Chauvel, the French Ambassador.

Returning to Paris, Jean Cocteau declared that contrary to

expectation he had eaten very well in England. In fact, he always ate sparingly, leaving on his plate a large part of what he was served. He liked shellfish, raw or grilled, and certain simple dishes such as calf's head, and the everyday Italian food served in the popular *trattorie* of Nice and Menton. But he was an excellent host, pressing delicacies upon his guests and giving them generous helpings with his own hands.

Louis Aragon was awaiting Cocteau's return to Paris to collaborate with him in *Entretiens sur le Musée de Dresde*, a commission from *Editions du Cercle d'Art*. This was a random collection of the views of two poets on certain painters, opening with a recorded discussion between them, in which Cocteau reminded Aragon that the breach between himself and the surrealists had not stopped them from "turning their eyes" towards the same painters. Nevertheless they did not always agree; Cocteau, for instance, affirmed that art was a reflection of the individual while Aragon declared that it was a reflection of the epoch. Increasingly now Cocteau liked to make use of recording facilities to speak his work instead of writing it.

After this brief sojourn in Paris Cocteau returned to Santo-Sospir and continued his work on the interior and exterior of the Saint-Pierre chapel. He could be seen in his overalls climbing the scaffolding, helped by the painter Jean-Paul Brusset, already well known in the United States, drinking wine with the fishermen, some of whom had known him since those youthful days when he frequented the Hôtel Welcome and the bars of Villefranche, and lunching in the little restaurant Chez Germaine, where he had become an habitué.

On the inside walls of the chapel he introduced drawings which he had made from famous pictures, from the photographs of gipsies by Lucien Clergue, the Arles photographer, and of angels who were none other than rugby players from the sporting journals, gaily embellished with wings.

Except for a journey to Baalbek in August to attend the opening of *La Machine Infernale*, in which Jeanne Moreau played the Sphinx, and to receive the Order of the Cedar, and a few brief visits to Paris to which he declared each time he never wanted to return—"Paris devours me"—he spent the rest of the summer and the following winter at Santo-Sospir and soon, at the request of the Mayor, made designs for decorating the *salle des mariages* in the Mairie at Menton. "A *salle des mariages*, a chapel," he joked. "There's nothing left for me to do but get married."

He began work at the Menton Mairie in the spring of 1957, taking much trouble not only with his murals, but with the doors, the furniture and the lighting of this square *salle*. The paintings were allegorical; the one on the main wall facing the public representing the bridal couple wearing hats of local tradition. It was a large undertaking, but although the result was spectacular, it had nothing of the perfection Cocteau achieved in the little chapel of Saint-Pierre.

He was also engaged with lithographs, making great prints in black and in colour of his designs for the chapel and the *salle des mariages*. Also, following Picasso's recent enthusiasm, he began learning pottery in the workshops of Madeline-Jolly above Villefranche, to which he was driven almost every day either in the old Citroën or in one of Madame Weisweiller's cars. At first he only decorated ready-made plates and dishes, but before long he began to make these for himself. In fact, at this moment, at least in the South of France, the Academician and Doctor of Letters was better known as a visual artist than as a writer, although he was still working on poems of a rigorous nature, of which the best found their way into the volume *Paraprosodies*.

In March of this year he received a new distinction in being made an honorary member of the New York National Institute of Arts and Letters, the number of foreign members being limited to fifteen, among which were already Henri Sauguet and Darius Milhaud. His diploma was bestowed on him in June by the American Ambassador at the Embassy in Paris. This month too

Jean Cocteau and Edouard Dermit in the mountains (*Private Collection*)

Jean Cocteau in his studio at Santo-Sospir (*photo Pierre Meunier*)

the young actress Toni Mag played in a revival of *Le Bel Indifférent* at the Théâtre de Lutèce, and the Festival of Saint-Malo included in its programme *Les Chevaliers de la Table Ronde*, *Antigone* and *Orphée*.

Jean Cocteau returned to Villefranche for the reconsecration of the chapel by the Archbishop of Nice, the first Mass, and the dedication of his own work with Madame Weisweiller, whose daughter Carole was portrayed on the walls, as "godmother". He now had another exhibition in Nice and expressed the view: "I am against exhibitions. The pictures are hung there. This kills them."

All these activities did not leave him much time to write; he had become the poet of messages, appeals, declarations: an appeal in *l'Humanité*, at Aragon's suggestion, to save the manuscript of Rimbaud's *Illuminations* being removed from France; a last salute in *Paris-Presse* on the occasion of the death of the Aga Khan; a postal flash for the Festival of Music at Menton. He appeared now to be unable to refuse any request from a friend, an acquaintance or even from a stranger. Dominique Ponchardier, the author of detective novels, proposed to write a sequel to *Les Parents Terribles* and Jean Marais envisaged making a film of *Les Monstres Sacrés*. Cocteau gave his permission to all these projects, although neither they nor his own plan for making a film of *La Machine à Ecrire* were realised.

On 1 October he was made Citizen of Honour of Villefranche. On the eve of this celebration a representative of the French Ambassador in London called on Jean Cocteau to invite him to decorate the Lady Chapel in the church, Notre-Dame-de-France, near Leicester Square. He consented: "They take me for a religious painter because I have decorated a chapel. Always the same mania for labelling people."

After this homage in Villefranche Jean Cocteau returned to Paris to sign the contract with Bernard Grasset for the publication of *La Corrida du Ier mai*, the first work, apart from his address, to be published by Cocteau the Academician, and one which did not please the critics. At the same time he had the pleasure of seeing André Fraigneau's book *Cocteau par lui-même* appear in *Editions du Seuil*. Meanwhile he himself was making a recording of *Les Mariés de la Tour Eiffel* with new music by Pierre-Philippe for Pathé-Marconi. When this record appeared the following year, General de Gaulle had just been triumphantly re-elected President, giving the General in *Les Mariés* an unexpected topicality which greatly amused Cocteau, without in the least detracting from his admiration for de Gaulle.

On 16 December, having finished his business in Paris, Jean Cocteau returned to Santo-Sospir with Dermit to enjoy the sunshine, the potteries and the constant stream of visitors to the Saint-Pierre Chapel. Distinguished neighbours, such as Sir Winston Churchill, Charles Chaplin, Prince Rainier and Princess Grace, he himself took round on private tours.

At the end of January 1958 Cocteau's sister, la Comtesse de la Chapelle, died suddenly and he immediately went back to Paris with Madame Weisweiller. Some refreshment, however, that he had on the train made him ill and he was unable to attend the funeral.

For ten years now Cocteau had been greatly interested in the sciences—in for instance the exploration of space—so he was delighted when the Prince de Broglie, a brother Academician, commissioned him to paint two enormous canvases for the planetarium of the exhibition "*Terre et Cosmos*", which was to be erected in June on the banks of the Seine beside the Tour Eiffel. Cocteau's great compositions were entitled *Hommage aux Savants* and *La Conquête de l'Inconnu*, and they satisfied his sincere desire to see poetry and science coming close together.

It was at this time that Jean Cocteau invited Jean-Jacques Kihm for a long visit to a little hotel in Villefranche to work on the book about Cocteau that he was writing. Kihm felt that they were all the time on holiday, talking endlessly as they strolled or sat in restaurants, but in fact they achieved a great deal.

After the opening in his presence at Nice of the ballet Serge Lifar had made from *Le Bel Indifférent*, Cocteau finished the script of *Paraprosodies précédées de sept dialogues*, in which he expressed a more lofty and more mystical conception of poetry than ever before, after which he returned to Paris to supervise the placing of his canvases in the Planetarium and to see his friends, particularly Jean Marais, whom he was horrified to find wasting his time over a ballet and its handsome star, George Reich.

He was also exploring the prospects of materialising his dream, his farewell to the cinema, his testament, *Le Testament d'Orphée*. The director was to be Etienne Périer and Cocteau was to play the leading part in the film—as himself. But to find a producer was as difficult for an Academician as for a beginner, and Cocteau never ceased to complain that art had become a commercial affair in which the stars took precedence over the poets.

Meanwhile there were many distractions: in July he went to Vienna to speak the Chorus in a production of *Oedipus Rex*, conducted by Herbert von Karajan, after which he spent several weeks with Madame Weisweiller and Dermit in Venice, where they visited Diaghilev's tomb. At Murano Cocteau tried his hand at moulding glass, endearing himself to all the artisans, and he wrote the poem *Gondole des Morts* to accompany a series of drawings in coloured crayons, depicting the people on the beaches and in the bars of the Lido where they were staying.

On their return to Santo-Sospir, urged by his "father", Doudou started to paint industriously, preparing for an exhibition in the spring. He began his pictures in the sunshine among the flowers and finished them at night by artificial light which gave them a certain strange character.

In the middle of September Cocteau went to Brussels to give a *Discours sur la Poésie* before a vast audience at the Exposition Universelle. This lecture, which earphones enabled people to hear in Flemish, English and Russian, did not contain any new views of poetry, but included an evocation of Venice, "which one finds each time so young and active". It also put an end to his recent quarrel with Sartre who had referred to him in an article as a coiner, a counterfeiter.

> He calls me a counterfeiter, forgetting that poets strike coins bearing their own image, whereas counterfeiters strike theirs bearing the image of the Bank of France.

> "Barrès . . ., Gide . . ., Sartre . . .," Cocteau ended, "suffer in some sort from not belonging to the family of the cursed."

In other words they were not poets.

The next day, in the small auditorium of the Pavillon de la France, with loud-speakers relaying the speeches out of doors, Jean Cocteau, warmly introduced by Pierre de Gaulle, the General's brother, gave a lecture called *Les Armes secrètes de la France* before his admirer Queen Elisabeth of the Belgians. This developed the idea that France with her apparent lightness, her apparent anarchy, her apparent disorder was the miracle country, the country that adapted itself to exceptional circumstances and to forms of invention that were essentially poetic.

> I wish France to know that she fosters art rather than science and that a number of her scientists are poets.

This lecture, after the recent events in Algeria, was startling, and Cocteau emphasised the fact that it was written before the insurrection, at the invitation of General de Gaulle's brother.

> ". . . voilà," he said, "a fine coincidence, if such a thing exists, a lucky chance, if such an expression can exist in the vocabulary of poets."

This is one of the rare occasions on which Cocteau, in spite of his isolationism, expressed awareness of a political situation. But then the situation was extremely grave and Jean Cocteau now considered himself the national poet.

For the rest of the autumn, while continuing to work on the scenario for the *Testament*, Jean Cocteau devoted himself to his pottery with such effect that by November he was prepared to show himself with his best ceramics before the television cameras in the Lucie Weill gallery in rue Bonaparte. In a short time he had sold a large number of these works at a very high price; indeed he was to observe that he had made more money as a visual artist than as a writer.

During this visit to Paris, Cocteau approved as ready for publication by Gallimard the long book that Jean-Jacques Kihm had written about his work.

"Give me genius," Cocteau wrote to Kihm, "children and poets have no right to anything but this side-arm . . . this word genius the only one that counts for children, fools and poets and which they always deny me, believing me to have a many-sided talent that I do not possess."

This was very much what Cocteau had said to Bernard Faÿ thirty years earlier when he was preparing his *Panorama de la Littérature Contemporaine*.

Also during his stay in Paris, Jean Cocteau made great efforts to get Paul Morand elected to the Académie Française, designed a label for a beer de luxe and dined at the British Embassy on the occasion of Princess Margaret's official visit.

In December 1958, he made another quick visit to Paris from Santo-Sospir, where he was preparing the designs for the decoration of the little Chapelle-Saint-Blaise at Milly-la-Forêt, a tribute he had promised to his adopted home-town. He spent a few hours at the Opéra discussing the coming first production in France of his ballet *La Dame à la Licorne*, and a few more hours at the Opéra-Comique, where the excellent opera Francis Poulenc had made from *La Voix Humaine* was to be performed.

On 19 December he spent an enjoyable evening at the Opéra attending Maria Callas' performance at the Légion d'Honneur Gala, after which he went back to Santo-Sospir for the Christmas and New Year festivities.

Jean Cocteau had expected to return to Paris to supervise the productions of his ballet and the opera, but January found him struck down by a terrible internal haemorrhage and forbidden by the doctors to move or to work.

"Here I am under the label: 'Writing forbidden' and drunk with disobedience," he wrote to Kihm a few days later. "I am taking the opportunity, while floating on the river of the dead, to write this *Requiem* which I have not dared to embark on during the last few months. It is an unending poem and as much a river as the river on which I am drifting, motionless."

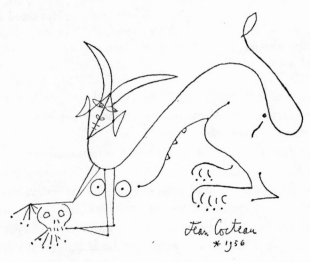

## CHAPTER XIV

## THE LAST MIRROR

"Nothing is more admirable than the silence of a sick-room," wrote Cocteau in the preface to *Requiem*. It was in this silence at Santo-Sospir in January and February 1959 that, in spite of the doctor's injunctions, he began to write this "endless" poem in which his imagination, unfettered by cleverness, roamed from the death so close to him to the death of his lost friends, and from people in the realm of half-sleep to memories of childhood.

> Où sont les secrets et les rites
> De vos souvenirs enfantins
> Mémoire de Maisons-Laffitte
> Que caresse le bruit des râteaux du matin.

As he wrote, his bed became smothered in pages of illegible writing which later on he had to decipher, like a work that one finds "on one's table in the morning, a work to which one has nothing to do except put it in order".

Meanwhile much of his earlier writing was now claiming attention. *Les Enfants Terribles* came out in a pocket edition and although Cocteau declared that the text was strewn with misprints, he was happy to have attained wide sales at last. At the end of January *La Dame à la Licorne* was presented at the Opéra, Cocteau following its fate with the closest concern. He was as ever involved in the technical details of the production and had summoned the technicians to his bedside to give them final instructions. When Jean-Jacques Kihm informed him that the banner in the final scene had remained in shadow, Cocteau replied: "When one reaches this point of perfection a mistake can only be a technical accident. A spotlight must have burnt out."

He had also, in spite of his illness, received Francis Poulenc to discuss the décor and lighting for *La Voix Humaine*, and Claude Pinoteau, his assistant in the preparation of the scenario for *Le Testament d'Orphée*, his "second Faust". On the morning of the public dress rehearsal of *La Voix Humaine*, created by Denise Duval, Cocteau telegraphed to Kihm:

> When opera perfect theatre then regains Chinese style and ceremonial language lost by realism.

This oriental desire for perfection pursued him. In March, at St Moritz with Francine Weisweiller and Dermit for his convalescence, he met the Count Bona Cossa and his wife, both of them professors of philosophy recently returned from Japan and India. The Count wrote to Kihm:

> The Zen leader said . . .: "Jean Cocteau is the only European writer who has penetrated deeply into Japan and India. Each one of his words is a spirit corresponding to oriental wisdom."
> And Zen is the best, the highest we have in this poor world. The Zen archer does not take aim. He thinks his arrow and his arrow goes of its own accord to the target.

Cocteau recounted these remarks of the Zen leader as a proof that he was right to refuse to be seen "through the small end of the opera glasses", and also as a proof of the universality of his work, which was one of his main concerns.

At Saint-Moritz, where he made good progress in the alternating sunshine and mists—returning quite bronzed, Cocteau finished *Requiem*, to which was now added the present landscape haunted by the ghost of Nietzsche:

> Le vent d'Engadine se rue
> Dans Sils Maria par le val
> D'ou montait à la découverte
> de l'Eternel Retour l'alerte
> L'infatigable chamois Nietzsche.

Jean Cocteau painting the Lady Chapel at Notre-Dame-de-France, London, November 1959 (*Collection Yves le Creurer*)

Inside the chapel Saint-Blaise-des-Simples at Milly-la-Forêt, 1960 (*Private Collection*)

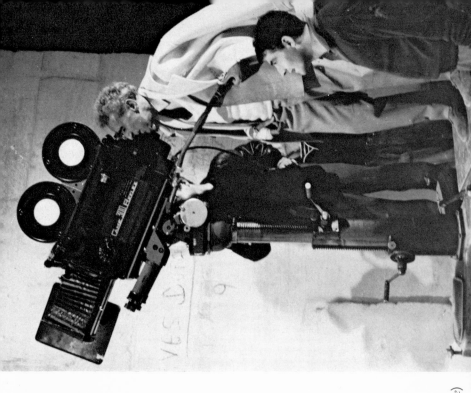

Jean Cocteau at the camera (*photo Lucien Clergue*)

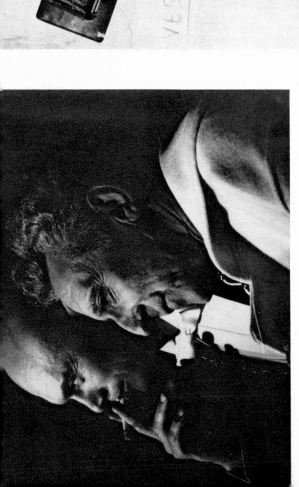

DURING THE FILMING OF *Le Testament d'Orphée*

Jean Cocteau and Yul Brynner (*photo Lucien Clergue*)

Nostalgic and uncertain of his future, farther on in the poem
Cocteau meditated:

> Reverrai-je avril sur le lit
> De la Belle au Bois qui s'éveille...

His wish was granted. He was able to return to Paris in reason-
ably good health for Edouard Dermit's exhibition in the Galerie
Montmorency in the rue Cherche-Midi, which opened on 19
March. Radiant and triumphant, supported by Francine Weisweiller, Jouhandeau and his wife, it was Jean Cocteau who
received the visitors as if the paintings were his own. He did
not try to hide his paternal pride—he had written the preface to
the catalogue, elegantly refusing to sign it, but everyone recognised his style and his desire to turn Edouard Dermit into a
Raymond Radiguet of painting.

> Edouard Dermit has developed in the midst of the most recent
> *audaces* without any doubt he has understood instinctively how these
> *audaces* would lead to their own destruction, for the thing about his
> own [paintings] is that they do not exhibit any...
> Why is this apparent conventionality the peak of unconvention-
> ality? It is not only because unconventionality has become official, it
> is because a modest appreciation of reality has led Dermit into a
> world as completely unreal as, for instance, that of Vermeer.

> It is not Sunday painter but Monday painter that one must say in
> front of his canvases. Only yesterday such paintings would have
> been impossible for any young artist. They would have been afraid
> of being thought *pompiers*. However, by a strange phenomenon, here
> is *audace* no longer starting a fire but putting one out and no longer
> profiting by the dramatic surprises of a blaze.

The critics greeted the new painter with reserve. It must be
admitted that to be presented by Cocteau had certain risks; each
time that any criticism had been levelled at one of his discoveries,
such as Radiguet and Desbordes, he had retaliated by laying too
much stress on their genius.

During his illness at Santo-Sospir Cocteau, with the help of Claude Pinoteau, had finished the cutting of the *Testament* scenario and he now completed the financial arrangements. As the film was not wholly commissioned by a producer, a great part of the costs was divided among individuals who were repaid by its eventual royalties.

At Milly Cocteau arranged for the inside walls of the little twelfth-century chapel Saint-Blaise-des-Simples, which had once been a sanctuary in this retreat for lepers, to be prepared ready for him to paint his frescoes during the summer months. After only a few weeks' rest at Santo-Sospir an exhausting period began, in which he constantly travelled backwards and forwards between Saint-Jean-Cap-Ferrat, Paris and Milly-la-Forêt.

His teeth, of which he had always taken the greatest care, were troubling him now, and he was forced to visit the dentist.

They put me to sleep after the Académie (which is quite good at starting that process) and the dentist works on my ghost.*

At the beginning of May he was once more installed at the Carlton Hotel in Cannes for the Cinema Festival, after which he started making maquettes of a Greek theatre which he had been asked to build for the Cap d'Ail, to stand on the hill between the sea and the pine-woods. "No more beautiful site even in Greece," he wrote to Kihm, happy to be at work on something less restricted than the walls of a chapel, happy particularly at the prospect of using his hands to make with stones and mosaics a building true to the ritual of theatre.

At the end of April, the novel by Roger Peyrefitte *L'Exilé de Capri* had come out with an introduction by Cocteau. He, who had refused to put his name to *Le Livre Blanc* or, even after his mother's death, to admit explicitly that he was its author, he who was always so prudent, so masked in his approach to sexual

---

* The Academicians meet every Thursday afternoon to work on the *Dictionnaire de l'Académie.*

subjects, had now provided a preface to a compromising book by one of the most unconventional of French novelists. Some of his more puritanical friends naturally deplored this gesture and his defence was weak, as everyone knew that he had not only made the erotic drawings for *Le Livre Blanc* but had written the text himself.

Although *L'Exilé de Capri* is a novel, many well-known figures appear in its pages, including Oscar Wilde, and the youthful Cocteau at the Hôtel Biron. Its young hero lives a life of debauchery, dreams of being a genius, and according to Cocteau:

> imagines finding in sexual deviations and their unacceptable decorativeness a compensation for his creative impotence.

Considering his own views, it is strange that Cocteau agreed to write the preface:

> If I show respect for certain of the great "damned", if it happens that for Oscar Wilde for instance, for Captain Alfred Dreyfus, the drama puts a halo on the victim, I have on the other hand always had an acute distaste for a certain little blue flower of hell.

And he doubly condemns Peyrefitte's hero, first for not having had the "genius of soul" which would have allowed him to rebel in another domain, and then for making his life of debauchery a real life of the damned.

> *Eros apteros* [Eros without wings]. This should have been the title of this work that the author dedicates grandly to one of those *Icares* whose wings were melted by the sun of vain-glory.

In fact, in this preface, Cocteau seems to be telling us that it was his creative genius that saved him from falling into the abyss of debauchery.

For the feast of St Peter in June, the fishermen gave Jean

Cocteau a golden sardine weighing 60 grammes, a reproduction of the best sardine caught at Villefranche during the year. This was a kind of revival of the fourteenth-century custom of depositing a silver sardine each year at the foot of the saint.

On Cocteau's seventieth birthday, which fell on 5 July 1959, he did not have a party. He went with Francine and her daughter, Dermit and the Picassos to Arles to see the fine Torero Dominguin, who was later to figure in the *Testament*, after which he went on to the Festival of Spoleto, where they were producing the ballet *Le Poète et sa Muse*, for which he had written the story and designed the décor and costumes, while Gian-Carlo Menotti had composed the music.

As Cocteau describes the ballet:

A young American poet appears tormented by his searchings. His muse appears in a ball dress and from behind her fan dictates him a poem in an unknown language. . . . In order to assure his fame, this muse, with the gestures of Tosca, makes him lie down and simulate suicide, and herself places funeral candles to the left and right of his face. A revolver shot attracts a group of young people in blue jeans who go into transports of hysterical admiration. After the departure of these young aesthetes a champagne cork, to celebrate the adventure, simulates a revolver shot and recalls the troupe. Thinking that they have been fooled, they torture the poet and insult the muse.

The muse throws the trampled manuscripts out of the window and disappears without glancing at the poet who commits suicide by following the route by which he came and leaping from some skyscraper into space.

The curtain falls as one hears the screaming of the police sirens.

This ballet was never shown in France.

He spent the rest of July at Milly, painting on the walls of the little chapel the scene of the Resurrection and the medicinal herbs cultivated in the surrounding country and now grown in the chapel garden; herbs such as mint, gentian, aconite, arnica and valerian, of which he had made a careful study, not from nature but from the plates in an album.

The chapel finished, except for the windows which were being made in Germany from his designs, Cocteau returned to Santo-Sospir to make a great many drawings and gain strength for filming the *Testament*.

The first take was on 17 September 1959 at Les Baux-de-Provence, in that rugged countryside which Cocteau found more beautiful than Greece, more beautiful even than Spain—Dante must, he thought, have lived here and must have found inspiration for his *Inferno*. The filming was exhausting—for many night scenes had to be shot in the damp caves—the weather was unsettled the whole time, rare for September in this region, and the limited budget made it essential to keep to the time-table. Cocteau, the scrupulous technician, was more than once troubled by the complaint of the camera-man that the film was being made in too much of a rush. The camera-man was an artist himself who understood how, in this film without a story, the images themselves must evoke the atmosphere. The whole company admired Cocteau and was devoted to him and to Claude Pinoteau, who had worked from the beginning on the scenario and to whom Cocteau entrusted the delicate task of making everyone understand what he wanted. One important member of the company was Madame Janet, discovered by Francine Weisweiller at Balenciaga, where she dressed the windows, and who came to make the properties for the film. They had many difficulties in constructing these objects devised by Cocteau—for example a mask in which the eyes had to open and close and the moving wings of the Sphinx from *Orphée*, which costume, owing to lack of extras, Edouard Dermit had to don for the scene in which the Poet meets the Sphinx.

Cocteau himself acted the part of the poet Orphée-Cocteau. He said:

> It is very difficult to make one's début at seventy. At twenty one has charm and weapons . . . I wasn't thinking of playing the part myself when I began to write the part of the poet. And then

suddenly, this morning, I saw that I had an enormous rôle and that I wasn't an actor . . . And so I took the plunge.

Among the properties that Madame Janet had to make were a pair of false eyes which Cocteau, like the Princess in *Orphée*, stuck on his eyelids for certain scenes, because the Poet and Death see what others do not see. The other leading part in the film was taken by Dermit, who found it hard to learn his lines, but who, out of devotion for his "father", had agreed to play Cégeste, the same part that he had taken in the film *Orphée*. Cocteau tried to justify Dermit's part by declaring:

> Somebody whom we know well and who knows us equally well is far more suited to play our characters than an actor about whom we know nothing but his physique and his talent.

As they were always on the set together in the same scenes, Cocteau was never able fully to direct Dermit, which accounts for his performance not being stronger.

The *Testament*, to which Cocteau gave the sub-title *Ne me demandez pas pourquoi*, is not a well-constructed picture like the earlier *Orphée*. It is, as he said himself, "a strip-tease, in which bit by bit I remove my body and reveal my soul quite naked". To this purpose he threw together some of the most important characters of his work and of his life. Thus, in the farcical sketch that opens the film with Cocteau suddenly appearing in Louis XV costume, a little boy in short trousers is seen who at once recalls Dargelos; then there are the gipsies of the Spanish poems, camping among the rocks, the Judith and Holofernes tapestry, Oedipus and Antigone, the Villa Santo-Sospir, the Princess from *Orphée* with her attendant Heurtebise—Maria Casarès and François Périer playing their original rôles—the Saint-Pierre chapel and the streets of Villefranche as they were in Cocteau's youth, the motor-cyclists, who bear down upon the poet, but who, he realises, are not "the black angels" of *Orphée* but simply the police, and who frighten the Poet, although they do nothing but ask, as a matter of routine, to see his papers. There is also a Picasso invention: the two bathers who pretend to be a dog which looks like one of the Antibes fauns. Picasso, present at the filming of this scene in the garden at Santo-Sospir, was highly amused by it.

The meeting between the Poet and his characters is one of the most important aspects of this mirror-picture. Another is the phoenix motif—like the phoenix the poet must die many times and be reborn. At the end of the sketch that serves as a prologue, he kills himself in his Louis XV costume in order to be reborn in modern dress—a suede jacket and light trousers. Descending into the other world and appearing before the tribunal of the Princess, the Poet dies once more, transfixed by Minerva's spear, and comes back to life while the gipsies are mourning him.

Pretend to weep, my friends, for poets only pretend to be dead.

Finally, at the end of the film, urged by Cégeste to disappear, the Poet vanishes among the rocks and Cégeste comments:

"The earth after all is not your domain."

In the course of the film, objects too die and are reborn, like the hibiscus flower, which Cégeste brings back from the depths of the sea, from which he himself appears, and offers to the Poet:

It is made of your blood and it follows the hectic line of your destiny.

Unable to paint the flower—his own image appears instead—the Poet pulls it to pieces, then dons the gown and mortar-board of the Oxford Doctor of Letters and resuscitates it. As love is only present in one sequence and that an ironic one—the lovers noting, as they embrace, the experiences they are having—*Le Testament d'Orphée*, which Cocteau declared to be his last film, is seen to be imbued with death in all its forms. With its same central figure, it is far closer to *Le Sang d'un Poète* than to *Orphée*. While it was being taken, a representative from the Radio Française asked Cocteau if the film was "an exact image" of himself and he replied:

> This film will be a kind of shadow-play of my life. Many times they have asked me for one of those films that they make on the life of a poet or a painter. My own, alas, could not be told in any anecdotal manner. It is a long drama, a long fight against customs, against others, against myself, a terrible mixture of consciousness and unconsciousness, of disorder and austerity. I have crossed the path of more people and more events than you would believe and, besides this, I am the sole survivor of a crew that shared work . . .
>
> One must not tell *me*. One must, by allusions and the day to day fable, show those who esteem me a silhouette like those eighteenth century ones cut out in black paper.

The difference between the mirror and the shadow-play is that the former reflects every detail, whereas the latter only portrays the essential outline, but this too is a mirror of a special kind.

The filming presented innumerable problems, the objects being even more difficult to direct than the cast—when the eyelid of Tirésias refused to close, it took Madame Janet an hour to repair it.

All the parts except those of the Poet and Cégeste, being short, each actor or extra had only a few hours filming to do. Cocteau prided himself in getting actors of great talent, as in American films, to play small parts. Out of affection and respect for him they agreed to this and so, from 7 to 22 September, there was an unending flow of stars at Les Baux, of whom none was mentioned in the list of characters. The curious flocked, gazed, photographed. Madame Weisweiller, living with the cast at the Hôtel Val d'Enfer, took care of Cocteau. A caravan followed him as they worked, so that he always had somewhere close at hand to rest. Lucien Clergue went with him everywhere and made a photographic record of the filming as it progressed.

Yul Brynner was there for the first take, lasting two nights; Charles Aznavour and Serge Lifar were there for a single scene; Picasso and Jacqueline Picasso, the torero Dominguin and his wife, Lucia Bosè, were all in the box from which they watched the death of the Poet. Jean Marais, who was playing in Paris, arrived by air for his only free day.

On 24 September certain scenes began to be filmed in the studio de la Victorine at Nice, alternating with others in Villefranche and at Santo-Sospir. Francine Weisweiller, in a marvellous Second Empire dress by Balenciaga, supported by her own butler, played the part of the lady who mistakes the period in the garden of the villa, and it was in her yacht Orphée II that the Iseult scene was taken, while the scene in which Cégeste comes out of the sea to give the hibiscus flower to the Poet was filmed close to the lighthouse of Cap Saint-Jean.

On 19 October, after a final session at Les Baux, the company dispersed and Cocteau and Dermit returned to Paris to film the central scene with the Princess and Heurtebise. Early in November Francine Weisweiller, Dermit and Cocteau left for London, where they stayed at Claridges, Cocteau going each day to the French Church, Notre-Dame-de-France, to decorate the Lady Chapel. He was helped in this work by a painter from Nice and his son, who prepared the walls and the outline of the paintings for him. The ceiling being very low Cocteau showed only the lower part of the crucifix with the feet of the Christ, on His right the Virgin Mary and on His left the artist himself, who felt that his Christian name gave him some right to figure as the traditional Saint Jean. On the panel to the left of the chapel he painted the Annunciation, with the Angel very clear and the Virgin very pale, because she was not yet the Mother of God, and on the opposite side the Assumption, and he signed the work "Jean

Cocteau, 1960", as he was to come back in May of the following year for the official unveiling of the frescoes. During this visit, on 4 November, Cocteau once again spoke the part of the Chorus in a very successful performance of *Oedipus Rex* at the Festival Hall, conducted by Stravinsky himself.

Back in Paris, Cocteau was still busy with the sound-track and the final editing of the *Testament*, and by the end of the year the film was ready to show to a few chosen friends, among whom were Madame Weisweiller, Dermit and Picasso, in a cinema at Nice. For a long time Cocteau had been submerged in the film's technicalities; now he was able to sit back and contemplate himself and his creations in this extraordinary mirror.

The first showing of *Le Testament d'Orphée* in Paris was a private one in the B.B.C. studios, to which so many people came that Cocteau himself had to sit in the gangway, refusing to take the seat of any guest. Before it was seen again he was already engaged in new work. This was for a film of *La Princesse de Clèves* which Jean Delannoy was to make. Cocteau had already written a scenario of this novel to which he had been enthusiastically introduced by Raymond Radiguet nearly forty years earlier. Now he improved the scenario and wrote the dialogue, but although Jean Marais had a leading part in the film and Delannoy too was a good friend of Cocteau's, the latter did not take part in the actual filming, those concerned feeling that his presence was bound to be disturbing. Nor was he present at the filming of the short documentary made at Saint-Blaise-des-Simples by a group of young film-makers—the scenario and commentary being by Jean-Jacques Kihm—except to make one short appearance in this picture which alone mirrors his work as a painter. He had dreamt of a film trilogy:—the Villefranche chapel, the Menton Mairie and the Judith and Holofernes tapestry, and out of this project had come the *Testament*, but the trilogy was never made.

In January 1960 Jean-Jacques Kihm's book *Cocteau* was

published by Gallimard. Cocteau had read, either in script or in proof, more than half of this long study, but when the volume appeared—a mirror held up to him by another's hand—Cocteau found the image not only untrue but disfiguring. For eight days the author received an avalanche of letters and telegrams:

> "If your book is read," Cocteau wrote, "it will ruin me with a mass of people who might have discovered me through later serious analyses."

His two chief complaints were that the book brought to light "follies that the critics had forgotten, follies that time had obliterated", and also the sexual motive that had inspired many of his works. "Behaviour worthy of a Mauriac," Cocteau fumed. "I have hidden the book so that Francine and Doudou can't read it." Less than a fortnight later Cocteau agreed to discuss the book with the author on the Télévision Française, still, it is true, affirming that the model was not to be found in the portrait, but nevertheless demanding de luxe copies of the volume to give to Francine, Doudou and Maurice Goudeket.

Cocteau, now in better health, stayed on in Paris, awaiting with impatience the first public showing of the *Testament*. On 10 February it was presented at two select cinemas—L'Avenue and La Pagode—the producer deciding that this was the best way of launching the film. The critics were, naturally, cool and the film only ran at L'Avenue for two weeks although, thanks to a young audience, it lasted for nine weeks longer at La Pagode, after which it was not seen commercially, but only in the small *avant-garde* cinemas and ciné-clubs. Even here it was not considered a good film, although a revealing document.

After the unveiling of his frescoes, an intimate occasion in the chapel at Milly on 20 April, Cocteau left Paris again for Saint-Jean, where he continued his work for the theatre at the Cap d'Ail, while making a French adaptation of Jerome Kilty's play

*Dear Liar*, based on the letters of Bernard Shaw and Mrs Patrick Campbell, which was to be performed at the Théâtre de l'Athénée by Pierre Brasseur and Maria Casarès.

Although the *Testament* had not had the success he expected, Cocteau was doing very well. During this summer came the film Jacques Demy had made of *Le Bel Indifférent*, and in September Edwige Feuillère appeared once more at the Théâtre Sarah-Bernhardt, although this time without Marais, in *L'Aigle à deux Têtes*. Meanwhile the Télévision Française was preparing a production of *Les Parents Terribles*.

In June at the *Foire aux poètes de Forges-les-Eaux*, Cocteau was named "Prince of Poets". Jules Supervielle, who at the beginning of May had succeeded Paul Fort, Prince of Poets since 1913, had died a few days after his election, and Jean Cocteau was crowned at this "fair" as his successor, which caused a considerable controversy. The press accused Cocteau, who was certainly not guilty on this occasion, of always pushing himself to the fore, and André Breton took the opportunity to attack him once again. *Le Figaro* organised a referendum—there was almost as much fuss as over the "Bacchus affair". Finally Cocteau entered the fray, declaring that he should be elected as he had a letter from Paul Fort naming him as his successor. But even this move failed.

"I don't see why this should trouble me," Cocteau wrote to Jean-Jacques Kihm. "I have seen the others and my *gloire* is not of the same world as that of these gentlemen . . . They have not thought of the frightful situation into which they will be putting the fellow who takes my place."

Finally Saint-John-Perse, who had won the 1960 Nobel Prize for literature a few months earlier, was given the title the Prince of Poets, a further blow for Cocteau who had seen the Nobel Prize bestowed not only on him, but on Gide, Mauriac and Camus with some heart-searchings.

Only Louis Aragon devoted the first page of his weekly *Les Lettres Françaises* of 20 October to condemning the election of Saint-John-Perse.

"No vote, no majority," he wrote, "no parody of democracy can cut anyone out of that strange hierarchy of poets that the centuries and the generations bring forth. But in the end, since, as by a burlesque ceremony the same people who ought to laugh at princes and dukes have raised this false tempest . . . there must be an end . . . And so, taking my voice as the equivalent of that mob plus a poet, I am by no means saying here that I vote for Jean Cocteau.

No! I am content to crown him with authority Prince of Poets, since Prince of Poets, O frogs, you have wished him to be.

And this cannot be contested."

On the same page Aragon published an important poem by Jean Cocteau: *La Partie d'Echecs* which ends with these four significant lines:

> "Puisse l'art de mal vivre être ma seule étude
> Et de mon propre chef mettre ma tête à prix
> Afin que votre haine orne ma solitude
> C'est à moi que je rends les pions que j'ai pris."

In October Jean Cocteau, accompanied by Dermit, went to present *Le Testament d'Orphée* in Warsaw. It was to his friendship with Aragon, official writer of the French Left, that he owed this invitation to Poland. Later he went to Cadiz to give an address there at the opening of the University. It was partly this journey that inspired *Le Cérémonial espagnol du phénix*, a long poem in which the evocations of Spain mingle with the theme of death and rebirth—the phoenix, which was the central theme of *Le Testament d'Orphée*:

> La mort m'est douce-amère et son amour m'évite
> Phénix l'ennui mortel de l'immortalité.

These final words of the *Cérémonial* are also the final words of the film *Le Sang d'un Poète*.

While *L'Aigle à deux Têtes* was still running in Paris, other productions were bringing Jean Cocteau more laurels. On 15 November the Télévision Française presented *Les Parents Terribles* by Jean-Paul Carrère with the popular young actor Jean-Claude Brialy; a few days later Cocteau once again spoke the Chorus in the oratorio *Oedipus Rex* on the Paris radio, and during November and December there was an important exhibition at the Musée de Nancy, showing no less than one hundred and fifty-three of his works. Cocteau was present at the opening and spoke to the students. He invited questions, but when one young woman cast doubt on the poetic value of his paintings and drawings, he quickly brought the proceedings to a close.

While he was spending mid-winter at Santo-Sospir, the Radio Française arranged a broadcast of Jean-Jacques Kihm's adaptation of *Thomas l'Imposteur*, approved of by Cocteau, as nothing of the text was changed, and there was also a television production of Kihm's adaptation of Cocteau's *La Farce du Château* in which Edouard Dermit played an important part.

A further honour was now bestowed on Cocteau, which gave him infinite pleasure; on 1 March 1961, at the suggestion of André Malraux, he was made Commander of the Légion d'Honneur. The decoration was bestowed on him a little later at the Préfecture of Nice by Dominique Ponchardier in the presence of the Begum Aga Khan and the Prince de Polignac, father of Prince Rainier of Monaco.

Meanwhile, Cocteau had made a short journey to the Canaries and thence to Spain where he stayed for several weeks at the Casa Ana at Marbella. These were troubled days; he was grieving for the death of Francis Poulenc and harassed by Kilty, who was claiming damages and royalties amounting to ten million francs, for what he declared to be Cocteau's travesty of his play. Later he dropped the charge.

Needing more help now in his extensive affairs, Jean Cocteau had succeeded in finding an ideal secretary—Pierre Georgel, a great amateur of painting and poetry, who was henceforth to be with him much of the time and who organised all the forthcoming exhibitions, of which the most important would be held in Tokyo in 1962.

At the end of July Cocteau was present at the opening of an exhibition of his paintings and pastels at Cannes, after which he set off for Spain with Madame Weisweiller and Dermit. At the Madrid airport the police refused him entry and he was forced to return to Nice. The Spanish police asserted that they had acted from "humane and not political motives", and the French newspapers recalled, correctly, that Cocteau had signed a manifesto in support of the Spanish refugees, admitting his own sympathy for the Left. This was very upsetting for Cocteau who at this time was anxious to be in good favour with Catholic and bourgeois circles. "What would the Catholics say?" he would ask, when refusing to have *Le Livre Blanc* quoted among his works. In fact, after a long detour, he was returning to the social and religious conformity of his youth.

While waiting for the transactions between the Quai d'Orsay and the Spanish authorities to permit him to visit Spain, Cocteau had the great pleasure of selling a picture in Cannes to President Kennedy's mother. On 10 August he was at last able to leave, and now, sometimes in Madame Weisweiller's yacht and sometimes at Marbella, he completed a short book of reminiscences entitled *Le Cordon Ombilical*, dedicated to Denise Bourdet who had begged him to write it. This opens and ends with poems, and in the book he attempts to relate his work and his life—the umbilical cord attaching the artist to his reactions. Also at Marbella he painted four pictures called "Flamenco"—he described the inspiration of this work in *Le Cordon Ombilical*.

It is interesting to note that, returning as ever to the subject of

Dargelos, in this book Cocteau declares that "he took nothing of him but the name", whereas in *Portraits-Souvenir* he had made it clear that Dargelos *was* the character in *Les Enfants Terribles* and who appears again and again in his work. The reasons for this contradiction were twofold: first, between the publication of these two books, Jean-Jacques Kihm had discovered that far from being the dunce described, Dargelos was a brilliant pupil at the Condorcet. And second, during these last months friends of Cocteau's had discovered Pierre Dargelos living peacefully with his wife in the environs of Paris. Cocteau wrote to him and his old schoolfellow replied politely but reticently. Clearly it was wiser only to admit the use of his name in that first youthful and never-to-be-forgotten experience of falling in love with human beauty. Another link too with Cocteau's youth was broken in this year 1961 by the death of his brother Paul.

Returning from Spain in October, Cocteau made a brief visit to Paris, then settled down at Santo-Sospir. But his relations with Francine Weisweiller were no longer so happy; for some time now, in spite of their long and fruitful friendship, there had been difficulties between them. On Cocteau's side there was the pull between his love of luxury and his love of liberty, and Madame Weisweiller had her own reasons for wishing to be in less close contact with Cocteau and his adopted son.

For the first time for several years Cocteau did not spend Christmas at Santo-Sospir, but with Dermit at Milly, during which period he wrote the short and brilliant play *L'Impromptu du Palais-Royal*, in which he put Louis XIV and his court on the stage. This was written for the Comédiens Français and was intended to be shown at the Petit-Théâtre de Gabriel at Versailles. In fact, it was only produced during the tour of the Comédiens Français in Japan the following May, and although Cocteau wrote another version of it during the summer, it has never been seen in France.

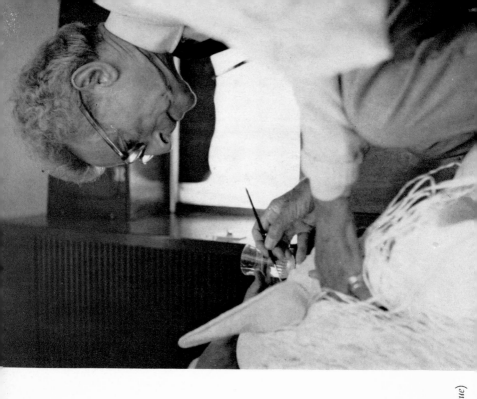

DURING THE FILMING OF *Le Testament d'Orphée*

Jean Marais and Jean Cocteau (*photo Lucien Clergue*)

Jean Cocteau painting the mask of the Sphinx (*photo Lucien Clergue*)

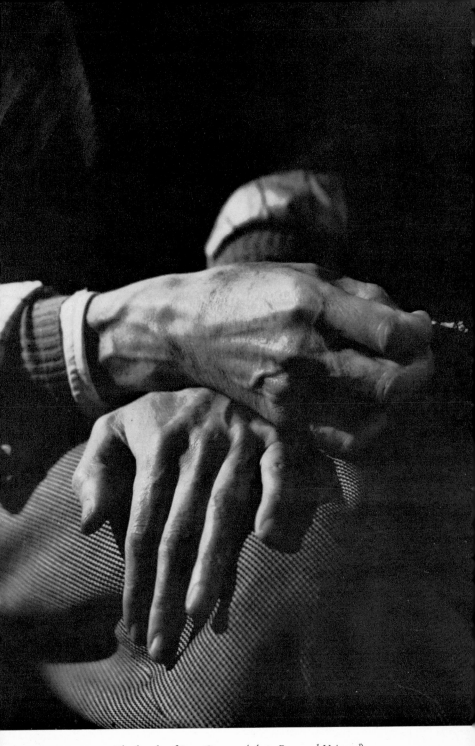

The hands of Jean Cocteau (*photo Raymond Voinquel*)

In January 1962 there was a revival of *La Voix Humaine* at the Comédie-Française with Louise Conte, and Cocteau started work on an adaptation of Paul Osborn's *The World of Suzy Wong* for Marie Bell, although this was never performed.

In spite of all these activities and the wide fame that he now enjoyed, Jean Cocteau was lonely. As spring came and gave the poet a longing for the sunshine and the sea, this time it was not to Saint-Jean-Cap-Ferrat, but to Villefranche, to the Hôtel Welcome, haunted by memories of his youth and the friends of his early days, that Jean Cocteau returned with Doudou. From here he supervised the leisurely completion of the theatre at Cap d'Ail and also, at the request of the Mayor that he would start a Jean Cocteau museum at Menton, he decorated the Bastion for this purpose—with Pharaoh painting his own sarcophagus. About the break with Madame Weisweiller, he contented himself with saying politely to importunate journalists: "We have had enough of one another. We do not expect to meet again."

On 22 May he went to Metz alone with Dermit for a glittering revival of Debussy's *Pelléas et Mélisande* for which he had designed the décor. For this work, which he did not greatly admire, his scenery was not really suitable, being far too linear, but he had been unable to resist linking his name for all time with that of Claude Debussy.

In spite of his announcement to the press, Jean Cocteau and Francine Weisweiller were soon quietly reconciled; he returned to Santo-Sospir, inaugurated the Bastion at Menton and the Cap d'Ail theatre and was invited by the Chevaliers du Saint-Sépulcre to decorate a chapel at Fréjus.*

This year he refused to go to the Festival at Baalbek because Francine Weisweiller's daughter Carole was unable to obtain a visa on account of her Jewish origin. In the autumn he returned to Paris, this time with no other project in view but the preparation with Roger Stéphane, Roland Darbois and Paul Seban of a

* Edouard Dermit finished this work after Cocteau's death.

long *Portrait-Souvenir* for the Télévision Française. This was really a further *Testament d'Orphée*, a testament without mythology and in which the poet has become a man.

The film was made during the first weeks of 1963. Consciously or not Cocteau was holding up the mirror to himself for the last time, and this reflection would not be seen by the public until after his death. Although exhausted he was more brilliant than ever and threw himself wholeheartedly into the work.

Meanwhile a French company took *Orphée*, the play, on a tour of the American universities, and a comprehensive exhibition of Jean Cocteau's work opened at the Institute of Contemporary Artists in New York.

After a few more days at Santo-Sospir, early in April Cocteau went to Fréjus to start work on the chapel, but before long he returned to Paris. At nine in the morning of 22 April, he had another heart attack, far more severe than the previous ones. For several hours he was in agony; Dermit fetched the doctors and Madeleine put a notice on the door: *"Défense de sonner"*. Silence and solitude descended on the little apartment accustomed to the footsteps, the conversation and the constant laughter of Jean Cocteau and his friends.

As soon as he was a little better Francine Weisweiller, Jean Marais and a few other intimate friends were allowed to pay him short visits.

"I have stopped at a red light," he joked with them, "and I am wondering if it will ever turn green again."

Presently he was moved to the house of Jean Marais, still his faithful Galahad, at Marnes-la-Coquette, where the latter took affectionate care of him. None the less he remained very weak and it was with apprehension that his friends watched his slow recovery. It was here that Marianne Singer visited him for the last time. On 5 July, his seventy-fourth birthday, Jean Cocteau was moved by ambulance to Milly-la-Forêt.

"It's my birthday," he said. "Instead of blowing out candles, I am blowing out the red lights."*

Jean Cocteau had suddenly become an old man and led the life of an old man, although as he flitted about his room, finding things of interest to show them, he still gave his few visitors an impression of energy and of being, as always, an *enfant terrible.* He read detective novels, wrote a few letters and was driven in his Jaguar by Dermit to see the radiologist at Fontainebleau and to visit the little cinema in Milly. He thought for a while of returning to Fréjus, then ceased to think of this and never left Milly again. He was protected by Dermit and the married couple, who kept all work away from him and chased the journalists from the door.

On 1 October 1963 Jean Cocteau enjoyed watching *La Machine Infernale* on television. On the 11th, early in the morning, while he was still asleep, the telephone, still kept in the kitchen, rang and was answered by one of the staff. Edith Piaf had died during the night, the caller said, and the Radio Française wanted an interview with Jean Cocteau. This was refused and the news of the singer's death was kept from Cocteau, who was in no state to bear any emotional strain. But the telephone continued to ring and the caller to importune. Presently, when he was up, Cocteau answered the telephone himself, heard with profound grief of Edith Piaf's death and agreed to the interview.

Towards noon he recorded a few words about the singer, after which, feeling very ill, he added: "The death of Edith Piaf is choking me again." The reporters left and Jean Cocteau went back to bed. His staff never left him. He could not find any comfort in bed and wanted to get up again. He was in pain and said: "The boat is sinking." Jean Cocteau knew then that he was dying.

* "*Au lieu de souffler des bougies, je soufflerai des feux-rouges.*" To pass a red traffic light is "*souffler un feu rouge*" and ambulances do this.

The doctor and the curé were immediately sent for. They arrived a few moments later—too late. Jean Cocteau was dead. Above his head hung the Gustave Doré mirror that Francine Weisweiller had given him and which, despite the custom of veiling mirrors in the presence of death, was left uncovered and reflected the image of the dead poet.

They clothed him in simple black, put on his *cravate of Commandeur de la Légion d'Honneur* and laid him on a couch in the salon with his Academician's sword beside him. Jean Marais and a few close friends joined Francine Weisweiller, Edouard Dermit and Madeleine at Jean Cocteau's side. The next day, following his own instructions, he was embalmed. He looked beautiful, serene and younger than in life. Now came the photographers, the journalists and even schoolchildren, all eager to gaze upon the poet, already a legend in his lifetime, and to be inside the very house where he had lived.

Jean Cocteau had wanted to be buried in the garden of his home, but this the authorities would not allow. On 15 October he lay in simple state in the Mairie at Milly and on the following day the villagers, young and old, followed with his few relatives (among them his cousin Marianne), his many friends and the representatives of the Government, of the French and Belgian Academies and of La Comédie-Française. He was buried in the churchyard of Saint-Blaise-des-Simples, but on 24 April 1964 his body was moved to the interior of the chapel to lie under a great stone slab—the gift of the Mayor of Menton—inscribed in Jean Cocteau's own handwriting and decorated with his star:

Je reste
avec vous.
*

cela fait que j'ai ma St Charlemagne -
J'ai reçu beaucoup de livres très jolis
je t'embrasse tendrement et je fais
bien des amitiés à la soeur
ton petit fils
Jean Cocteau

HANDWRITING: Letter from Jean Cocteau to his grandmother, 1899

Madame Maurice Lecomte
Jean Cocteau.

HANDWRITING: On a fan box, about 1907

Immeubles
votre boucle insulte le silence
La foule perce neige et les bustes de sel
bonnet phrygien
Le au bout des fers de lance
Et ,
au musée.
Le système nerveux
Jean Cocteau
× 1956

HANDWRITING: Picasso had advised him to simplify his handwriting:
extract from a poem, 1956

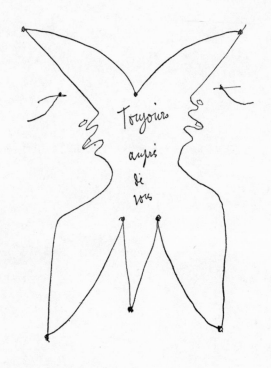

Toujours
auprès
de
vous

# BIBLIOGRAPHY
## AND
# PRINCIPAL WORKS CONSULTED
## OR QUOTED

*

# INDEX

# BIBLIOGRAPHY

First and current editions of Jean Cocteau's works,

*French Edition*

1909 LA LAMPE D'ALADIN, poèmes (Société d'Editions)
1910 LE PRINCE FRIVOLE, poèmes (Mercure de France)
1912 LA DANSE DE SOPHOCLE, poèmes (Mercure de France)
1918 LE COQ ET L'ARLEQUIN, notes autour de la musique (Editions de la Sirène)
1919 LE CAP DE BONNE-ESPERANCE, poème (Editions de la Sirène)
     ODE A PICASSO (F. Bernouard)
     LE POTOMAK (Société Littéraire de France). (Edition définitive: Stock, 1934)
1920 CARTE BLANCHE (Editions de la Sirène)
     ESCALES, poèmes (Editions de la Sirène)
     POESIES (1917–20) (Editions de la Sirène)
1921 LA NOCE MASSACREE (Souvenirs) I. Visite à Maurice Barrès (Editions de la Sirène)
1922 LE SECRET PROFESSIONNEL (Stock)
     VOCABULAIRE, poèmes (Editions de la Sirène)
1923 DESSINS (Stock)
     LE GRAND ECART (Stock)

LES MARIES DE LA TOUR EIFFEL (Les Oeuvres Libres, Gallimard)

PLAIN-CHANT, poèmes (Stock) (Gallimard)
LA ROSE DE FRANÇOIS (F. Bernouard)
THOMAS L'IMPOSTEUR (Gallimard)

# BIBLIOGRAPHY

not including collections to which he contributed.

*Corresponding English and American Editions*

COCK AND HARLEQUIN, trans. by Rollo H. Myers (Egoist Press, London, 1921)

THE GRAND ECART, trans. by Lewis Galantière, (Putnam, London and New York, 1925)

THE MISCREANT, trans. by Dorothy Williams (Peter Owen, London, 1958)

THE WEDDING ON THE EIFFEL TOWER, trans. by Michael Benedikt (in MODERN FRENCH PLAYS, Faber and Faber, London, 1964)

THE EIFFEL TOWER WEDDING PARTY, trans. by Dudley Fitts (in THE INFERNAL MACHINE and OTHER PLAYS, New Directions Books, New York, 1963)

in French, edited by Bernard Garniez (Macmillan, New York, 1964)

THOMAS THE IMPOSTER, trans. by Lewis Galantière (Appleton, New York, 1925)

THE IMPOSTER, trans. by Dorothy Williams (Peter Owen, London, 1957, Citadel, New York, 1960)

1924 FERAT (Crès)
PICASSO (Stock)
POESIE. 1916–23. Le Cap de Bonne-Espérance. Discours du Grand
Sommeil. Poésies. Vocabulaire. Plain-Chant. (Gallimard)
1925 CRI ECRIT (Montpellier, Impr. de Montane)
LE MYSTERE DE L'OISELEUR, reproductions de manuscrits inédits
(E. Champion)
PRIERE MUTILEE (Ed. des Cahiers Libres)
1926 L'ANGE HEURTEBISE, poème (Stock)
LETTRE A JACQUES MARITAIN (Stock)

MAISON DE SANTE, dessins (Briant-Robert)
LE RAPPEL A L'ORDRE. Le Coq et l'Arlequin, Carte blanche. Visite
à Maurice Barrès. Le Secret Professionnel. D'un ordre considéré
comme une anarchie. Autour de Thomas L'Imposteur. Picasso.
(Stock)
ROMEO ET JULIETTE (Au Sans Pareil)
1927 ANTIGONE, Les Mariés de la Tour Eiffel (Gallimard)
OPERA, oeuvres poétiques, 1925–7 (Stock)
ORPHEE (Stock)

1928 LE MYSTERE LAÏC (Giorgio de Chirico) (Editions des Quatre-
Chemins)
OEDIPE-ROI, Roméo et Juliette (Plon)
LE LIVRE BLANC (sans nom d'éditeur) (Morihien)
1929 LES ENFANTS TERRIBLES (Grasset)

25 DESSINS D'UN DORMEUR (Mermod)
UNE ENTREVUE SUR LA CRITIQUE AVEC MAURICE ROUZAUD (Abbe-
ville, Impr. F. Paillard)
1930 OPIUM (Stock)

LA VOIX HUMAINE (Stock)

1932 ESSAI DE CRITIQUE INDIRECTE (Grasset)
MORCEAUX CHOISIS, poèmes (Gallimard)

Long extracts in THE JOURNALS OF JEAN COCTEAU, edited and trans. by Wallace Fowlie (Criterion Books, 1956)

A CALL TO ORDER, trans. by Rollo H. Myers (Faber and Gwyer, London, 1926)

ANTIGONE, trans. by Carl Wildman (MacGibbon and Kee, London, 1962)

ORPHEUS, trans. by Carl Wildman (Oxford University Press, 1933)
ORPHEUS, trans. by John Savacool (in THE INFERNAL MACHINE and OTHER PLAYS, New Directions Books, New York, 1963)

THE WHITE PAPER (Olympia Press, Paris, 1957)
ENFANTS TERRIBLES, trans. by Samuel Putnam (Brewer and Warren, New York, 1930)
THE CHILDREN OF THE GAME, trans. by Rosamund Lehmann (Harvill Press, London, 1955)

OPIUM, trans. by Ernest Boyd (Longmans, London and New York, 1932, Allen & Unwin, London, 1933)
OPIUM, new trans. by Margaret Crosland and Sinclair Road (Peter Owen, London, 1957)
THE HUMAN VOICE, trans. by Carl Wildman (Vision Press, London, 1951)

1934 LA MACHINE INFERNALE (Grasset)

MYTHOLOGIE, poème (Editions des Quatre-Chemins)
1935 PORTRAITS-SOUVENIR, 1900–1914 (Grasset)

60 DESSINS POUR "LES ENFANTS TERRIBLES" (Grasset)
1936 LE FANTOME DE MARSEILLE (Gallimard)
1937 LES CHEVALIERS DE LA TABLE RONDE (Gallimard)

MON PREMIER VOYAGE (Tour du Monde en 80 jours) (Gallimard)

1938 LES PARENTS TERRIBLES (Gallimard)

1939 ENIGME (Editions des Réverbères)
1940 LA FIN DU POTOMAK (Gallimard)
LES MONSTRES SACRES (Gallimard)

1941 ALLEGORIES, poèmes (Gallimard)
DESSINS EN MARGE DES CHEVALIERS DE LA TABLE RONDE (Gallimard)
LA MACHINE A ECRIRE (Gallimard)

1943 LE GRECO (Au Divan) (Gallimard)
RENAUD ET ARMIDE (Gallimard)
1944 SERGE LIFAR A L'OPERA (Champrosay)
LES POEMES ALLEMANDS (Krimpeer, The Hague)
1945 LEONE, poème (Gallimard)
PORTRAIT DE MOUNET-SULLY (F. Bernouard)
1946 L'AIGLE A DEUX TETES (Gallimard)

LA BELLE ET LA BETE, Journal d'un film (Janin)

in French (Nelson and Son, London, 1944)
in French, edited with introduction and note by W. M. Landers
(Harrap, London, 1957)
THE INFERNAL MACHINE, trans. by Carl Wildman (Oxford University
Press, 1936)
THE INFERNAL MACHINE, trans. by Albert Bermel (New Directions
Books, 1963)

PARIS ALBUM. 1900–1914, trans. by Margaret Crosland (W. H. Allen,
London, 1956)


THE KNIGHTS OF THE ROUND TABLE, trans. by W. H. Auden (New
Directions Books, 1963)
ROUND THE WORLD AGAIN IN EIGHTY DAYS, trans. by Stuart Gilbert
(Routledge, London, 1937)
MY JOURNEY ROUND THE WORLD, trans. by W. J. Strachan (Peter Owen,
London, 1958)
INTIMATE RELATIONS, trans. by Charles Frank (MacGibbon and Kee,
London, 1962)


THE HOLY TERRORS, trans. by Edward O. Marsh (MacGibbon and Kee,
London, 1962)


THE TYPEWRITER, trans. by Ronald Duncan (Dennis Dobson, London,
1947)




THE EAGLE HAS TWO HEADS, adapted by Ronald Duncan (Vision Press,
London, 1948)
THE EAGLE WITH TWO HEADS, trans. by Carl Wildman (MacGibbon and
Kee, London 1962)
DIARY OF A FILM. La Belle et la Bête, trans. by Ronald Duncan (Dobson,
London, Roy, New York, 1950)

1947 LA CRUCIFIXION (Morihien) (Gallimard)
DEUX TRAVESTIS (Fournier)
LA DIFFICULTE D'ETRE (Morihien) (Editions du Rocher)

L'ETERNEL RETOUR (Nouvelles Editions Françaises)
LE FOYER DES ARTISTES (Plon)
RUY BLAS (Morihien)
1947-1950 OEUVRES COMPLETES (Marguerat, Lausanne, 10 vols.)
1948 DROLE DE MENAGE (Morihien) (Editions du Rocher)
POEMES. LEONE. ALLEGORIES. LA CRUCIFIXION. NEIGE. (Gallimard)
REINES DE LA FRANCE (Darantière) (Grasset)
LE SANG D'UN POETE (Marin) (Editions du Rocher)

THEATRE (Gallimard, 2 vols.)
1949 DUFY (Flammarion)
LETTRE AUX AMERICAINS (Grasset)
MAALESH, Journal d'une tournée de théâtre (Gallimard)

THEATRE DE POCHE (Morihien) (Editions du Rocher)
UN TRAMWAY NOMME DESIR, adaptation de la pièce de Tennessee
Williams (Bordas)
1950 MODIGLIANI (Hazan) (Gallimard)
1951 JEAN MARAIS (Calmann-Lévy)
1952 BACCHUS (Gallimard)
LE CHIFFRE SEPT, poèmes (Seghers)
GIDE VIVANT (Amiot-Dumont)
JOURNAL D'UN INCONNU (Grasset)

LA NAPPE DU CATALAN (Impr. Faguet et Badier)
1953 APPOGIATURES (Editions du Rocher)
DEMARCHE D'UN POETE. Der Levensweg eines Dichters (Bruckmann, Munich)
DENTELLE D'ETERNITE, poème-objet (Seghers)
1954 CLAIR-OBSCUR (Editions du Rocher)
1955 COLETTE, discours de Réception à l'Académie Royale de Belgique
(Grasset)
DISCOURS DE RECEPTION A L'ACADEMIE FRANÇAISE (Gallimard)
1956 ADIEU A MISTINGUETT (Dynamo, Liège)
LE DISCOURS DE STRASBOURG (Impr. de la S.M.E.I. Metz)

THE DIFFICULTY OF BEING, trans. by Elizabeth Sprigge (Peter Owen, London, 1966, Coward McCann, New York, 1967)

THE BLOOD OF A POET, trans. by Lily Pons (Bodley Press, New York, 1949)

MAALESH. A theatrical tour in the Middle-East, trans. by Mary C. Hoeck (Peter Owen, London, 1956)

BACCHUS, trans. by Mary C. Hoeck in *The Infernal Machine and Other Plays* (New Directions Books, New York, 1963)

THE HAND OF A STRANGER, trans. by Alec Brown (Elek Books, London, 1956)

Extracts, with other portraits, in MY CONTEMPORARIES, trans. and edited by Margaret Crosland (Peter Owen, London, 1967, Chilton, New York, 1968)

1956 LE DISCOURS D'OXFORD (Gallimard)

POEMES 1916–1955 (Gallimard)
TEMOIGNAGE (Bertrand, Flers-de-l'Orne)
1957 LA CHAPELLE SAINT-PIERRE, VILLEFRANCHE-SUR-MER (Editions du Rocher)
LA CORRIDA DU PREMIER MAI (Grasset)
ENTRETIENS SUR LE MUSEE DE DRESDE avec Aragon (Editions du Cercle d'Art)
ERIK SATIE (Dynamo, Liège)
THEATRE, ill. par l'auteur (Grasset, 2 vols.)
1958 PARAPROSODIES, précédées de 7 dialogues (Editions du Rocher)
LA SALLE DES MARIAGES, Hôtel de Ville de Menton (Editions du Rocher)
1959 GONDOLE DES MORTS, poèmes (Milan, All'Insegna del Pesce d'oro)
POESIE CRITIQUE I. (Gallimard)
1960 GUIDE A L'USAGE DES VISITEURS DE LA CHAPELLE SAINT-BLAISE-DES-SIMPLES (Editions de Rocher)
NOUVEAU THEATRE DE POCHE (Editions du Rocher)
POESIE CRITIQUE II (Gallimard)
1961 CEREMONIAL ESPAGNOL DU PHENIX. Suivi de LA PARTIE D'ECHEC, poèmes (Gallimard)
ORPHEE, film (André Bonne)
LE TESTAMENT D'ORPHEE, film (Editions du Rocher)
1962 LE CORDON OMBILICAL. SOUVENIRS (Plon)
DISCOURS A L'ACADEMIE ROYALE DE BELGIQUE, Commémoration Maeterlinck (Dynamo, Liège)
L'IMPROMPTU DU PALAIS-ROYAL (Gallimard)
LE REQUIEM, poème (Gallimard)
1963 ANNA DE NOALLIES OUI ET NON (Librairie Académique Perrin) [posthumous]

POETRY AND INVISIBILITY, trans. by Jean Stewart (In the London Magazine, January 1957)

# PRINCIPAL WORKS CONSULTED OR QUOTED

BEATON (Cecil): *The Glass of Fashion* (Weidenfeld & Nicolson, 1953, Doubleday & Co., Inc., 1953).

BIBESCO (Princesse Marthe): *Requiem pour Jean* (in *Les Nouvelles Littéraires*, 17 October 1963).

BOISDEFFRE (Pierre de): *Une histoire vivante de la littérature d'aujourd'hui* (Le Livre contemporain, 1958).

BOURDET (Denise): *Edouard Bourdet et ses amis* (La Jeune Parque, s.d.).

— *Images de Paris* (in *La Revue de Paris*, March 1966 and May 1959).

CHANEL (Pierre): *Catalogue de l'Exposition de Nancy*, notes de Jean Cocteau (1960).

COLETTE: *Le Fanal bleu* (Ferenczi, 1949).

CROSLAND (Margaret): *Jean Cocteau* (Peter Nevill, London, 1955).

DAUVEN (Jean): *Jean Cocteau chez les Sirènes* (Ed. du Rocher, 1956).

DESBORDES (Jean): *J'adore* (Grasset, 1928).

— *Les Tragédiens* (Grasset, 1931).

— *La Mue* (Stock, 1936).

DUBOURG (Pierre): *Dramaturgie de Jean Cocteau* (Grasset, 1954).

FAY (Bernard): *Les Précieux* (Librairie Académique Perrin, 1966).

FRAIGNEAU (André): Jean Cocteau: *Entretiens à la radio avec* . . . (Bibl. 10/18, 1965).

— Jean Cocteau: *Entretiens autour du cinématographe* (André Bonne, 1951).

— *Jean Cocteau par lui-même* (Ed. du Seuil, 1957).

GARROS (Roland): *Mémoires de* . . . publiées par Jacques Quellennec (Hachette, 1966).

GEORGEL (Pierre): *Jean Cocteau et son temps.* Catalogue de l'Exposition (Imprimerie Nationale, 1965).

GHEON (Henri): *La Danse de Sophocle* (in *La Nouvelle Revue Française.* No. XLV, 1913).

GIDE (André): *Incidences* (Gallimard, 1924)

— *Journal, 1889–1939* (Gallimard, 1949).

— *Les Faux-Monnayeurs* (Gallimard, 1926).

— *Si le grain ne meurt* (Gallimard, 1927).

GILSON (René): *Jean Cocteau* (Seghers, 1964).

GOESCH (Keith): *Radiguet* (La Palatine, 1955).

GOUDEKET (Maurice): *Près de Colette* (Flammarion, 1956).

GOUDEKET (Maurice): *La Douceur de vieillir* (Flammarion, 1965).

HAGAN (Friedrich): *Zwischen Stern und Spiegel: Jean Cocteau als Zeichner* (Wilhelm Anderman, München-Wien, 1956).

HUGO (Valentine): *Il y a trente ans* (in *La Parisienne*, December 1953).

JACOB (Max): *Lettres à Jean Cocteau (1919-1944)* (Morihien, 1949).

JULLIAN (Philippe): *Robert de Montesquiou* (Librairie Académique Perrin, 1965).

JUNGER (Ernst): *Journal de guerre et d'occupation. 1939-1948.* (Julliard, 1965).

KIHM (Jean-Jacques): *Cocteau* (Gallimard, 1960).

— *Pages oubliées de Jean Cocteau* (R.T.F., 1959).

— *Jean Desbordes ou le poète d'avant le mal* (R.T.F., 1962).

LANNES (Roger): *Jean Cocteau* (Seghers, 1945).

LANOE (Julien): *Une querelle sur l'amour* (La Ligne du Coeur, Nantes, 1928)

LIFAR (Serge): *Serge de Diaghilev* (Putnam, London and New York, 1940).

MARITAIN (Jacques): *Réponse à Jean Cocteau* (Stock, 1926).

MARITAIN (Raïssa): *Les Grandes Amitiés* (Desclée de Brouver, 1947).

MARTIN DU GARD (Maurice): *Les Mémorables*, 2 vols. (Flammarion, 1957).

MAURIAC (Claude): *Jean Cocteau ou la Vérité du mensonge* (Odette Lieutier, 1945).

— *Conversations avec André Gide* (Albin-Michel, 1951).

MEUNIER (Micheline): *Méditerranée ou les Deux Visages de Jean Cocteau* (Debresse, 1959).

— *Présence de Jean Cocteau* (Vitte, Lyon, 1964).

MILLECAM (Jean-Pierre): *L'Etoile de Jean Cocteau* (Ed. du Rocher, Monaco, 1952).

MONNIER (Adrienne): *Mémorial de la Rue de l'Odéon* (in *Le Littéraire*, 19 June 1953).

MOURGUE (Gérard): *Jean Cocteau* (Ed. Universitaires, 1915).

MORAND (Paul): *Journal d'un attaché d'ambassade* (Table Ronde, 1949).

MYERS (Rollo H.): *Erik Satie* (Dobson, 1948), (Gallimard, 1950. Preface Jean Cocteau).

NADEAU (Maurice): *Histoire du Surréalisme* (Ed. du Seuil, 1945).

— *Documents surréalistes* (Ed. du Seuil, 1948).

OBERLE (Jean): *La Vie d'artiste* (Denoël, 1956).

PAINTER (George D.): *Marcel Proust*, 2 vols. (Chatto and Windus, London, 1959-65; Atlantic Monthly-Little Brown, Boston, 1965).

PEETERS (Georges): *Les Monstres Sacrés du ring* (Table Ronde, 1959).

PILLAUDIN (Roger): *Jean Cocteau tourne son dernier film* (Table Ronde, 1960).

RADIGUET (Raymond): *Oeuvres complètes*, 2 vols. (Club des Libraires de France, 1959).

SACHS (Maurice): *Le Sabbat* (Corrêa, 1946).

— *La Décade de l'illusion* (Gallimard, 1950).

SALMON (André): *Souvenirs sans fin*, 3 vols. (Gallimard, 1955–61).

SERT (Misia): *Memoirs of... Two or Three Muses*, translated by Moura Budberg (Museum Press, 1953).

SIMON (Pierre-Henri): *Mauriac par lui-même* (Ed. du Seuil, 1953).

SPRIGGE (Elizabeth): *Gertrude Stein, Her Life and Work* (Hamish Hamilton, Harpers, New York, London, 1957).

STEPHANE (Roger) et DARBOIS (Roland): *Portrait Souvenir: Jean Cocteau* (R.T.F., and Jules Tallandier, 1963).

THOMSON (Virgil): *Virgil Thomson* (Alfred A. Knopf, New York, 1966, Weidenfeld & Nicolson, London, 1967).

## VARIA

*Adam*, No. 300, 1965.

*L'Avant-Scène*. Théâtre. Spécial Cocteau. (Paris, 1–15 October 1966).

*Emprentes* (Brussels, May, June, July 1950).

*Images de Jean Cocteau* (Nice, Matarasso, 1957).

*Table Ronde* (Paris, October 1955).

*Journal Le Mot* (1914–15).

*Journal Le Coq* suivi du *Coq Gaulois* (1921).

(Journaux français de la période 1945–63).

# INDEX

Bacchus 197

Mas de Fourques, Jean Hugo's home at,
  118, 133
Massine, Léonide, 64
Massis, Henri, 102
Mauriac, Claude: *Conversations avec
  André Gide*, 143; *Jean Cocteau ou
  la vérité du mensonge*, 201
Mauriac, François, 62, 80, 208, 212,
  244; *Lettre à Jean Cocteau* (the
  "Bacchus affair"), 198–200, 201;
  *L'Agneau*, 208
Maurois, André, 211, 219
Maurois, Simone, 211
Max, Edouard de, 36–8
Melville, Jean-Pierre, 183–4, 188–9
Mendès, Catulle, 43, 52
Menotti, Gian-Carlo, *Le Poète et sa
  Muse*, 236
Menton, 223; the Mairie, 224, 242;
  Festival of Music, 225; the
  Bastion, 249
*Mercure*, 81
Metz, 249
Meudon, 98, 101–2
Milhaud, Darius, 61*n*., 73, 79, 80, 83–4,
  89, 224; *Le Boeuf sur le Toit*, 76,
  78; *Le Train Bleu*, 96
Miller, Lee, 120
Milly-la-Forêt, 152, 157, 169–70, 172,
  175, 177–8, 184, 188, 192, 194,
  204, 248, 251; chapel of Saint-
  Blaise-des-Simples, 229, 234, 236–
  237; Cocteau buried at, 252
Miró, Joan, 122
Mistinguett, 33, 34, 72
Modigliani, Amedeo, 62
Molière, *Fourberies de Scapin*, 177
Mondor, Professor Henri, 211
Monnier, Adrienne, on Cocteau, 71–2
Montargis, 138
Monte-Carlo, 94
Montherlant, Henry de, 197
Montmartre, 18, 74, 77
Montmorency, 188
Montmorency, Galerie, 233
Montparnasse, 61, 62
Montrouge, 62
Morand, Paul, 73–4, 77, 89–90, 123,
  152–3, 229
Morihien, Paul, 161, 166–70, 172–3,
  203
*Mot, Le*, 58
Mugnier, Abbé, 93

Munich, 201, 204
Murano, 227
Mürren, 30, 113

Nancy, Musée de, 246
Naples, 64, 81
Natanson, Thadée, 46
Neuilly, 144
Neuilly, Maurice Barrès' home at, 55
New York, 130–1, 170, 176; Institute
  of Contemporary Artists, 250
Nice, 196, 223, 225, 241, 247
Nicolau, Dr Pierre, 148, 151
Nicolau, Jacques, 149, 150
Nietzsche, Friedrich, 58, 160, 232
Nieuport, 58
Night-clubs. See Cafés, Night-clubs,
  etc.
Nijinska, 96
Nijinsky, Vaclav, 44, 47, 49–51, 60,
  64, 96
Noailles, Anna Comtesse de, 41–3, 49,
  181, 211, 216
Noailles, Charles de, 106, 118–20,
  124–5, 154
Noailles, Marie-Laure de, 125
Nobel Prize, 244
Normandie Oscar, 189
*Nouvelle Revue Française, La*, 49, 66–7,
  77, 92, 116
*Nouvelles Littéraires*, 91, 109

Offranville, 45, 48, 51
Olivier, Laurence, 166
Opium smoking, by Cocteau, 94–5,
  102, 106, 111, 149
Osborn, Paul, *The World of Suzy Wong*,
  249
Oxford, 89; University, 220, 221–2

Painter, George D., quoted 59
Palais de Glace, Champs-Elysées, 33
Palais-Royal, 144; Cocteau's apart-
  ment in, 147, 153–5, 157, 161, 164,
  167, 169, 188, 192, 204, 208–10,
  215, 220
Paley, Nathalie, 148–9
*Paris-Presse*, 225
*Paris-Soir*, 127, 128
*Parti Populaire Français* (fascist paper),
  151
Pathé-Marconi, 226